T0243394

Strike of the *Sailfish*

Also by Stephen L. Moore

Blood and Fury: The World War II Story of Tank Sergeant Lafayette "War Daddy" Pool

Patton's Payback: The Battle of El Guettar and General Patton's Rise to Glory

Battle Stations: How the USS Yorktown *Helped Turn the Tide at Coral Sea and Midway*

Rain of Steel: Mitscher's Task Force 58, Ugaki's Thunder Gods, and the Kamikaze War off Okinawa

Uncommon Valor: The Recon Company That Earned Five Medals of Honor and Included America's Most Decorated Green Beret

As Good as Dead: The Daring Escape of American POWs from a Japanese Death Camp

The Battle for Hell's Island: How a Small Band of Carrier Dive-Bombers Helped Save Guadalcanal

Texas Rising: The Epic True Story of the Lone Star Republic and the Rise of the Texas Rangers, 1836–1846

Pacific Payback: The Carrier Aviators Who Avenged Pearl Harbor at the Battle of Midway

Battle Surface!: Lawson P. "Red" Ramage and the War Patrols of the USS Parche

Presumed Lost: The Incredible Ordeal of America's Submarine POWs During the Pacific War

Relic Quest: A Guide to Responsible Relic Recovery Techniques with Metal Detectors

Savage Frontier: Rangers, Riflemen, and Indian Wars in Texas, Volume IV: 1842–1845

Last Stand of the Texas Cherokees: Chief Bowles and the 1839 Cherokee War in Texas

War of the Wolf: Texas' Memorial Submarine, World War II's Famous USS Seawolf

Savage Frontier: Rangers, Riflemen, and Indian Wars in Texas, Volume III: 1840–1841

Spadefish*: On Patrol with a Top-Scoring World War II Submarine*

Savage Frontier: Rangers, Riflemen, and Indian Wars in Texas, Volume II: 1838–1839

Eighteen Minutes: The Battle of San Jacinto and the Texas Independence Campaign

Savage Frontier: Rangers, Riflemen, and Indian Wars in Texas, Volume I: 1835–1837

Taming Texas: Captain William T. Sadler's Lone Star Service

The Buzzard Brigade: Torpedo Squadron Ten at War (with William J. Shinneman and Robert Gruebel)

Strike of the *Sailfish*

Two Sister Submarines and
the Sinking of a Japanese Aircraft Carrier

Stephen L. Moore

CALIBER

CALIBER

An imprint of Penguin Random House LLC
penguinrandomhouse.com

LIBRARY OF CONGRESS CATALOGING-IN-PUBLICATION DATA
has been applied for.

ISBN 9780593472873 (hardcover)
ISBN 9780593472880 (ebook)

Printed in the United States of America
1st Printing

BOOK DESIGN BY ELKE SIGAL

Dedicated to Bill Dillon for sharing his story
for future generations to appreciate

Contents

Prologue		1
One	*Sculpin* on the Warpath	9
Two	Running from Targets	21
Three	"A Clean Slate"	45
Four	"They Have Us"	65
Five	Battle Surface!	86
Six	"A Living Hell"	103
Seven	"Chance of a Lifetime"	121
Eight	Carrier Passage to Japan	137
Nine	First Strike	149
Ten	*Chuyo* in Peril	160

Contents

Eleven	Third Strike of the *Sailfish*	171
Twelve	Carrier Down	180
Thirteen	*Sailfish* on the Prowl	199
Fourteen	Prisoners of War	213
Fifteen	Wolf Pack	223
Sixteen	The Mines of Ashio	252
Seventeen	Lifeguard League	258
Eighteen	The Last Nine Months	284
Epilogue		297
Acknowledgments		305
Appendix A:	Roster of USS *Sculpin* (SS-191) for Ninth War Patrol	309
Appendix B:	Muster Roll of USS *Sailfish* (SS-192) for Patrols 10 to 12	313
Notes		319
Bibliography		343
Index		355

Strike of the *Sailfish*

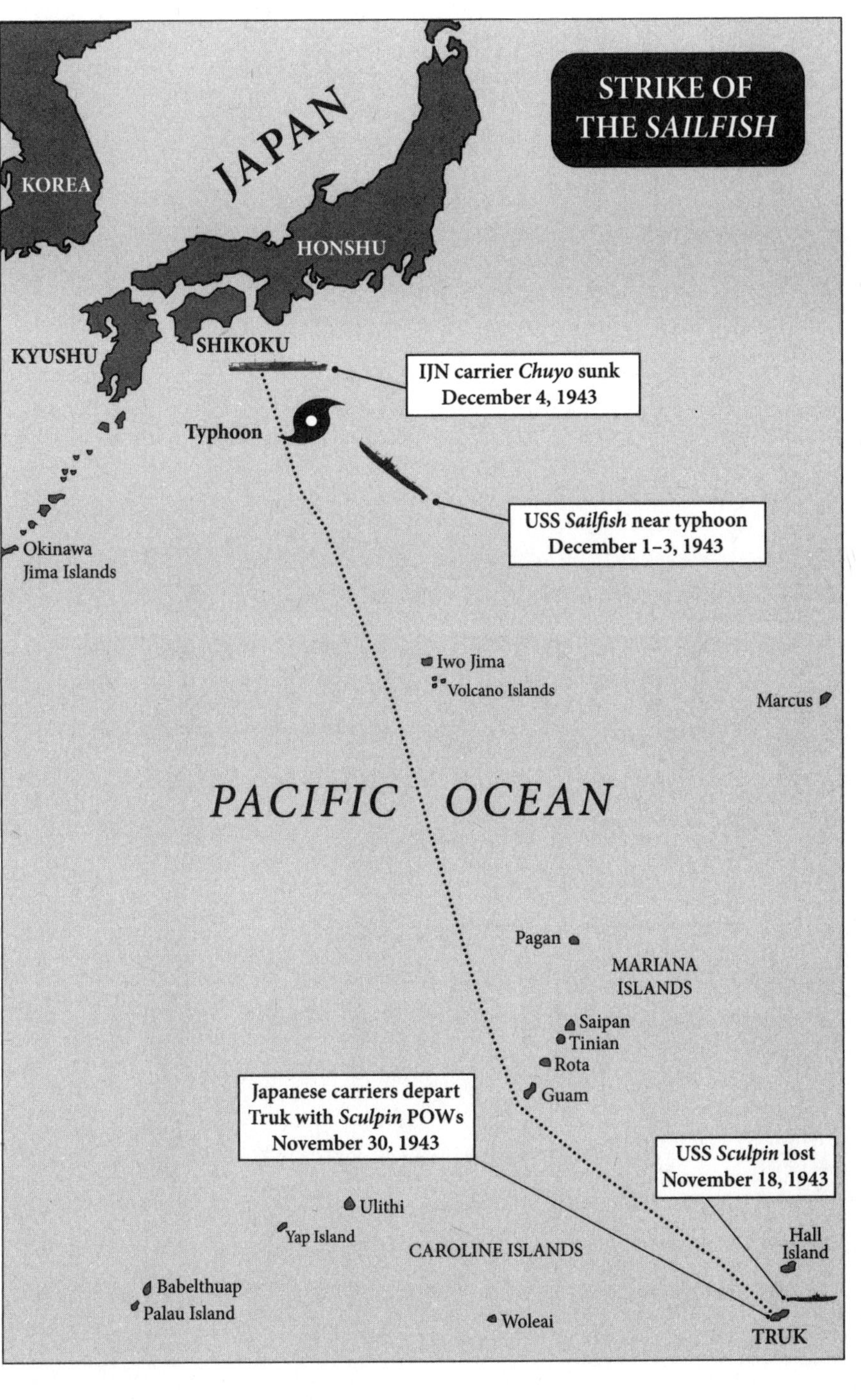

STRIKE OF THE *SAILFISH*
JAPAN
KOREA
HONSHU
KYUSHU
SHIKOKU
IJN carrier *Chuyo* sunk
December 4, 1943
Typhoon
USS *Sailfish* near typhoon
December 1–3, 1943
Okinawa
Jima Islands
Iwo Jima
Volcano Islands
Marcus
PACIFIC OCEAN
Pagan
MARIANA
ISLANDS
Saipan
Tinian
Rota
Guam
Japanese carriers depart
Truk with *Sculpin* POWs
November 30, 1943
USS *Sculpin* lost
November 18, 1943
Ulithi
Yap Island
CAROLINE ISLANDS
Hall
Island
Babelthuap
Palau Island
Woleai
TRUK

Prologue

May 23, 1939

Just off Portsmouth, New Hampshire

"The engine rooms are flooding!"

The call from Yeoman Second Class (Y2c) Charles Kuney—the battle stations talker connected via headset to other compartments throughout the ship—hit every sailor like a depth charge. The worst possible scenario was coming true. The submarine USS *Squalus* was in the process of completing a routine checkout dive off America's East Coast. Her new skipper, thirty-five-year-old Lieutenant Oliver Naquin, hoped to impress his superiors by shaving seconds off his boat's crash-dive time, the length of time it took to fully submerge his submarine.

All indications had been normal. In the control room, the vessel's watertightness was measured by an electronic board of lights known as the Christmas Tree indicator. Naquin had *Squalus* run up to full speed and gave the order to dive. Vent valves were opened to allow the icy cold water to begin flooding ballast tanks to help pull the vessel below the seas. In quick order, sailors shut down the diesel engines, closed the main induction valve, and switched on battery-powered motors. Just below the conning tower, in the control room, every red light on the Christmas Tree had switched to green, indicating all was safe to dive. Air was bled into the boat to confirm its airtightness as the ballast and bow buoyancy tanks were flooded to take her down.[1]

But as *Squalus* passed fifty feet, a blast of air pressure swept through the control room. Something had gone terribly wrong. Thousands of gallons of water rushed through the main induction air valve and began flooding the engine and maneuvering rooms. Men screamed as icy water began climbing above their knees and continued to rise. Skipper Naquin and his diving officer ordered men to blow compressed air through the ship's ballast tanks to force water back out. It was imperative that *Squalus* resurface immediately to check the potential disaster in progress.

The rush of compressed air forced enough water out of the submarine to allow her bow to briefly broach the surface, but *Squalus* had simply swallowed too much ocean. The weight of the water pouring into her engineering spaces pulled the vessel down like a mighty anchor, forcing her to slide backward into the empty depths of the Atlantic Ocean.

Men raced to slam watertight doors, but the inrushing water was too much for some compartments. Sailors fled toward the forward torpedo room, but seventeen men were drowned as the water filled the aft compartments. Other crewmen acted swiftly to securely dog down the hatches to ensure watertight integrity in their more forward compartments. Naquin shouted at electrician's mate Lloyd Maness from North Carolina to close the watertight door between the control room and the after battery.

Maness paused in swinging the three-hundred-pound steel door closed as men shouted at him to wait. Six sailors sloshed through into the control room, followed by a ship's cook who had paused long enough to peer through the glass eye port into the next flooded compartment aft. He charged through waist-high water toward the control room and was the last man from the back half of the boat to stagger in before Maness dogged down the heavy hatch.[2]

"There was no big bang when we hit the bottom," recalled electrician's mate Gerald McLees. At that moment, he had been in a three-foot-high crawl space beneath the main deck in the forward battery compartment, taking readings on his battery cells. On the surface, *Squalus* ran on four V16 diesel engines able to generate 5,500 horsepower and push the boat to a top speed of 21 knots (24 mph). Two auxiliary generators and four electric motors could produce 2,740 horsepower while submerged, these driven by two massive 126-cell batteries maintained by McLees and his fellow electricians. At 2 knots' speed, *Squalus* could operate up to forty-eight hours on battery power. At full 8.75-knot submerged speed, these batteries would be depleted in just over an hour. McLees could hear the high-pressure air system as men in the control room tried to expel water ballast to bring *Squalus* back to the surface, but she continued to settle stern first. "It was a losing battle," he remembered. McLees and others struggled to maintain footing against the sharp up angle until his submarine nestled upright on the ocean floor.[3]

By the time *Squalus* settled two hundred forty feet below the surface, skipper Naquin knew the dreadful truth. He took the phones and mouthpiece from talker Kuney, but his calls to the after engine rooms and after torpedo room went unanswered. Twenty-six of his officers and men in the after half of his submarine had drowned.

Thirty-two officers and men, plus one civilian observer, remained alive from the control room up to the forward torpedo room.

As commander of the vessel, Naquin decided it was paramount to work on saving the other half of his men. "Only one man mentioned the people aft, and I shut that off real fast," Naquin later related. "If one or two men had panicked, the whole thing might have gone up in smoke."[4]

The fight to survive and return to the surface was just beginning.

Naquin ordered gunner's mate Gene Cravens to fire one of the ship's forty distress rockets from the control room overhead. One of his officers released a bright yellow marker buoy that floated to the surface, trailing a long telephone line between the buoy and the sunken submarine. "Submarine Sunk Here. Telephone Inside" was stenciled in black letters on the bright buoy. Naquin could only hope that they would soon be found if someone spotted the exploding rocket and its cloud of red smoke.[5]

As fate would have it, good fortune would shortly arrive in the form of the sister submarine of *Squalus*, USS *Sculpin* (SS-191). Built at the Portsmouth Naval Shipyard in Kittery, Maine, the twin three-hundred-ten-foot submarines had been launched within seven weeks of each other in the summer of 1938. Both were *Sargo*-class boats, built with seven watertight compartments in addition to their conning towers. Their 11⁄16-inch steel pressure hulls made them capable of a "test depth" of two hundred fifty feet—considered to be the edge of a *Sargo*-class submarine's safe limits. This test depth was fifty feet deeper than the rating of the older *S*-class U.S. submarines, but two hundred fifty feet was a depth that many *Sargo*-class boats would greatly exceed in times of duress, such as during enemy depth charge counterattacks. In the months following their launching, the new crews of *Sculpin* and *Squalus* had lived together on base and had trained together. While off duty, the two crews played one another in softball games and their two skippers had become close friends.

Within two hours of *Squalus* failing to return to the surface from her dive, *Sculpin*'s skipper, Lieutenant Warren Wilkin, was directed to proceed to the location and conduct a search. Around 1245, as *Sculpin* neared the site, one of her officers spotted a distress rocket fired from the sunken vessel. Wilkin conned his boat toward the emergency telephone buoy and dropped anchor as his sailors pulled it on board.[6]

In *Squalus*'s forward torpedo room, Lenny de Medeiros—a muscular torpedoman third class (TM3c) of Portuguese descent—had closed the watertight door to his compartment once his submarine began flooding. During the hours that followed, he worried about the fate of two of his close friends, electrician's mates Lloyd Maness and Gerry McLees. De Medeiros spent the next hours standing watch on the marker-buoy telephone line. He and others had raised spirits as they heard the propellers of *Sculpin* arrive 243 feet overhead and halt.

Lieutenant Wilkin took the emergency phone and made a call. De Medeiros heard his voice clearly: "Hello, *Squalus*. This is *Sculpin*. What's your trouble?"[7]

De Medeiros handed the headset to Lieutenant John Nichols, who quickly relayed the disaster and the flooding on his submarine. Nichols then handed the headset to his skipper, Oliver Naquin, so he could speak with his fellow commander, Wilkin. "Hello, Wilkie," he greeted him. Naquin quickly stated that he believed a rescue diver could close the high induction valve and hook salvage lines to the flooded compartments to help bring his ship to the surface. Shortly into this conversation, *Sculpin* rose on a wave and the telephone cable—tied to a cleat on *Sculpin*—snapped. Voice communication with the sunken submarine was lost.[8]

But a massive rescue operation was already in progress. From New London, Connecticut, the naval rescue and salvage tug *Falcon* was dispatched to the location. Lieutenant Commander Charles "Swede" Momsen, who had toiled for years developing submarine escape and rescue equipment, and a team of deep-sea divers were flown in and raced to the scene in other vessels. While more rescue equipment and a diving bell were ferried to the scene, another vessel managed to drag grapnels and hook the sunken *Squalus*. During this time, survivors communicated with the rescuers on the surface by using a hammer to bang out Morse code messages. "Beating on the hull was our only means of communication," recalled electrician's mate Judson "Jud" Bland. Within eight hours of their sinking, *Squalus* sailors learned that rescue divers were en route.[9]

Captain Naquin and his thirty-two surviving comrades lay silently shivering in wait, trying to conserve energy and oxygen as the air temperature inside *Squalus* plunged into the thirties. The drama was already playing out in the press, as newspaper reporters had made their way to sea in fishing vessels to document the efforts of the ragtag armada of vessels assembled above the sunken submarine. By midday on May 24, a mighty bell-shaped rescue chamber was being lowered from the *Falcon* down to the forward deck of *Squalus*. Once the chamber was securely attached, the submarine's upper hatch was opened and rescuers passed emergency supplies to the crew. Seven survivors were helped into the rescue bell, the submarine's hatch was closed again, and a forty-five-minute ascent to the surface commenced.

Among those helped out onto *Falcon*'s deck from the first ascent was Gerry McLees, who had been sent up due to being nauseous. Shortly after the first group of survivors emerged from the bell on *Falcon*'s deck, the rescue chamber began its next descent. During the hours that followed, two more ascents were made, bringing up Lenny de Medeiros and others from the sunken *Squalus*. McLees was still on board *Falcon* when the second bell arrived on deck carrying nine more men to the surface. Among those stepping out was electrician's mate Jud Bland; McLees was still in the process of paying him for a green Plymouth coupe. "I got $250 from him, $50 down, and $50 per day," Bland remembered.[10]

As McLees happily watched his shipmate emerge from the rescue bell, he was struck with a sudden realization: *Damn, there's Jud! I'm going to have to finish paying for that damn car!*

The final rescue was plagued with difficulties, as a cable jammed, forcing *Falcon*'s crew to lower the diving bell back to the bottom of the ocean. "We started to swing and spin around," recalled machinist's mate Carl Bryson. "Some of us started wishing we were back inside the submarine."[11]

A diver cut away the shredded cable and attempted to attach a new one. But, with hours ticking away, the *Falcon* crew was ultimately forced to haul the rescue bell up by hand, praying that the final frayed cable would hold long enough to do so. The rescue bell finally broke the surface at 0038 on May 25, almost thirty-nine hours after *Squalus* had made her last dive. Emerging from the depths in the last haul to freedom were the final eight survivors, including yeoman Kuney, Bryson, gunner's mate Cravens, and skipper Oliver Naquin.[12]

The dramatic rescue played out live over millions of radios and the *Squalus* saga filled the pages of newspapers across the world. Four of the rescue bell operators and divers were sent to Washington to be decorated with Medals of Honor. Salvage efforts began immediately to raise the sunken submarine, and teams worked for fifty days to lift *Squalus* from the depths with cables and pontoons for buoyancy. The first effort on July 13, 1939, failed. The submarine rose too fast, slipping her cables and causing her dripping black nose to burst through the surface for ten seconds, with her hull number 192 clearly visible on her bow. *Squalus* shook her cables like a wounded beast and sank to the ocean floor again. The next lift three weeks later was successful, and the sub was towed into Portsmouth on September 13 and formally decommissioned two months later.

The vessel was completely overhauled during the next year, and the Navy decided to rename her to diminish her past legacy. Submariners were a superstitious lot by nature, and half the crew had perished on this boat. So, in May 1940, she became USS *Sailfish*. The name was inspired by President Franklin Roosevelt, an avid sport fisherman who had seen the award-winning photo of *Squalus* bursting to the surface during her first failed lift from the bottom. FDR thought she looked like a tethered sailfish fighting for its life. Three months later, *Sailfish* was properly recommissioned, with Lieutenant Commander Morton Mumma as her new skipper.[13]

While he had plenty of former *Squalus* sailors eager to return to service on the new *Sailfish*, he allowed only four survivors back on the boat: Gerry McLees, Lenny de Medeiros, Lloyd Maness, and Gene Cravens. Maness would be transferred off before the boat entered service for World War II, but three *Squalus* survivors would do war patrols on *Sailfish*.

With a new lease on life and a new name, *Sailfish* was destined for great accomplishments in World War II. But her crew and that of her sister submarine, *Sculpin*, would face challenges during that time that defied imagination.

ONE

Sculpin on the Warpath

June 9, 1943

George Brown felt a sudden rush of adrenaline. Peering through his binoculars, the lieutenant stared a moment longer before reaching for the sound-powered telephone on the bridge. Brown, a lean, dark-haired New Yorker making his ninth war patrol, was the submarine's officer of the deck this night.

"Captain to the bridge!" he called over the 1MC announcing system.

In less than a minute, Lieutenant Commander Lucius "Lu" Chappell scrambled up the conning tower ladder to the bridge. It was right at midnight as he eagerly swept the horizon with his own binoculars to where Lieutenant Brown was pointing. Sure enough, thanks to the clear, starlit sky, he was able to discern the distinctive shapes of a pair of enemy warships—ones that he had been anxiously expecting to encounter. They were a pair of loaded aircraft carriers, dream targets for any World War II submarine skipper.

Chappell's *Sculpin* had been directed toward this fateful rendezvous thanks to top secret U.S. intelligence efforts. In the four years that had passed since *Sculpin* had helped save half of the crew of her sister submarine, *Squalus* (now *Sailfish*), America had gone to war against Japan and the other Axis powers, and *Sculpin* was making her seventh war patrol in enemy waters. Cryptanalysis experts working with the Combat Intelligence Unit at Pearl Harbor had broken the Japanese military's code, and now routinely deciphered radio transmissions regarding their enemy's fleet movements.

Such intelligence was carefully guarded, but when appropriate, American submarines could be directed toward capital ships known to be moving toward precise locations at precise times. This data was transmitted to fleet submarines, but the contents of these so-called Ultra messages were allowed to be seen only by a boat's commanding officer and his second-in-command. When *Sculpin*'s radioman received this particular communication at 2245 on June 6, the first word decoded was "Ultra." Lieutenant Frank Alvis, the communications officer, quickly decoded the message, writing out the words on a scrap of paper that he hastily carried to skipper Lu Chappell and *Sculpin*'s executive officer (XO), Lieutenant Al Bontier.[1]

Chappell had conned his submarine toward the reported path of the Japanese carrier fleet and lain in wait through late evening of June 8. Now, hours later, as the night rolled into the morning of June 9, Lieutenant Brown had the prized carriers in sight. The crew, unaware of the source of the intelligence that put their boat directly in the enemy's path, was excited at their prospects.

The two warships *Sculpin* was stalking were the twenty-thousand-ton escort carriers *Unyo* and *Chuyo*, which had departed Truk Island on June 5 bound for Yokosuka, Japan, in Tokyo Bay. *Sculpin* found them making 19 knots on course 330 degrees, in company with an escorting destroyer, *Hagikaze*. The two carriers were making one of their many ferrying runs between Truk and the Japanese mainland to deliver supplies, aircraft, and troops. By the early-morning hours of June 9, the sister flattops were just hours away from reaching safe anchorage.[2]

Sculpin raced forward at emergency flank speed, her four diesel engines roaring to push the boat across the smooth black sea.

For some, it was like buck fever—the anticipation a hunter experiences before his or her first kill. Riding on board *Sculpin* for this patrol was Lieutenant Commander Ignatius "Pete" Galatin, an experienced submariner who was slated to take command of his own boat. Prior to doing so, such officers often made one run as a prospective commanding officer (PCO) to observe the attack procedures of a successful crew. As such, Galatin would monitor and assist Chappell's officers on this run, and he hurried to the bridge with Chappell and Bontier. Galatin was so excited that his knees were jerking up and down.[3]

Officer of the deck (OOD) George Brown quickly relayed to his senior officers that *Sculpin*'s radarmen had solidly locked onto the Japanese carriers. The distance was a range of 11,500 yards, and a third vessel—appearing to be either a light cruiser or a large destroyer—was the only other ship in company with the important target ships. Brown directed his three lookouts, perched on their platforms atop *Sculpin*'s conning tower, to confine their looks to their respective sectors to keep watch for any other unseen enemy escort ships.[4]

Chappell relayed orders below via his battle stations telephone talker, Yeoman First Class Aaron Reese. Both torpedo rooms were ordered to make ready their war fish, and the battle stations tracking party was called to the conning tower and control rooms below. Every member of the crew stood ready at their respective positions for the approach and potential attack.

Thus far in the war, no other American submarine had managed to sink a Japanese aircraft carrier. A number of opportunities had presented themselves. At the Battle of Midway in June 1942, the old *Nautilus* had stalked and attacked the crippled Japanese carrier *Kaga*. Pounded by U.S. dive-bombers, *Kaga* was dead in the water when *Nautilus* made her strike. But American torpedoes were notoriously faulty in the first year of the war, often running eleven feet deeper than their intended settings. Even worse, the Mark 14 torpedoes had magnetic exploders that were prone to set off a detonation prematurely, allowing precious target ships to escape unscathed.

Further, even when the magnetic exploders worked as designed, many torpedoes failed to detonate upon impacting a ship due to poor design of the contact exploder's firing pins. Such was the case with the torpedoes fired by *Nautilus*. The first malfunctioned and failed to leave its tube. Two ran erratically to miss astern and ahead of the target. The fourth torpedo slammed into *Kaga* amidships without exploding and broke in half, leaving its air flask and tail assembly bobbing in the water.[5]

Now, with his own chance to sink an enemy carrier in hand, Lu Chappell rang up emergency flank speed, hoping to chase down the enemy fleet, which was moving at a healthy speed of almost 20 knots. The closest he could get was seven thousand yards. Carriers *Chuyo* and *Unyo* were at extreme range for a torpedo attack, but such opportunities were so rare that it was deemed worth the expense. Lieutenant Corwin Mendenhall, manning *Sculpin*'s old Mark I torpedo data computer (TDC) down below in the control room, calculated that the torpedo run would be 7,800 yards. Mendenhall knew that his target would continue to pull away as the torpedoes approached.[6]

Chappell had torpedomen set their Mark 14s to run at slow speed (31.5 knots) in order to reach as far as nine thousand yards. At 0016 on

June 9 (2316 on June 8 in Tokyo time), he gave the order: "Fire one!" Waiting seconds between each launch, he fired three more torpedoes, all out of *Sculpin*'s forward tubes. But just thirty seconds after firing them, one exploded prematurely only three hundred yards from the sub.

In desperation, Chappell swung *Sculpin* for a stern shot, but it was too late. The Japanese carriers were quickly opening up the range and did not offer him a fortuitous course change for a prayer shot. About eight minutes after firing, Chappell's crew heard three explosions and prayed they were hits. But radar continued to track the carrier fleet out to 14,300 yards. The bridge watch saw considerable signaling by lights between the ships immediately after the explosions.[7]

For Chappell, it was the second time in two consecutive patrols that his *Sculpin* had fired at and missed an aircraft carrier. Such opportunities for a sub skipper were few and far between, and it would be many months before a U.S. submarine would finally succeed in downing an Imperial Japanese Navy flattop.

As fate would have it, *Sculpin* and her sister submarine, *Sailfish*, had not seen the last of sister carriers *Chuyo* and *Unyo*.

* * *

Lu Chappell continued his aggressive assaults with *Sculpin* during the week that followed. On June 14, he sighted a convoy of five ships and fired four torpedoes at the largest merchant vessel. Once again, one of his Mark 14s exploded prematurely, but one torpedo did hit his target forward of amidships. *Sculpin* was forced down by a charging escort, eliminating any further attempts to hit this convoy.

With nothing better than Japanese fishing vessels in sight during the next few days, Chappell finally elected to work out his gun crews on June 19 against a sampan-type patrol boat. *Sculpin* burst onto the surface at 0325 and her gunners raced for their weapons as the foamy white seas receded. Twenty minutes later, Chappell ordered his men to open fire as the range narrowed to eight hundred yards. Within a quarter hour, the sampan was shot to ribbons, its deckhouse a mass of brilliant orange flames.

Chappell cleared the area and patrolled submerged through the day. During the late afternoon, he approached another seventy-five-ton fishing sampan and surfaced at 1625 to conduct another gun attack. In the next hour, *Sculpin* made three firing passes. By 1730, the sampan was engulfed in flames and its afterdeck was awash. Chappell decided to send a boarding party onto the vessel in hopes of salvaging its machine guns and perhaps even some important papers.

The five-man boarding party—led by Lieutenants George Brown and Joe Defrees—waited on *Sculpin*'s bow, ready to jump across as the submarine snuggled alongside the burning sampan. To junior officer Mendenhall, the group looked "like pirates with knives tucked in their belts and .45-caliber pistols in their hands." Each man had to time his jump across due to a long swell. Defrees, being a short man, mistimed his jump and splashed into the ocean among Japanese men who were clutching at timbers. Fearful of *Sculpin* gunners, who were taking pot-shots at the Japanese, Defrees hollered, "Don't shoot me! Don't shoot me!"[8]

Brown's party encountered two Japanese men armed with rifles in the forecastle and quickly shot them down. The only survivor in the water refused to accept assistance while Defrees swam for *Sculpin*'s stern and scrambled back onto his boat. Brown's raiders returned after a harrowing ten-minute search of the vessel. During that time, ammunition exploded in the sampan's bridge house machine gun and in its ready ammunition locker. Raging fires prevented the men from recovering any papers of value, but they did note the name *Ibarakiken Daiichi*

Miyashoma Maru painted on its bow. The party returned to *Sculpin* with two rifles and one wooden dummy machine gun as booty.[9]

Chappell found other merchant ships that were worthy of torpedoes during the week that followed, but his poor luck with faulty war fish prevailed. Yet another premature explosion on June 22 allowed *Sculpin*'s targeted freighter to dodge the other three Mark 14s. Chappell wrote in his patrol report that he was "thoroughly discouraged by the fatally unsatisfactory performance of torpedoes," and he sent a report to Vice Admiral Charles Lockwood—commander of all U.S. submarines in the Pacific Theater, or "ComSubPac"—requesting permission to deactivate the exploders on his remaining weapons.[10]

By the time *Sculpin* returned to Midway Island on July 4, Chappell had fired all twenty of his torpedoes. He had obtained only two direct hits on enemy shipping and had suffered three premature torpedo explosions. *Sculpin* was credited with damage to two freighters and the sinking of two sampans with her guns. The faulty torpedo performance experienced by *Sculpin* was a serious concern that had been voiced by numerous other skippers.

Charlie Lockwood took on the task of exploring the issue during the late summer and early fall of 1943. A World War I veteran, Lockwood had commanded five submarines of his own prior to ascending to the role of Commander, Submarines Pacific in early 1943. One of his staff members was Captain Swede Momsen, who had orchestrated the *Squalus* crew rescue in 1939. Momsen directed the submarine *Muskallunge* to fire torpedoes into the sheer cliffs of Kahoolawe; the smallest of the eight Hawaiian Islands was uninhabited, and currently being used as a bombing range. Divers recovered one failed Mark 14, whose nose was crushed although its firing pin had failed to detonate its explosives. Other tests, including dropping warheads from a crane onto a steel plate, proved to Lockwood that his boats were going to sea with torpedoes incapable of exploding on a regular basis when they struck target ships solidly. Warheads that struck targets at 45-degree angles, however, failed only half the time. ComSubPac's staff set to work on reengineering the faulty firing pin design, one that had allowed countless enemy ships to escape during the first twenty-one months of war.[11]

When *Sculpin* was ready to head back to sea on July 22 for her eighth war patrol, the Mark 14 torpedo issue was still months from its remedy. Skipper Lu Chappell had a different challenge at the moment. The emergency deck hatch leading topside from the crew's after battery compartment had developed a leak when the boat was deeply submerged. Repairs had been made at Midway while alongside the submarine tender *Sperry*, but when *Sculpin* submerged to test depth this day outside of the atoll, the hatch continued to allow water to spew into the boat.

Sculpin returned alongside *Sperry* that afternoon and repairs commenced again. The following morning, the boat put to sea again and made another dive to test depth. "After battery hatch leaked at all depths," the skipper wrote in his patrol report. The crew worked to isolate the leak, but could not find the source. Chappell returned to the surface, set course for Midway again, and radioed the base commander that he recommended the flanged joint simply be welded.[12]

Repairmen removed the upper hatch trunk for closer inspection and found cracks at the weld between the upper trunk and its flange. The remedy for the time being was simply to replace the upper trunk with a flat iron plate bolted to the lower flange, welding it in place to ensure watertightness. This hatch would simply remain out of service until *Sculpin* could return Stateside for a proper yard overhaul. In the event of an emergency at sea, all hands in the aft sections of the boat would have to make their way forward to escape.

With the work tested and complete by July 25, *Sculpin* finally stood out from Midway at 0830 for another dive to test depth. This time, the sealed hatch proved to be watertight, so the skipper surfaced at 1000 and proceeded in company with her sister boat, *Sailfish*, under cover of air escort. *Sailfish* and *Sculpin* parted ways at 1230 and *Sculpin*'s eighth war patrol was underway.

★ ★ ★

"I'll take the first boat that comes in."

Those were the words twenty-one-year-old Bill Cooper had told the sub base yeoman at Midway. The first to arrive in early July 1943 had been *Sailfish*, but in the standard shuffling of personnel between patrols, Cooper was ultimately assigned to *Sculpin*. After three runs on *Greenling*, he had reached the rank of quartermaster third class, before being shuffled off to the relief crew. He was itching to return to submarine combat.[13]

Raised in Chattanooga, Tennessee, as the middle of seven children, Bill Cooper had enlisted in the Navy on December 31, 1941, shortly after the Pearl Harbor attack. He had worked at Kay's Ice Cream in Chattanooga since age fourteen, but had decided to go into the life insurance business in the fall of 1941. As he wrestled with the cost of obtaining his insurance license, Bill instead suddenly found himself among many young Tennesseans who were eager to enlist and fight the Japanese. "Some of 'em I don't think had ever even been to town before," Cooper recalled. After boot camp and submarine training, he had been assigned as a relief crewman on the sub tender *Fulton*, which operated from Pearl Harbor during early 1942. Shortly after the Battle of Midway, Cooper made three runs on *Greenling*, during which time his boat was credited with sinking six Japanese ships. Afterward, he served briefly on the submarine *Halibut*, but had since spent months as a relief crewman again on the tender *Sperry*.[14]

Cooper was pleased to report on board *Sculpin*, where he assumed the duties of assistant navigator with the executive officer, Bontier. Soon after *Sculpin* departed on patrol, he was informed by a Bureau of Personnel dispatch that he had attained the rating of quartermaster second class. Cooper, a curly-haired, smiling man of faith who avoided the heavy drinking some of his shipmates enjoyed while on liberty, soon became a solid member of *Sculpin*'s torpedo-attack team.[15]

Cooper's new boat began her patrol off the southeast coast of Nansei Shoto and made her first torpedo attack on August 9. Skipper Chappell dived to avoid an escort, heard one torpedo hit, and returned to the surface a half hour later. His target ship, the 3,183-ton freighter *Sekko Maru*, was badly hit, down by the bow, and in the process of abandoning ship. Escorts again forced *Sculpin* deep, but when she returned to the surface, Chappell witnessed his target sink before he had time to fire more torpedoes.

During the following week, *Sculpin* sighted a number of patrol boats, fishing boats, and sampans, none worthy of a torpedo. During the early-morning hours of August 16, while running on the surface near Formosa, Chappell's bridge crew spotted a small ship coming out of a rain squall. Chappell ordered full speed and tried to outmaneuver the small vessel. Moments later, the Japanese opened fire with point-detonating ammunition, forcing *Sculpin* to dive.

Sculpin made another torpedo attack the following morning on a small freighter, but her torpedoes failed to explode. That evening, Chappell began tracking another small ship on the surface until he realized he was on the tail of a patrol boat. He turned *Sculpin* to evade, but quickly found two enemy anti-submarine vessels approaching. "Both patrols in hot pursuit," Chappell wrote. At full speed, his submarine was able to open the distance on the southern patrol boat, but the other to his westward began gaining on him.[16]

Because of brilliant moonlight, there was little chance of getting away. As the western patrol boat closed the distance, he suddenly opened fire. Cooper was on the bridge, hoping for a fast dive. Instead, his skipper casually stood his ground, relating a story in his soft Georgia drawl of the Philippines before the war as gunfire boomed in his wake. Cooper became alarmed as shell explosions began landing closer to *Sculpin*, and he was much relieved when Chappell finally dived ship to ride out the ensuing depth charge attack.[17]

On August 21 and September 1, *Sculpin* fired spreads of torpedoes at Japanese merchant ships, but there were no explosions. Her officers were convinced that in each case, at least one dud torpedo struck their target. On the latter attack, Chappell actually watched one of his torpedoes slam into his target and fail to explode. Water was thrown as high as the main deck rail, just aft of the center of the target. Chappell was so convinced of success that he shouted, "Hit!" before he realized there was no ensuing explosion.[18]

Sculpin returned to Midway on September 17, her crew thoroughly frustrated with the performance of their torpedoes. The Submarine Force commander, Captain Leon Blair, credited *Sculpin* with one ship sunk and added, "Although touchdowns only are counted, had the torpedoes exploded when they hit the target, no doubt the kill for this patrol would have been much larger."[19]

From Midway, *Sculpin* was ordered back to Pearl Harbor for a lengthy overhaul during early October. During that time, Chappell was detached after having commanded the boat since the start of the war. Whereas most skippers were reassigned after five command patrols, he had made eight. Chappell wished his crew well, and departed with prized keepsakes in the form of the ship's bell and a hand-sewn battle flag. Exec Al Bontier also departed to assume his own first command, of the celebrated *Seawolf.*

Bill Cooper enjoyed liberty ashore in Hawaii during the yard overhaul. *Sculpin*'s sister boat, *Sailfish*, had arrived in Pearl Harbor one day behind *Sculpin*, and both crews had time to catch up on their recent events. The *Sculpin* crew learned that *Sailfish* would also have a new skipper coming on board, but for different reasons. The *Sailfish* crew was demoralized from enduring a patrol in which their commanding officer shied away from making torpedo attacks.

Sweeping changes were in store for both *Sculpin* and *Sailfish* before they departed Pearl Harbor on their next patrols.

TWO

Running from Targets

August 5, 1943
Near the Bonin Islands

Bill Dillon was sleeping soundly when the duty messenger nudged him. It was shortly before midnight, and he had been dozing for only a few hours. He was used to the routine: four hours on and eight hours off duty. But during those eight hours off, he stood a variety of duties. As a member of his submarine's radio gang, Dillon had spent some of the evening hours in the radio shack, a tiny compartment at the aft end of the control room. There, he copied messages off the "Fox schedule"—the nightly encrypted messages sent from Vice Admiral Charlie Lockwood's staff at Pearl Harbor to all submarines.

It took a special skill to decipher the five-digit coded letters that came across the radio waves. Dillon and other radiomen on *Sailfish* copied the digits they heard, even as more characters were already being received. The copied Fox schedule code then required it be translated into coherent phrases by the submarine's communications officer,

Ensign Irving Earl Wetmore, using a special electric code machine (ECM). This device, known as a Sigaba, resembled a typewriter that utilized three banks of five rotors to encipher every character that radiomen like Dillon copied. Using the proper code key of the day, Wetmore was able to type in the code characters and produce the message in plain language, which was then delivered to the ship's skipper.

Following his stint in the radio shack, Dillon had stepped through a watertight hatch opening. He moved aft, past the tiny ship's galley and through the crew's mess to reach the crew's berthing quarters. He crawled into his assigned bunk, the first one on the left side in the middle. Sleeping was a luxury on a World War II submarine, and the *Sailfish* crew practiced "hot bunking," a system wherein men rotated turns sleeping in the same canvas bunk when off duty. With only three dozen bunks stacked three high in the main crew's quarters, there were simply not enough berths to go around for sixty-nine enlisted men. Although some two dozen men slept in either the chief petty officers' quarters or the two torpedo rooms, the crew's quarters still required hot bunking.

Hours later, he was being shaken awake to stand his four-hour shift on the radar gear. Dillon shuffled forward to the crew's mess area and grabbed a quick cup of coffee before moving forward to the control room. He climbed the steel rungs of the ladder into the conning tower and assumed his position at the radar gear. His job duty was a specialized one, consumed with operating one of the newest technological advances in submarine warfare.

In 1942, the U.S. sub fleet had seen the introduction of two different radar sets: the SD air search radar and the SJ surface search unit. "The SD set was omni-directional," Dillon recalled. "It could give you the range to a target but not the azimuth, or horizontal direction of a compass bearing." The SD radar, operating on frequencies close to those used by Japanese radio and radar gear, was highly susceptible to direction finding, a tactic used by enemy forces for anti-submarine attacks. *Sailfish*'s newest radar gear, the SJ surface search unit, provided more precise input on the targets it contacted.[1]

Dillon was one of two radar specialists on board who had been specifically trained in the operation of such highly classified radar gear. Watch duty consisted of a four-hour shift monitoring both the SD and SJ sets for contacts. The newer SJ utilized an "A" scope for measuring range, which was displayed on a planned position indicator (PPI) viewing scope in *Sailfish*'s conning tower. In ideal conditions and weather, the SJ could detect a single merchant ship at roughly 17,500 yards (nearly ten miles), and a small warship at 10,500 yards (about six miles), although much larger ships and multiple-ship convoys could be detected at greater distances.[2]

The amplified return signals by radar were shown on the crude PPI display scope in the form of green vertical lines, which were known as "pips." The display pips spread out across the tube according to the time they were received. Most nights, the PPI scope remained clear while *Sailfish* was on war patrol. But Dillon remained vigilant through his watch, and three hours into it, he had a target.

"Radar contact! Range 4,000 yards," Dillon announced. "Call the skipper."

A minute later, Lieutenant Commander William Robert Lefavour appeared in the conning tower. Only weeks prior, on July 17, Dillon and his fellow crewmen had stood on deck for the change-of-command ceremony as Lefavour read his orders and became *Sailfish*'s fourth wartime skipper. Unlike the captain he relieved, thirty-three-year-old Lefavour had little wartime experience. He had made only one war patrol, and that had been as an observer in the role of PCO on *Sawfish*.

Prior to that, he had been serving as the communications officer on Rear Admiral Freeland Daubin's staff in the Atlantic and had previously commanded the destroyer *Brooks*.[3]

In his heavy New England accent, Lefavour asked Dillon for the latest update on radar. The enemy contact was now less than four thousand yards away and appeared to be closing. Lefavour scrambled up the ladder to the bridge and asked his lookouts whether they had a visual on the target ship through their binoculars.

"No, sir," a sailor replied. "Nothing yet."

Lefavour called down on the voice-powered telephone to the control room, ordering his helmsman to put the target astern of *Sailfish*. He called for full speed ahead, and the boat's mighty diesels responded accordingly. Within minutes, *Sailfish* began opening up the distance from the unknown vessel.

From below, Dillon reported that the pip was similar to one that would be obtained on a submarine, and that strong radar interference could be detected on the unknown vessel's bearing. As the range opened up to 6,100 yards, Dillon and fellow radar operator Frank Dieterich were able to synchronize to the pulse rate of the other ship's radar, an indication of the likelihood of another SJ set. "Concluded contact was on a friendly submarine," Lefavour wrote in his patrol report.[4]

Some World War II skippers might have more aggressively stalked this unseen ship to determine if it was indeed another American submarine or instead a Japanese sub or even a small, radar-equipped warship. But Bill Lefavour, just two weeks into his first command patrol, was content to ignore the suggestions of his junior officers to more doggedly investigate this contact. *Sailfish*'s SJ radar continued to pick up intermittent interference from the other ship until dawn, when Lefavour dived his boat for the day and resumed course toward his patrol station. His twenty torpedoes remained unused.

Bill Dillon hoped his new skipper would assume a more offensive attitude against the next blip that appeared on his PPI scope.

★ ★ ★

When Dillon was first assigned to *Sailfish* in January 1943, three and a half years had passed since the tragic sinking of the former *Squalus*. Raised from the depths and repaired, *Squalus* had been recommissioned as *Sailfish* in May 1940.

Oliver Naquin, the surviving skipper of *Squalus*, had petitioned to President Roosevelt that his shipmates who so desired be allowed to return to submarine service. As for his former boat, he was chagrined to find that the new *Sailfish* skipper, Lieutenant Commander Morton Mumma, was haunted by the *Squalus* saga and so superstitious that he blacklisted Naquin from setting foot on her. Naquin believed in luck, and that even when one had a reversal in life, it had the potential to turn out for the best. He returned to duty in surface ships, and was serving as the engineering officer of the battleship *California* when Pearl Harbor was attacked and his ship was sunk. In 1942, he was awarded the Bronze Star for navigating his cruiser *New Orleans* back to port after she lost a hundred fifty feet of her bow to a Japanese torpedo. Lucky Naquin would spend thirty-four years in naval service before retiring as a rear admiral.[5]

Mort Mumma had forbidden the use of the name *Squalus* again, leading some to instead refer to their ship as "Squailfish." This term was just as quickly dismissed when Mumma threatened to court-martial anyone heard using it.

Sailfish's first war patrol under Mumma in December 1941 had been less than stellar. He attacked a pair of Japanese destroyers and fired two torpedoes from a mere five hundred yards' distance as they charged toward his *Sailfish*. As Mumma took his boat deep to evade,

Sailfish was rocked by a heavy explosion fifteen seconds after his torpedoes had been launched. Although the blast was likely the result of a premature torpedo detonation or an enemy depth charge, Mumma mistakenly decided that he had hit and likely sunk one of the destroyers. In the ensuing vicious depth charge attack, Mumma suffered a nervous breakdown.[6]

He turned command of the boat over to his executive officer and locked himself in his stateroom. Once his XO was able to send a radio dispatch that stated "commanding officer breaking down," *Sailfish* was ordered back to the sub base in Manila. There, Mumma was relieved of command and *Sailfish* was handed over to a new skipper, Lieutenant Commander Dick Voge, whose own boat had been destroyed weeks earlier by Japanese bombing attacks on Manila. During his four patrols in command, Voge proved to be competent and more aggressive than Mumma. On *Sailfish*'s third run, Voge fired four torpedoes at a target he deemed to be the Japanese aircraft carrier *Kaga*. Two hits were obtained and the ship went down, but Voge was mistaken on her identity. Rather than *Kaga*, his victim was instead the 6,440-ton aircraft ferry *Kamogawa Maru*—still a prized kill.

During the fall of 1943, *Sailfish* made two more war patrols, now under Lieutenant Commander John Raymond "Dinty" Moore, an intelligent Tennessean who had amassed a successful record while commanding his previous boat, *S-44*. Among his three kills on *S-44* had been the 8,800-ton Japanese heavy cruiser *Kako*, the first major combatant ship lost to U.S. submarines in the war. But Moore's first two runs in command of *Sailfish* were not successful. Postwar analysis failed to credit him with any sinkings.[7]

Worn down from a solid year at sea against the enemy, *Sailfish* was sent to the Mare Island Naval Shipyard in California for a complete overhaul in January 1943. Significant modifications took place during the months that followed, including the installation of two vapor compression stills to provide additional fresh water while on patrol. *Sailfish*'s 3-inch deck cannon was moved from aft to forward of the conning tower, and twin 20mm antiaircraft guns were installed on the bridge. But most important to Dinty Moore was the addition of an SJ radar set, affording him much greater precision in tracking enemy vessels both day and night than his older, omnidirectional SD air search radar gear had provided.[8]

Radioman Third Class (RM3c) Bill Dillon had orders to join *Sailfish* to help run both the SD set and the new SJ gear. Before permanently reporting on board his new ship, Dillon was consumed with completing an advanced radar training school that spanned late January and the majority of February 1943. His electronics schooling took place on Treasure Island, an artificial island built in San Francisco Bay during the late 1930s to hold the 1939 Golden Gate International Exposition. Connected by a nine-hundred-foot causeway to Yerba Buena Island, Treasure Island and the land adjacent to it comprised only 576 acres.

During 1942, the U.S. Navy took control of this man-made isle and commissioned it Naval Station Treasure Island, making it a bustling electronics and radio communications training school. There, seventeen-year-old Dillon spent weeks living on the cramped base, his days filled with countless classroom hours of training on how to operate, dismantle, repair, and rebuild both the SJ and SD radar sets. The knowledge he gained at the school would give him a leg up on other sailors manning the newest technology on the boats for tracking enemy targets. He was a long way from his home in rural Pennsylvania, and Dillon's world was changing fast.

William Joseph Dillon had been born on September 6, 1924, in a modest suburban home in Turtle Creek, Pennsylvania, a town of about twelve thousand just east of Pittsburgh. He was already well adapted to cramped living, having shared two bedrooms with eleven siblings in his youth. Brothers Jack, Bob, Bill, Bernard, Tom, Jim, and Charles resided in one bedroom. The older boys slept in a large bed while the younger kids slept on wooden cots. Their five sisters slept in the other bedroom. It was the Great Depression, and the Dillon kids appreciated what they had.[9]

Bill's father, John Henry Dillon, who worked at Westinghouse in nearby East Pittsburgh, was a staunch believer in his fellow man. He risked his career to help form one of the first salaried-employee unions to fight for fair pay and better benefits. Bill's mother, the former Mary Ellen O'Donnell, was a dedicated housewife who worked diligently at raising a dozen kids, preparing their daily meals, baking eleven loaves of bread every other day, and tending to countless details that kept their family fully prepared. Beggars came to the door of the Dillon house, and Mary Ellen always had something for them.[10]

Bill's mother passed away from surgical complications shortly after her youngest daughter, Marilyn, was born. His eldest sister, Eleanor, sacrificed her youth to help raise her younger siblings while her father worked to keep food on the table, still finding time to coach the softball team that his son Bill played on. There was never extra money for a meal at a restaurant, and John Dillon also served as his family's barber. During his youth, Bill made money by caddying with brothers Jack and Bob, and each became crack golfers in their own right. Through the Great Depression, young, nonprivileged men like Bill—later dubbed the "Greatest Generation"—defined themselves through hard work, earning every opportunity they received. "Everyone in this country was united in doing one thing, and one thing only," Dillon recalled. "That was to get the country back to work."

Although an average-sized man at five foot six and 134 pounds, Bill Dillon was a rugged athlete who lettered in high school track and football. He became an accomplished right halfback, though he proved to be more nimble at avoiding tackles than in handling blocking duties. His Union High School team in Turtle Creek went undefeated in 1941. During a key game against their rival Homestead, Pennsylvania, football team, Dillon scored two touchdowns in a driving rainstorm and was nicknamed the "Flash" by the *Pittsburgh Post-Gazette*.[11]

With America swept into World War II, Bill dropped out of high school in 1942 before ever reaching his senior year. He had decided to enlist in the U.S. Navy upon turning seventeen on September 6, largely motivated by the death of one of his close high school friends killed in service on Guadalcanal. His older brother Bob was already in training with the Army as Bill shipped out to boot camp. He was disillusioned to find that his first month's pay of twenty-one dollars had to be used to buy all of his basic gear, underclothing, duffel bag, and toiletries.

Following basic, Dillon went through RCA radio school in New York City. His superiors—amazed that he could read code as fast as it was transmitted—tried to convince him to go to work in a nonmilitary role with a classified organization. But Dillon turned down this offer, as he had made up his mind that he wanted to volunteer for submarine service. *I'm going into service in one piece,* he theorized. *If I come back, I want to be in one piece.*

His subsequent three months of training at the Basic Enlisted Submarine School in Groton, Connecticut, were intensive. The program was presided over by Chief Torpedoman (CTM) Charlie Spritz, a former Bronx policeman, a veteran master diver, and the Navy's version of a Marine master sergeant.[12] Spritz was tough on any recruit who failed to perform, leaving many to hate their new world of "Spritz's Navy." But many of those who survived Submarine School would later respect the discipline and teamwork that Spritz had instilled in them.

For Dillon, the toughest challenge was making the emergency submerged ascent from the bottom of New London's hundred-foot submarine escape tower. Students started in a pressurized chamber that was slowly flooded to armpit level on most men. Dillon and his fellow students, each wearing a Momsen lung, put on spring-loaded nose clips and began the slow climb up an ascending line toward the top of the 240,000-gallon tank. Dillon wrapped his feet around the line and climbed upward. At several points, each escapee had to pause at a series of knots in the line and count to ten while breathing in and out of the lung to decompress the air in their bodies. Halfway up, he struggled to "crack," or equalize, the pressure in his ears. *I'm not flunking this course!* he thought as the pressure in his ears became piercingly painful. *I want to be on submarines!* Finally able to crack his ears from the pressure, Dillon passed the test and proceeded.

Assigned to *Sailfish* in January, Radioman Third Class (RM3c) Dillon was first sent for advanced radar training at Treasure Island before he could settle onto his new submarine. When he formally reported on board his boat, it was February 28, 1943, and Commander Dinty Moore's *Sailfish* was still in the midst of her intensive overhaul at Mare Island. Among the dozen other new enlisted men coming on board this day was Seaman Second Class (S2c) Edwin Karl Frederick Keller, a twenty-one-year-old who hailed from southern New Jersey.

The tall, 175-pound sailor possessed a booming voice that caused some of his comrades to dub him "Whispering Ed." Raised by his aunt after losing both parents early in his life, Keller had enlisted in the U.S. Navy in 1942. Like Dillon, he had gone through basic training and survived Spritz's Navy—submarine school at New London. Upon completion, he and other men received orders to travel cross-country by train to California for assignments to the boats. En route, Keller became friends with another second class seaman named Tom Brown, who hailed from Philadelphia. Keller had relatives in Philly, and the two found that they had run around in the same places at times in their youth.[13]

At the Mare Island Naval Shipyard, Brown was assigned on February 15 to the submarine *Sculpin*. Two weeks later, Keller received orders to report on board *Sailfish*, still under overhaul beside *Sculpin* in the yards. "She was all tore up," Keller recalled of *Sailfish*. "She didn't look very pretty." Countless hoses for water, air, welding, and other repairs snaked through her open hatches as yard workers loaded new batteries into the boat. Keller was eager to join a submarine family, even though he heard stories that his new *Sailfish* was the "ill-fated" former *Squalus*. Not one to dwell on the past, Keller optimistically engaged himself in the daily routines of prepping his boat for its next war patrol.

By early April 1943, the veteran members of the crew who had been allowed to take leaves back home had returned, and Moore took *Sailfish* out for two days of sea trials. Ensured that all was in order, he headed his boat out from California on April 22, bound for Pearl Harbor and another war patrol in the Pacific. By this time, Bill Dillon had become intimately familiar with *Sailfish*'s sonar gear, radio equipment, SD radar, and her newly installed SJ set. It was a far cry from the electronics he had trained on in the old R-boats and S-boats at sub school. "Whereas everything had been manual on the S-boats, *Sailfish* had hydraulics," Dillon recalled. "It was like a fleet boat."[14]

The newer "fleet submarines," designed to operate as adjuncts to the Navy's main battle fleet, were larger, stronger, and more heavily armed. *Gato*-class submarines, which were commissioned into service beginning in late 1941, were 311 feet in length—five feet longer than *Sailfish*. *Gato*-class boats sported six forward torpedo tubes versus only four in the older *Sargo*-class boats. They were loaded with two dozen torpedoes instead of twenty, and stronger hulls pushed their test depth from two hundred fifty feet to three hundred feet.

Dillon's radio gang was a tight bunch. *Sailfish*'s senior operator was Chief Radioman (CRM) Ray Doritty, who had made all seven prior patrols and hailed from Dillon's home-state area in Pennsylvania. Radioman First Class Bob Johnson, a tall, quiet Californian who had also been on board *Sailfish* since the start of the war, spent considerable time training young Dillon. "Even under the most stressful situations, Johnson always remained calm and collected," Dillon recalled.

The only other new man in the communications group was Radio Technician Second Class (RT2c) Frank Dieterich, who joined *Sailfish* at the last minute on April 22, fresh from the Treasure Island radar school. At age thirty-eight, Dieterich became the oldest man on the boat. Prior to enlisting in the Navy, he had been a self-employed film director in Los Angeles. Like Dillon, he would also be making his first war patrol. Together, the two freshly schooled radarmen would prove to be an efficient team.

Another of the new hands, Ed Keller, was striking for an electrician's mate rating. En route to Pearl Harbor, he stood a variety of watches, and was assigned occasionally to topside lookout duty. As *Sailfish* made her final approach to the Hawaiian Islands one afternoon, Keller was standing on the cigarette deck, sweeping the horizon with his binoculars as an after lookout. In the distance, he noted a four-engine U.S. Army B-24 Liberator bomber circling far astern. "I reported him and they said to keep an eye on him," Keller recalled.[15]

Although *Sailfish* was flying her U.S. ensign, the plane turned and began coming in. The officer of the deck ordered the duty quartermaster to flash recognition signals, but the Liberator crew had apparently decided they had found an enemy submarine. "As he came over the top, the bomb bay doors opened and he dropped two bombs," Keller recalled. "They straddled us forward." Fortunately, the bombs were only close enough to rattle the nerves of the *Sailfish* crew. The anger felt by skipper Moore regarding the "friendly fire" bombing attack, as Keller later heard, was soon vented toward the Army aviators ashore in Hawaii.

Upon reaching Pearl's sub base on April 30, *Sailfish* underwent additional Navy yard work for nearly two weeks to refit her stern torpedo tubes, make repairs to her TDC, and overhaul her No. 2 auxiliary engine. For Dillon, the extra time in port allowed him the chance to get his first liberties in Hawaii. "We young single guys believed the stories of guys who had been to Hawaii that the Hawaiian women wore no tops," Dillon recalled. "We were sorely disappointed when we found they did."[16]

Although not a big drinker, Dillon went ashore with several buddies who managed to convince him to drink enough of a seemingly harmless clear liquor called vodka to produce ill effects. "I passed out and they carried me back to the boat," he remembered. "But submariners can be real sons-of-bitches. They threw me in the captain's quarters."

Lieutenant Commander Moore, fully aware of the fun that enlisted men liked to have on liberty, did not reprimand young Dillon. Upon finding the radioman passed out in the skipper's bunk, Moore simply told one of his chief petty officers, "Get him the hell out of here!"

Dillon's poor luck continued just days later. Being from Pennsylvania and unaccustomed to the strength of the Hawaiian sun, he made the mistake one day of lying on deck in only shorts and falling fast asleep. "When I woke up, I was badly sunburned and had to be treated by the pharmacist's mate," he remembered. "They wanted to dishonorably discharge me for neglect, but I begged them to keep me. In the end, they found getting a new radioman for a submarine was not easy at that time. I was in pain for a long time after we went to sea, and ended up with scars on my chest."[17]

At the completion of his boat's yard work, Moore then spent five days running his crew through training prior to departing on his third patrol in command of the boat. During this period in early May, a number of enlisted men were shuffled to other duties, including seaman Ed Keller. Having spent fewer than three months on *Sailfish*, he was frustrated to be sent to the relief crews. He hoped to quickly make his way onto another submarine, perhaps even *Sailfish*'s sister boat, *Sculpin*, which had returned from her Mare Island overhaul just a week behind *Sailfish*. But both boats soon headed to sea, leaving young Keller stuck at Pearl, still wishing to make his first patrol.

One of the new hands coming on board *Sailfish* for her eighth patrol was a familiar face. Motor Machinist's Mate First Class (MoMM1c) Montie Dewitt Walkup, a lean twenty-three-year-old from Lynchburg, Virginia, had enlisted in the Navy in 1938 to escape the Great Depression. His early service had been on the cruiser *Honolulu*, until he answered a call at Pearl Harbor in August 1941 for submarine volunteers and found himself assigned within hours to *Sailfish*.[18]

Walkup had made the first four war patrols on *Sailfish* before being transferred to the Pearl Harbor relief crews in June 1942. He had spent the ensuing months working at the sub base in Hawaii, and was looking forward to being transferred back Stateside to a new submarine under construction. Walkup was enjoying a beer in early May at the sub base swimming pool area when he ran into Chief Motor Machinist's Mate (CMoMM) Bill "Pop" Ziel, a *Sailfish* plank owner (a sailor who had been with a ship since it was put into commission) he had known well during his previous patrols.[19]

Ziel explained that he was in short supply of qualified engine room personnel. Firemen and motor machinist's mates referred to themselves as the "black gang," the Navy jargon dating back to the soot and coal dust that fouled the air for men working in the days of coal-fired steamships. During the early-morning hours of April 22, while racing back to the boat in time to make her departure that day from Mare Island for Pearl Harbor, five members of *Sailfish*'s black gang had been involved in a severe automobile accident on the Yolo County Causeway. Two had been killed, among them MoMM1c Leander Haug, who had previously served as Walkup's throttleman during his early runs on the boat. Haug had taught him a lot, and Walkup now felt an obligation to his buddy.

He explained to Ziel that he really wanted to go to new construction, but agreed to go back out for one more run on *Sailfish* to help train their new hands. Walkup was pleased to see many familiar faces still on board. He found Lieutenant Commander Moore to be kindly and solid as his CO, and he assumed the duty of running *Sailfish*'s forward engine room.[20]

Bill Dillon was eager for action as his *Sailfish* departed Pearl on May 17 for her eighth war patrol. In the months he had spent on the boat, he had heard plenty of stories of the 1939 *Squalus* disaster. One of the survivors, Gerry McLees, was transferred to other duties just as Dillon joined *Sailfish*, but two other *Squalus* men remained. Chief of the boat Willard Blatti had narrowly escaped death by missing the departure of *Squalus* on that fateful morning, but he had served on the renamed *Sailfish* since she was recommissioned. The only survivor still serving on *Sailfish* for her eighth run who been rescued with the diving bell was Chief Torpedoman Lenny de Medeiros, now in charge of her forward torpedo room gang.

Aside from Blatti and de Medeiros, only six other *Sailfish* sailors remained on board since the renamed boat had been put back into commission: Chief Electrician's Mate (CEM) Lester Bayles, Chief Quartermaster Claude Braun, Chief Radioman Ray Doritty, Chief Motor Machinist's Mate Pop Ziel, MoMM1c David Gebhart, and Electrician's Mate First Class (EM1c) Walton Young. A large man with a hefty waistline, Young was known to all as "Round Belly." During liberties between patrols, he had a talent for enjoying his liquor and raising hell. And it was Round Belly who tagged Dillon with his lifelong nickname. Young was listening to Dillon explain how he could extend the range of his radar gear by skipping the signals off the ocean surface.

"That's a nifty trick there, Skippy," said Young with a hearty laugh. In short order, Dillon was being called either "Skippy" or "Skip" by his shipmates, and the names would stick.

* * *

Skip Dillon's first patrol under Commander Dinty Moore was eventful. After a quick stop at Midway Island to refuel, *Sailfish* proceeded to her war patrol station off the Japanese island of Honshu. Patrolling waters as shallow as a hundred fathoms, or six hundred feet, Moore was unable to make successful approaches on his first shipping contacts due to fog and foul weather. With visibility almost nil, *Sailfish* was navigated by radar ranges against landmasses to maintain her position. Honshu could be detected as far as eighteen miles away via the SJ set.

Moore spent more than a week dodging small vessels and fishing boats that were unworthy of a torpedo. On June 15, he commenced his first attack against two ships off Todogasaki, the easternmost tip of Honshu. He fired three stern tubes and obtained one direct hit on the 3,617-ton freighter *Shinju Maru*, which proceeded to break up and sink. Dillon could clearly hear the death throes of crunching metal as their target ship collapsed into the sea. The three-hour enemy depth charge attack that followed was far less thrilling, as he sweated out the ordeal on his sonar headset while *Sailfish* silently evaded her stalkers.

Once clear from the enemy counterattack, Dillon felt satisfied. His boat had destroyed an enemy ship, making this a successful patrol. Each man aboard would therefore be eligible to receive the Submarine Combat Patrol Insignia pin. Ten days later, on June 25, skipper Moore made another successful torpedo attack against a Japanese convoy. This one consisted of three merchant ships accompanied by a subchaser escort ship and an airplane flying cover. Firing his stern tubes again from a close 1,200-yard range, Moore obtained one hit. It was enough to sink the 3,291-ton *Iburi Maru*.

Three patrol craft worked *Sailfish* over for the next hour, dropping twenty-six depth charges. When Moore returned to periscope depth at sixty-four feet to check on his latest victim, *Sailfish* was suddenly rocked by the near-miss explosion of a bomb dropped by an unseen airplane. In the conning tower, Lieutenant Joe Tucker, the executive officer, was knocked flat on his back. Below in the control room, radioman Ray Doritty was slammed in the head by a ventilation fan that broke loose in the radio shack. Light bulbs were shattered throughout the boat, and overhead cork insulation rained down like snow.[21]

Moore noted in his log that this explosion was "a good one," powerful enough to fracture the lens of his No. 2 periscope and create two small leaks. As he took *Sailfish* deeper, two more aircraft bombs exploded close enough to rock his ship heavily, but fortunately they were not as close as the first bomb had been. Escort vessels raced in to pound *Sailfish* again. Sound operators Doritty and Johnson spent the next eight hours tracking the Japanese anti-submarine vessels as they made occasional runs to drop their depth charges. Packed with a two-hundred-twenty-pound charge of explosives, the cylindrical Japanese anti-submarine weapons were dubbed "ash cans" by submariners. Some explosions were closer than others, but the endless hours submerged made for miserable conditions below.

Bill Dillon, who had move to the sonar set in the forward torpedo room, was sweating profusely as his boat ran slowly for hours to conserve her batteries. "So, we just sat there and got the shit kicked out of us," he recalled. During silent running, all air-conditioning and ventilating blowers were shut down to eliminate noise, but it also created dangerous oxygen levels over time. Men stripped to their skivvies, their bodies streaming sweat in the balmy confines of their steel submersible. Carbon dioxide absorbent was spread to help reduce the concentrations, but some men still suffered from headaches. Moore noted in his patrol report that all hands took it pretty well, although a few showed "signs of nervous strain."[22]

Sailfish survived her pounding. For Dillon, the most amusing highlight of this depth charging came that night when he picked up a radio transmission from the female radio announcer known as Tokyo Rose. This English-speaking propagandist—one of several female broadcasters used during World War II—often called out American ships by name. In this case, she announced that Japanese warships had attacked and destroyed *Sailfish.* Amused, Dillon switched the radio transmission onto the boat's 1MC announcing system so all could jeer Rose as she reported the loss of *Sailfish.*

Moore remained on station off Honshu for one more day, using only his No. 1 periscope to search for targets. With his other scope broken, he terminated his patrol on June 27 and headed for the barn. By this point in the patrol, *Sailfish* had run out of toilet paper "but pulp magazines carried us," Moore noted in his report.[23]

Sailfish reached Midway Island on July 3, just one day ahead of her sister boat, *Sculpin*. Although *Sailfish* had sunk two Japanese warships, neither sinking had been visually confirmed. Vice Admiral Lockwood only allowed credit for two ships having been damaged, and Moore was not credited with having been aggressive enough on this patrol. Division Commander Karl Hensel, fresh from the submarine school at New London, came down critically on Dinty Moore. Having sighted thirty-one ships better than an escort, he had fired on only two and was credited with only damaging them. (In fairness to Moore, postwar analysis would prove that both of *Sailfish*'s target ships sank.)[24]

Exec Joe Tucker recalled that Moore refused to defend himself against Hensel and was relieved to go back to Pearl Harbor to serve on Lockwood's staff as engineering and maintenance officer. Tucker asked Moore to get him off *Sailfish*, which he did, with Tucker later moving on to help instruct at the New London sub school. The new skipper assigned to *Sailfish* on July 17 was Lieutenant Commander William Robert Lefavour, a 1933 Naval Academy graduate with only one prior war patrol to his credit.[25]

When *Sailfish* departed on her ninth war patrol on July 24, the boat's sinking record under three prior skippers stood at five ships claimed as sunk and several damaged by torpedo hits. Lefavour was untested as a commander, but Dillon considered his new exec, Lieutenant Ben Jarvis, to be solid. A former football and wrestling star at the Naval Academy, Jarvis had graduated from Annapolis ranked first in his class. Having served under Dinty Moore previously, Jarvis knew the traits of a successful skipper, and he would soon come to have his doubts about Lefavour.

Radar operators Dillon and Dieterich had their own concerns after their August 5 encounter with another submarine detected on the surface. Lefavour quickly put on speed and cleared the area without attempting to fully ascertain whether the target was friendly or not. *Sailfish*'s assigned patrol area for her ninth run was the target-rich waters in the Formosa Strait and near Okinawa. But missed opportunities and friction between skipper Lefavour and his second-in-command would only continue to pile up as the weeks played out.

Upon entering her patrol area, *Sailfish* encountered typhoonlike weather that forced Lefavour to keep his boat more often than not at hundred-twenty-foot depths to ride out the storm. But when the weather calmed, the new skipper seemed equally content to keep his boat at safe depths, avoiding aircraft contacts and small fishing vessels. To his junior officers, Lefavour appeared to be letting good target opportunities pass him by if there appeared to be the chance of any danger involved.

Even somewhat easy targets were avoided. On September 2, the topside watch picked up smoke on the horizon off *Sailfish*'s port bow. Dillon and Dieterich were soon able to pick up an enemy merchant ship on their radar at the extreme range of twenty thousand yards. Moments later, a second vessel was detected astern of the freighter, but *Sailfish* never came within visual distance. Lefavour cautiously kept his boat submerged, monitoring the target ships from afar until they were simply out of firing range. His crew was disheartened, but their poor luck was only beginning.

The following day, September 3, distant smoke was sighted in the afternoon. Dillon tracked the ships by radar, but with two hours to go until dark, Lefavour kept his boat down. "Decided a surface chase was not feasible," he wrote. In his report, he added, "Having spent 29 days in area with no contacts except a trawler, several junks and one small freighter that we did not have a chance of getting in on, the morale of all hands is low."[26]

Sailfish made two more ship sightings on September 9 and 10, but Lefavour decided they were too small to attack. Each patrol boat was clearly tracked on radar, but the skipper let them pass, hoping for larger game. The following day, September 11, he set course for Midway, having made zero torpedo or gun attacks. Dillon was certain that he and his fellow radarman had reported far more potential torpedo targets in the past month than Lefavour had opted to log in his patrol report.

Sailfish remained at Midway only long enough to transfer her unused torpedoes to the tender *Sperry* and to refuel. Lefavour had her underway the same afternoon for Pearl Harbor, where she arrived on September 20. She had steamed 9,766 miles and burned 90,200 gallons of fuel with zero results. In his patrol report, Lefavour wrote, "The extremely low percentage of contacts was most disheartening, and it is regretted that no opportunity to inflict damage on the enemy was found." He added, "The lack of an SD radar in which confidence could be placed was keenly felt." Radar operator Dillon would have been livid had he been privileged in September 1943 to read this last remark. "We saw more targets on radar on that patrol than probably any other," he remembered. "With each one, we expected that we were going to make an approach to go after them. But we didn't. Each time, we turned around and ran away from the contacts."[27]

Admiral Lockwood's staff at Pearl Harbor was equally critical of *Sailfish*'s performance under Lefavour. In his notes attached to the patrol report, Captain Freddy Warder, commander of Submarine Division 122, noted that Lefavour complained of the lack of a fully functional SD radar set. "This influenced him unduly and caused him to operate submerged in an area which demanded surface operation in order to obtain adequate coverage."[28]

Captain John Griggs, commander of Submarine Squadron 12, fully concurred with the remarks made by Warder. Charlie Lockwood added his own endorsement to the patrol report, noting that worthwhile targets in the area were likely traveling in shallow water close to the shorelines, and that Lefavour could have obtained better coverage in the area only "by surface patrolling over much of it." Lockwood considered the patrol unsuccessful and denied the Submarine Combat Patrol Insignia award for *Sailfish*'s crew. "It was an embarrassment not to be awarded a battle star for that patrol," Dillon recalled.[29]

While submarine command brass began digging into the state of affairs with the *Sailfish* wardroom, her crew was taken ashore for liberty at the Royal Hawaiian Hotel on Waikiki Beach. Constructed of stained pink sandstone and opened in 1927, the so-called Pink Palace had been requisitioned by Admiral Chester Nimitz to be used during the war as a rest camp exclusively for submariners and aviators. Submarine officers paid only two dollars per day, despite the posted prewar rate of a hundred five dollars per day. Enlisted men like Dillon generally slept four to a room but spent more time roaming the bars, brothels, and beaches than they did sleeping.

Dillon had no desire to visit the brothels, choosing instead to rent a camera to take photos of his luxurious Hawaiian vacation. During his second day ashore, on September 23, he happened upon Admirals Nimitz and William "Bull" Halsey outside the Pink Palace. Noting the starstruck eighteen-year-old sailor staring at them, Nimitz's wife invited Dillon to pose for photos with the admirals. It was a chance encounter and one he would relate with great pride to his shipmates—many being skeptical of Dillon's story until he produced the developed images.

While the crew enjoyed their liberty at the Pink Palace, Lieutenant Jarvis stormed ashore with a bone to pick. On Admiral Lockwood's

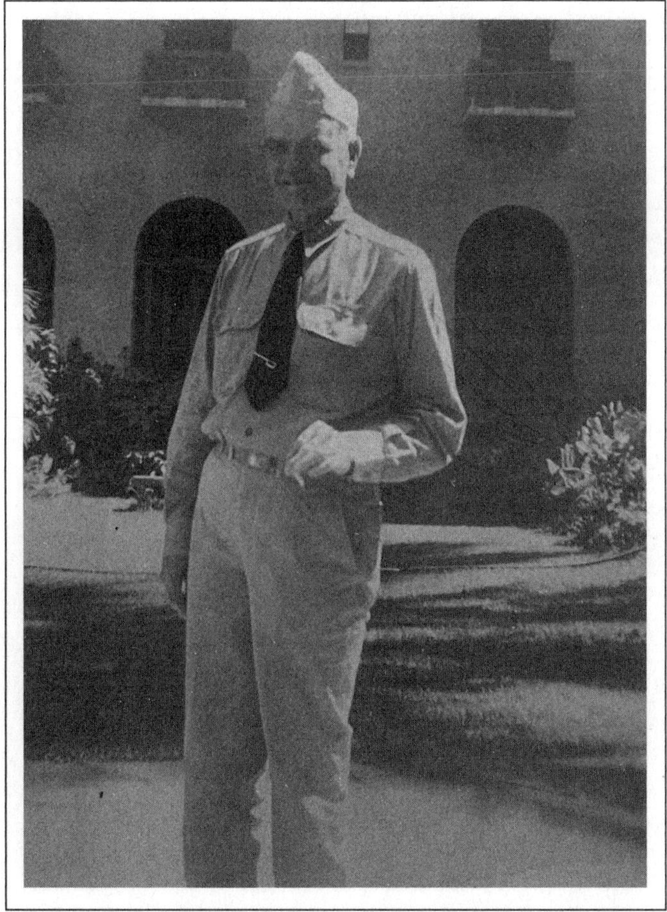

Radioman Bill Dillon snapped this photo of Admiral Bill Halsey outside the Royal Hawaiian Hotel in September 1943. | *Bill Dillon*

staff, he had willing ears in the form of two former *Sailfish* skippers. Commander Dinty Moore, who had taken *Sailfish* on three previous patrols, was now serving as Lockwood's engineering and maintenance officer. Captain Dick Voge, who had commanded *Sailfish* for four of her early runs, was Lockwood's operations officer.

Jarvis went to see Moore and spelled out for him in no uncertain terms that things were dismal on *Sailfish.* Lefavour had squandered chances to attack enemy shipping, and the crew's morale was low. Jarvis said that another patrol under Lefavour would produce no better results and would further damage the mental state of an otherwise good boat. Moore then advised Lockwood about the situation on *Sailfish* and assigned a division commander, Leon Blair, to conduct an official investigation of the state of affairs. After taking testimony from Jarvis, Lefavour, and others, Blair noted of the condition of *Sailfish*, "It was a real mess."[30]

Changes were inevitable for the *Sailfish* wardroom.

THREE

"A Clean Slate"

Lieutenant (jg) William Lee Bruckart had little idea what kind of turmoil he was stepping into. It was October 6, 1943, as the twenty-four-year-old officer crossed the gangplank onto the deck of *Sailfish*. The battle-scarred pigboat was in the midst of a full overhaul in one of Pearl Harbor's graving docks, adjacent to an equally weathered-looking heavy cruiser. At six foot and a hundred eighty pounds, Bruckart was a strong, athletic type, eager for his first experience on a World War II submarine as he advanced across the deck with his duffel bag in hand. The skipper, Lieutenant Commander Bill Lefavour, had little to say to the new officer, so Bruckart consulted with the exec, Lieutenant Ben Jarvis.

Bruckart explained that he was reporting on board as *Sailfish*'s new radar officer. While his war patrol experience was nil, his schooling in electronics was solid. Born in Washington, DC, in 1919, Bruckart had been with the Naval Reserves since 1937. Although he had won an appointment to the Naval Academy, he had been disqualified for not having perfect vision. Bruckart instead secured his degree in metallurgical engineering from the University of Kentucky in 1942, and then went on to Fire Control School at the Washington Navy Yard. Bruckart was then sent through radar schooling at Bowdoin College and MIT. While attending the Navy Fire Control School at Pearl Harbor in 1943, he volunteered for submarine school.[1]

Freshly graduated from sub school, Bruckart had orders to *Sailfish* in the new role of radar officer, pushing her wardroom complement from seven officers to eight. But he found things were not kosher in his new boat. Admiral Lockwood's staff was completing an extensive investigation into the dismal performance of Lefavour on *Sailfish*'s prior patrol. In the proceedings, Jarvis had spoken critically of his skipper to Lockwood's staff. To Bruckart, Jarvis confided that *Sailfish* had found plenty of worthwhile shipping targets during her ninth patrol. When enemy shipping was being tracked, a skipper would normally confer with his assistant approach officer on the "normal approach course" for attack. Instead, Jarvis told Bruckart that Lefavour often asked his exec for a "normal escape" course "when enemy shipping was being tracked, which was not what they were sent out to do."[2]

At the completion of Captain Blair's investigation of *Sailfish*, Lockwood's staff took the first steps in cleaning up the boat by dismissing its two senior officers. Skipper Lefavour was the first to go, sent to surface duty on the carrier *Franklin*, where he would perform more admirably. Second-in-command Jarvis was reassigned as exec of the veteran behemoth sub *Nautilus*, on which he served with distinction until making his own PCO run on *Bergall* and later commanding his own *Baya* in 1945.

The enlisted men had no qualms about Lefavour's departure. "We ran from everything we saw," recalled electrician's mate Royal

Harrison. "The crew was pretty disgusted with him, and we were happy to see him leave."[3]

With his two senior officers departing, Bill Bruckart was left anxiously awaiting the next steps. Who would be the next senior officers? And how would they overcome the dismal funk that now prevailed in the *Sailfish* crew?

* * *

Bob Ward had no interest in taking the easy route. When the chance was offered to him of taking command of either *Sculpin* or *Sailfish*, he choose the boat that had the greatest obstacles to overcome—*Sailfish.*

Lieutenant Commander Ward, an athlete and football star who graduated from the Naval Academy in 1935, was a perfectionist. His brown eyes burned with passion as he eyed his new command lying in the Hawaiian shipyard. Everything about his past pointed toward him being an efficient new captain. Born February 2, 1914, in San Acacio, Colorado, he had spent his teen years in California as an industrious farm boy. Ward delivered milk before and after school, and delivered newspapers, helping him to earn seventeen and a half dollars per month. During high school in Antioch, California, he lettered in football and other sports, and attained the rank of Eagle Scout.

Ward fell in love with green water and blue skies in 1928. At age fourteen, while he was enjoying a self-financed exploration of San Francisco, he took a cable car to the top of Nob Hill. Gazing in wonder at the ships steaming under the Golden Gate Bridge into San Francisco Bay, he decided right then and there that he wanted to be a ship commander. *Someday, I will bring my ship in through the Golden Gate,* he thought.[4]

Upon graduating from Antioch High School at age sixteen, he did not get an Annapolis appointment. Ward instead completed a semester at the University of California and enrolled in the Drew School in San Francisco to take practice exams for six weeks. He succeeded in securing an appointment to the Naval Academy in 1931, where he played for the Navy's football team and graduated in the top quarter of his class. In the Academy's *Lucky Bag* yearbook, Midshipman Ward was described as "willing and ambitious," and a man who left a trail of achievement in both athletics and academics.[5]

Early in his military career, Robert Elwin McCraner Ward used all three of his initials—R. E. M.—to avoid confusion. With so many Wards in the Navy, it was common to receive bills and letters meant for a different Robert Ward. Because Ward was prone to rising early and moving fast at all times, some of the men he commanded would insist his initials actually stood for "Run Every Minute."[6]

Following his graduation from Annapolis, Ward served two years on surface ships, on the battleship *Texas* and the cruiser *Augusta*. His Annapolis roommate set him up on a blind date with Frances Larco. The next year, she bought a round-trip ticket to the Orient and met with up Ward in Shanghai, where they were married during one of his stops while cruising with the Pacific Fleet.

Ward excelled as a junior officer, but he yearned for more responsibility. "The only place I could see getting additional responsibility and getting it fast was getting into small ships," he recalled. He volunteered for sub duty in 1939 with seventeen other officers and entered the submarine school at New London, Connecticut. Upon graduation six months later, he was assigned to an old S-boat, *S-26*, and Ward worked his way up to second-in-command during the next year.[7]

As America entered World War II, Ward's wife was still living in New London. Their first son, Robert, was born on December 12, 1941, while his father was en route to the Pacific on his first submarine, *S-26*. Like his future boat *Sailfish*, Ward was a survivor of a great tragedy.

Late on the evening of January 24, 1942, off Balboa in the Panama Canal Zone, *S-26* was rammed by an unlighted escort vessel fourteen miles off the coast. Ripped open along her starboard side, *S-26* plunged to the bottom three hundred feet below as water poured into the hole in her side and through her open bridge hatch. Forty-six men were lost, but four were thrown from her bridge at the moment of impact. Three survived—an enlisted lookout; the skipper, Lieutenant Commander Earle Hawk; and the executive officer, Lieutenant Ward. Shucking his shoes and clothing, Ward swam until a patrol craft rescued him. After being called to the bridge, he raised hell with the officers about their not following proper procedures to accurately mark the spot of *S-26*'s loss.

During his early years in submarines, Ward learned as much from negative influences as he did from positive. One of his first commanders was overly excitable in tense situations, and another indulged in alcohol enough to create some tough moments for Ward. He thus learned things not to do and the important traits for leadership that he aspired to uphold when he earned his own command.

In late 1942, Ward helped put the new boat *Gurnard* into commission, and he had served as her exec for two war patrols by July 1943. During *Gurnard*'s second patrol, Ward earned the Silver Star for helping to save the boat after she was hit by two bombs. *Gurnard* plunged toward the bottom, her bow planes stuck on hard dive. Only by running fifty men aft toward the after torpedo room was the crew able to check the boat's wild plunge at more than five hundred feet.

During post-battle damage inspections, Ward volunteered to crawl into the main induction piping. Being thin and wiry and standing five foot nine, he was just limber enough to strip to his skivvies, wriggle into the piping with a flashlight, and inch his way from the engine room toward the control room. The cramped tube was hot, stuffy, and "uncomfortable as hell" as salt-encrusted piping scraped his skin. He found the source of the bomb damage, but was unable to extricate himself when he got stuck on his return toward the engine room. Unnerved, he called for a cigarette and grease to smear on his body.[8]

"They passed it up and I smoked and calmed down," he remembered. "Then I maneuvered my body into the same position I'd used to get in the pipe and wriggled out." *Gurnard* completed her patrol, during which she was credited with sinking three ships and damaging five others, including an aircraft carrier. Skipper Herb Andrews was so impressed with the performance of his XO that he recommended Ward for his own command.[9]

Detached from *Gurnard* into the fleet's PCO pool, Ward was in Pearl Harbor on his second month of relief crew duty when both *Sculpin* and *Sailfish* returned from their disappointing patrols in September. Vice Admiral Charlie Lockwood offered Ward the choice of commanding either submarine, as both were due for new skippers. Ward learned from ComSubPac that *Sailfish*'s wardroom was under investigation for personnel problems and that several material defects were being overhauled. "If you want to succeed by growth of comparison, you pick the hard job," Ward later rationalized. "So, I took the *Sailfish* primarily because it offered a greater challenge."[10]

Lieutenant Commander Ward assumed command on October 20 without any ceremony. He merely walked aboard and called the remaining six officers together for a conference. "There's some decisions we need to have about problems on your last run," he started. "I don't want to know anything about it. I want to give this ship a chance."

Ward explained that he wanted his wardroom to go forward without any further criticism of the past in any direction. Anyone who preferred to move on to a new assignment was encouraged to go see ComSubPac. "You can pick a boat and a skipper to work with, and I'll take a whack at it," he promised. "I'll recommend you." Four of his junior officers did just that, going down to see Admiral Lockwood to put in for transfers. In addition to Captain Lefavour and Exec Jarvis, four other officers were transferred from *Sailfish*: Lieutenant Louis Farley, who later commanded *Billfish*; Lieutenant Raymond Brady; Ensign Robert Jones; and Warrant Machinist Thomas Bain.

In his follow-up with Lockwood, Ward told the admiral he was perfectly fine with their choices. He wanted officers who were as eager and excited to go on patrol as he was. "I've got to have a clean slate," Ward told Lockwood. The new skipper was then free to choose from the officer pool currently on hand at Pearl Harbor. During the next few weeks of work in Pearl Harbor's Navy yard, Ward would get the chance to properly size up the drive each of his officers possessed.

Only two officers who had been on board *Sailfish* under Lefavour were retained. Lieutenant (jg) Stan Cowin Jr., a twenty-four-year-old married man from Madawaska, Maine, would be Ward's engineering and diving officer. Blond-haired and small in stature, Cowin had made only *Sailfish*'s ninth patrol, and he was still working to attain his qualified-in-submarines rating, which would allow him to wear the gold dolphins insignia on his uniform.

The other wardroom veteran Ward retained was Lt. (jg) Wetmore, who had reported on board *Sailfish* in January 1943 as her most junior officer. Wetmore, known to his comrades as "Dutch," hailed from Michigan and was fully qualified in boats. He was a mustang, an enlisted man who had been advanced to the rank of officer due to the need to fill the Silent Service's ranks.

At age twenty-nine, Wetmore was older than most officers. His service in the boats had commenced as a radioman on board the old *Nautilus* in September 1937. By November 1942, he had completed three war patrols on *Nautilus* and was promoted from chief radioman to ensign. During his time on *Nautilus*, Wetmore earned two Navy Letters of Commendation for his work as sound and radar operator and as a member of the deck gun crew. With two patrols on *Sailfish* under his belt, Wetmore would be Ward's communications officer for the upcoming tenth patrol.

The other five officers rounding out *Sailfish*'s officer complement were all new to the boat. Lieutenant (jg) Bill Bruckart, who had arrived in the midst of the outgoing officers, had never made a patrol but would serve as the new radar officer based on his schooling. Ensign Edward Justus Berghausen II, a twenty-one-year-old who hailed from Glendale, Ohio, was a 1942 Princeton graduate fresh from sub school in New London. Having never served in a submarine before, Berghausen became "George," the nickname bestowed upon the lowest-ranking wardroom officer in a boat. As such, he was tasked with the duties of commissary officer and would have to work with others to become qualified to eventually stand deck watches on his own.

Warrant Electrician (WE) Wayne Anthony Evans was another mustang. He came aboard after more than two years of service on *Skipjack*, where had risen from electrician's mate to chief petty officer (CPO) to warrant officer by 1943. The husky, six-foot-two Evans, dubbed "Shorty" by Ward, would prove to be quite capable in his role as *Sailfish*'s new electrical officer and assistant engineer.

The final two new officers were both Academy graduates with previous submarine experience. For his executive officer, Ward received Lieutenant George Floyd Richardson, a husky Dutchman who hailed from New Jersey. After graduating from the Academy in 1938, "Bud" Richardson completed his obligatory two years of surface duty before volunteering for submarine service. After completion of New London's sub school in October 1940, Richardson had joined *S-46*, on which he was serving when World War II commenced.[11]

Richardson rose to second-in-command of *S-46* by February 1943, completing three patrols before he was reassigned during the boat's refit in Philadelphia. Assigned to the fleet boat *Pargo* in March 1943 as her gunnery officer and first lieutenant, Richardson earned a Bronze Star for his work as TDC operator during successful attacks on the boat's first war patrol.

Richardson was familiar with Bob Ward, having met him at the Naval Academy in the summer of 1934 when Ward was an upperclassman. Since that time, the two had bumped into each other in the Canal Zone and at New London as each was shuffling between different submarine assignments. After reporting to Ward, the two sat down to discuss expectations. "Of the eight officers aboard on that next patrol, six were new to the boat, including Bob and myself," Richardson recalled. "The boat had to be reorganized from the officers all the way down through the lowest seaman."[12]

The new skipper planned to run the boat with a heavy hand to remove any lingering morale issues from his predecessor. "I need someone to be the son of a bitch on *Sailfish*," Ward explained. "One guy has got to be the SOB, and if I've gotta be the son of a bitch, God help me!"[13]

Ward left his meeting confident that Bud Richardson would fit the bill in helping him to whip their crew into shape. He felt equal confidence in the final new officer he selected, Lieutenant Walter Patrick "Pat" Murphy Jr. Serving on board the cruiser *Nashville* when the war started, Murphy had applied for and was accepted into submarine school on April 1, 1942—one year after graduating from Annapolis. That date also marked the cancellation by the Navy of a long-standing two-year prenuptial waiting period for Academy graduates.[14]

Murphy quickly placed a call to his fiancée of eighteen months, Ruth Güenter, and assured her it was no April Fools' Day joke. They hurriedly prepared wedding plans and were married in New London on Saturday, April 18, at 0700, allowing Murphy just enough time to return to base for a full day of submarine training. Following classes, an awards ceremony, and dinner, the newlyweds were finally free to start their honeymoon that evening at about 2000. After a twenty-four-hour escape to nearby New Haven, the Murphys returned to New London Sunday evening and moved into their first home. Then Pat returned to classes on Monday morning.[15]

Upon graduation in June 1942, Murphy reported on board the submarine *Snapper* as a junior officer. "My first two patrols on *Snapper* were very disappointing 'zero runs' with an ultra-conservative skipper," Murphy recalled. "Plenty of ship contacts, few torpedoes fired, with no hits but our share of depth charges." Murphy's third patrol on *Snapper* saw a more aggressive skipper who sank a destroyer with a down-the-throat shot and bagged a large freighter in Apra Harbor at Guam. Detached from *Snapper* on October 7, 1943, Murphy was slated to head for new construction in New London. While awaiting transportation from Pearl Harbor, he received orders from Vice Admiral Lockwood to instead report immediately to *Sailfish*, where Bob Ward made him his new torpedo and gunnery officer and first lieutenant.[16]

Years later, Murphy would recall: "Although it was quite a disappointment at the time, it turned out to be one of the best things that ever happened to me."

★ ★ ★

Radar operator Bill Dillon was equally surprised in late October by the sweeping changes within his *Sailfish*. During the boat's overhaul at Pearl Harbor, his SJ radar set was partially converted to an SJ-1 set by the installation of a new transmitter utilizing all of the previous SJ components. The new unit would prove to be challenging for its technicians to maintain, but Dillon was pleased that the revamped multidirectional radar set would afford his boat new efficiency in tracking enemy shipping.[17]

In addition to equipment improvements, Dillon was also aware that *Sailfish*'s wardroom had been dismantled. Regarding the new batch of officers, he had legitimate concerns. "Two of them have never even made a damn war patrol!" Dillon complained to a shipmate. "They can't even spell *Sailfish*!"[18]

Dillon's ire was further raised as new skipper Ward set about working his crew tirelessly. One of the two junior officers retained, Lt. (jg) Stan Cowin, seemed only too eager to carry out his new captain's orders to make sure the boat was properly spit and polished. Dillon felt that Cowin, small in stature, had a Napoleonic complex and was prone to talking down to his enlisted men to make sure they knew who was in charge. "He was a real prick," Dillon recalled. "When we were chipping rust off the hull, he would come around and say, 'You missed a spot there.'"

In fairness to his crew, Lieutenant Commander Ward offered his enlisted men the same chance to transfer that he had given his wardroom. Dillon had no idea what was going on one morning when Chief Torpedoman Willard "Bill" Blatti began ordering the men to make their way topside and line up on deck.

At thirty-three years of age, Blatti was an old salt in the Navy, four years older than his new skipper. At the time of the loss of *Squalus* in 1939, he had been in charge of her after torpedo room. But as fate would have it, Blatti was late to arrive at the boat and missed her sailing. All of his comrades in the aftmost compartments had perished that morning. When *Squalus* was recommissioned as *Sailfish*, Blatti had been there, and he had subsequently made all nine prior war patrols. By the time *Sailfish* set sail on her tenth war patrol, only Blatti and one other man, CEM Lester Bayles, remained from the original commissioning crew.[19]

As the senior enlisted man on board *Sailfish*, Blatti held the key position known as chief of the boat. Equivalent to a top sergeant in the Army, the chief of the boat set the watch schedules for the crew and served as the senior enlisted adviser for the exec and skipper. Blatti had wide-sweeping latitude to handle any minor personnel issues that did not require an officer's intervention.

Dillon and his comrades waited anxiously on deck in Dry Dock No. 3 as their new skipper stepped forward to speak. Ward addressed the challenges his men had faced on their past patrol, and made it clear he did not want to hear any more critical talk about this moving forward. "I'll give you the same opportunity I gave the officers," he said. "If anyone wants off this boat, I will help you find a new ship."[20]

In the wake of the skipper's talk, only a handful of enlisted men approached Blatti or Exec Bud Richardson to request a transfer. But during the weeks *Sailfish* lay in Pearl Harbor on overhaul and in training, a full one-third of the crew was shuffled to new duties. It was a normal process for a percentage of experienced submarine veterans to move on to new boats to continue building a strong fleet. But Ward was faced with a much higher percentage of green hands. "The patrol was started with 48% of the crew having not qualified in submarines, 24% of the crew having never made a submarine war patrol, 23% having made only one previous war patrol, and 30% having made only two previous patrols," Ward wrote.[21]

The seventy-one-man crew was thus tasked with bringing the less experienced men up to speed on submarine operations. "School of the boat" was a normal process of qualifying both officers and enlisted men in submarines, and those who became qualified were eligible to wear the coveted submarine dolphin insignia on their uniforms. *Sailfish*'s thirty-seven qualified men would serve as the teachers for those were not yet qualified. Twenty-three new hands were received on October 31 alone, and more shuffling of personnel would continue up until the date *Sailfish* departed on her tenth war patrol.

Among those joining the boat this day from the Submarine Division 122 relief crew pool was twenty-five-year-old motor machinist's mate John Michael Good. A Pennsylvania native and sub school graduate, Good had helped work on *Sailfish* during her previous weeks of refit. During the course of her ninth patrol, the boat's black paint had blistered and worn off, leaving orange oxide in places and white crustacean growth in others. By the time Good was assigned to this boat, *Sailfish* had been repainted both inside and out, her exterior now a gleaming gray color.

"My transfer to the sub was met with mental apprehension and caution," Good later wrote. He was assigned to the forward engine room, where he would serve as an aide to MoMM1c Freddie Wheeler, an efficient, fully qualified engineman from Kansas who had a string of war patrols to his credit on *Sargo*, *Spearfish*, and *Sailfish*. Wheeler told Good that his first order of business toward earning his submarine dolphins was to learn the boat thoroughly, from stem to stern, and to become familiar with every operation a sailor must know at sea.[22]

For Bill Dillon, his radio and radar team also had new faces. He and RT1c Frank Dieterich had become a tight pair during *Sailfish*'s two prior runs. Radioman First Class Bob Johnson, having made all nine prior runs, would work closely with them to help break in their two rookies—radio technician Ben West and junior radioman Paul Kelly—and other nonrated sailors who were striking for a rating. Around the clock, it took a full team to man the SJ and SD radar sets, sonar gear, and the boat's radio gear.

Another enlisted man who stayed on board *Sailfish* did not do so by his choosing. Montie Walkup had been persuaded to temporarily rejoin the boat prior to her eighth run to lead her forward engine room and train new personnel for one run. But Captain Lefavour had not granted his transfer prior to the ninth run, one Walkup found to be overly frustrating. "When we made contact with enemy shipping, we did not press home for an attack," he recalled. "Instead, we eased away from the contact area."[23]

In the wake of the drama involving the *Sailfish* wardroom, Walkup—now a chief motor machinist's mate—remained on board. During the overhaul at Pearl Harbor, he was shocked one day to see the Navy yard crane lowering a massive hydraulic jack onto *Sailfish*'s forward deck. Months earlier, while talking to a CPO from another boat, Walkup had learned how a set of hydraulic jacks had helped save his friend's boat during an enemy depth charging. Walkup had then requisitioned a jack from a Navy supply catalog and had long since forgotten about it.[24]

The jack lowered onto *Sailfish* this day was far too large to be stowed below, leaving Walkup scrambling to remove it. The base supply personnel refused to take it back, but he was able to strike a deal with a dock foreman who had been looking for just such heavy-duty equipment for some time. Walkup then placed a new requisition for a smaller hydraulic jack and was pleased to obtain the last one they had in stock. Time would tell whether Walkup's new acquisition would earn its salt.

During his early days of working with new skipper Bob Ward, Walkup was summoned to the bridge one afternoon to see the skipper. "Walkup, as of today, you are in charge of the engine rooms," Ward announced.[25]

Walkup instead protested that he had been asked to make only one more run on *Sailfish*, but had instead now made two. Ward explained that he needed his experience as a seasoned chief petty officer. "When *Sailfish* makes her last run, you will have made yours," said Ward. His frustrated new senior enlisted engineer was given no choice but to remain on board as long as the skipper was on board. "I requested permission to go below," Walkup remembered.

Luverne Carl "Bud" Pike was one of two new yeoman who joined *Sailfish* at Pearl Harbor. While Pike was in boot camp in Illinois in 1942, his proficiency testing determined that he would make a good yeoman since he had two years of banking experience back in Austin, Minnesota. He completed a three-month Yeoman School in Boston and was rated as a yeoman third class. He was then offered three opportunities: service in Washington, DC, or on submarines, or in PT boats. Having no desire to work in Washington, Pike volunteered for submarines, "even though I didn't have the slightest idea what a submarine looked like."[26]

Pike was then shipped to submarine school in New London. During his qualification swim with a Momsen lung in the tower, he was guided up the hundred-foot ascending line by a master swimmer by the name of Carl Bryson. Only later would Bud learn that Bryson was one of the thirty-three survivors who had escaped from the sunken *Squalus* back in 1939.

By July 1943, Pike was stationed at Pearl Harbor, working in the relief crews and hoping for a chance to work his way onto a combat submarine. In October, he learned that sister subs *Sculpin* and *Sailfish* were both in need of new yeomen prior to their next runs. Yeoman 2c Del Schroeder, having seniority over Pike, was given first choice. Both men were aware that the old *Squalus* had been raised from the ocean floor and renamed *Sailfish*. "I don't care to go on board the *Sailfish*, as she is a jinxed boat," Schroeder explained.

Pike went on board *Sailfish* on October 31 and quickly set himself to work learning the requirements of his new skipper. He had the luxury of working with seasoned Chief Yeoman (CY) Bill Crytser, so Pike soon found himself in good standing with Bob Ward. Once *Sailfish* put to sea, Ward tapped Pike to serve as his battle stations telephone talker during mock-torpedo-attack approaches. During his off-duty hours, Pike became friends with radioman Bill Dillon and others in the forward torpedo room.

In time, Pike had little regret that Schroeder had chosen to be assigned to *Sculpin*. One-third of his crew was as new to the boat as he was, and Captain Ward had no place for anyone like Schroeder who believed in jinxes.

★ ★ ★

By early November, Lieutenant Commander Ward found that his *Sailfish* still needed a few more days at Pearl Harbor to correct various mechanical issues before he could run his crew through several days of prepatrol training at sea.

In shaping up his new wardroom, he and Exec Bud Richardson admittedly "worked their tails off." Ward challenged his junior officers to procure various items for use on the upcoming patrol, some of these things being more gimmicky than really necessary. "We did all kinds of screwball things, but it showed you the texture of the people you're leading, and what they'll go for and what they won't," Ward remembered.[27]

There were also plenty of serious needs that were in the final stages of being shored up. New torpedo officer Pat Murphy spent numerous hours working with the Navy yard crews who had just finished installing a new model Mark III torpedo data computer in *Sailfish*'s conning tower. The boat's outdated Mark I unit, previously operated from the control room, had been removed. Murphy's new TDC would prove to be a very worthwhile addition in a matter of weeks.

New junior officer Bill Bruckart had the chance to spend some time with his new skipper one afternoon. Ward took him to the north side of Oahu to enjoy a swim and to get to know his young radar officer a little better. He asked Bruckart to make sure that *Sailfish* had the best new radar in the fleet before the next patrol. It was his job to locate one, and he need not bother the skipper with details regarding how he procured it. "If you can find a better unit, we should have it," said Ward.[28]

With this mission in hand, Bruckart struck out through Pearl Harbor's Navy yard and located a brand-new SD radar unit. The liberated unit was carefully covered, hauled on board *Sailfish*, and deposited on Lieutenant Commander Ward's bunk. "No one searched for it there," Bruckart remembered. The new unit was an upgrade to his prior SD unit, and he hoped his new skipper would be pleased with his resourcefulness.

Upon leaving dry dock, *Sailfish* commenced shipboard drills to prepare the crew for the war zone again. This included operations at sea off Hawaii to practice crash dives, silent running, mock torpedo approaches, and surface gun actions. The new TDC and propeller shaft realignment had added unplanned days to the refit, but the long weeks in Pearl Harbor were coming to an end. Still, it was bittersweet for men like Bill Dillon when they noted their sister submarine, *Sculpin*, pulling away from her dock on the afternoon of November 5 to commence her ninth war patrol.

Nearly two more weeks would pass before *Sailfish* was ready to sail on her tenth run. The date was November 17, 1943, as new yeoman

Bud Pike hurried to get his freshly typed sailing list over the side. His complete roster of all officers and enlisted men was set. Seven new hands had been received at the last minute from the relief crews. By this time, only chief of the boat Bill Blatti and chief electrician Lester Bayles remained as men who had put the renamed *Sailfish* back into commission in 1940. Of the balance of the crew, only six others remained who had made all nine prior war patrols: EM1c Harry Blundell, RM1c Bob Johnson, CMoMM Bill Lyon, Gunner's Mate Second Class (GM2c) Lewis McCarty, CMoMM James McGrath, and MoMM1c Paul Traxler.

Fireman First Class Larry Macek, a twenty-three-year-old from Philadelphia, was one of the seven new hands received just hours before *Sailfish* departed. Macek went to work in the engine rooms, where his time around the new skipper was limited. But being a newbie, he quickly absorbed from others that this new skipper seemed to be a survivor and had plenty of positive energy. "The main thing that attracted you to Ward was his smile," Macek recalled. He found Ward to be outward, friendly, charismatic, and confident. The crew desired a leader who really knew what he was doing. "With Ward, you always had the feeling you would be coming back," said Macek.[29]

Junior officer Bill Bruckart felt equal confidence. "The Captain showed himself to be a true leader who had developed a fine state of morale after only two months as CO," he recalled.[30]

Twenty-year-old Torpedoman 3c Ray Bunt had joined *Sailfish* on November 9 from the Submarine Division 122 relief crew. Black-haired, muscular, and standing five foot ten, Bunt was eager to get back to war. He had made one run as an apprentice torpedoman on the submarine *Pargo*, but had spent the past month itching to get back on patrol. Raised in Cleveland by his mother after the death of his father, he had once been so crippled with polio that he was placed into an iron lung ventilator. Bunt's lungs had recovered well enough from this trauma that, following high school graduation, he served as a captain in charge of forty young men for the Cleveland Lifeguards.[31]

Bunt was then studying at Case School of Applied Science as a tool-and-die pattern maker. He left this behind in 1942 to enlist in the U.S. Navy, in which he proceeded to volunteer for submarine school at New London. A month removed from *Pargo*, Bunt learned of an opening on *Sailfish*. "A lot of the boys said she was a jinxed ship," Bunt recalled of the former *Squalus*, but he knew that her new XO was Lieutenant Richardson, freshly transferred over from his former boat, *Pargo*. Upon crossing the gangway to report below, Bunt took a moment to chat with some of the sailors who were topside on *Sailfish*. He found that new skipper Bob Ward had already raised morale on the boat. "A more jovial crew could not be found anywhere, full of hell and fight, just a gang of single men who didn't give a damn for nothing," Bunt remembered.[32]

Bunt learned from the sailors that this was a new crew, with a new "Old Man" to run the boat. Ducking below to the wardroom, Bunt found the skipper relaxing in the wardroom. Ward asked about Bunt's background and learned that he was a strong swimmer and a master diver. "He asked me if I was married, and what experience I had," Bunt recalled. "I told him, and he said he only wanted men on his boat that wanted to be on her. I was sold."

After a month of working with his new skipper, Exec Bud Richardson found Ward to be a true professional with a "driving personality." The former *Squalus*, "a resurrected boat as some say, from having been sunk and brought back up again," had been transformed "into a boat which was practically new except for the hull." By the time

Sailfish headed out for her tenth war patrol, Richardson believed she "was just as good as any of the new ones out now, and I think every officer and man on the ship felt that way."[33]

In the meantime, *Sailfish*'s onetime savior and sister submarine, *Sculpin*, had departed Pearl nearly two weeks earlier. Her new skipper had found plenty of enemy action, but it was not at all what he had hoped for on his first run.

FOUR

"They Have Us"

Fred Connaway assumed command of *Sculpin* on October 20, 1943—the same day that Bob Ward took over *Sailfish*. Both new skippers had boats lying near each other in Pearl Harbor's shipyard, finishing up yard overhauls. But Connaway had the upper hand for the moment: His crew was not overcoming a morale problem, and his *Sculpin* would ultimately be declared ready for sea weeks sooner.

Born in New Mexico in 1911, Connaway had been appointed to the U.S. Naval Academy in Annapolis from Arkansas. During his midshipman's cruise in June 1931, he served in the engineering department of the battleship *Wyoming* as it sailed for Copenhagen. In the midst of bitter cold and rough seas, his ship was called upon to help a broken-down submarine, *Nautilus*, to port in Ireland for repairs. Twice the tow lines parted, but finally *Nautilus* was able to limp along under her own power. As the warships entered a mighty winter storm, the seas threatened to finish her off as even *Wyoming* rolled as much as 25 degrees.[1]

"The poor *Nautilus* is being tossed around like a cork, and this afternoon her bridge was carried away," Connaway wrote. "I wouldn't be at all surprised to see it break up into little pieces pretty soon." *Wyoming* ultimately took *Nautilus* under tow again and hauled her into Cork Harbour in southern Ireland. Upon reaching Copenhagen, Connaway celebrated by spending fifty-five dollars on a new pair of binoculars. "They are something I shall always need in the service," he wrote to his mother.

Thirty-two-year-old Connaway came on board *Sculpin* carrying his prized binoculars, eager to make his first war patrol in the Pacific. It would mark his first command of a fleet boat after years of service on older and smaller S-boats. After his obligatory two years of surface duty on the battleship *Texas*, Connaway volunteered for submarine service, and thereafter worked his way through the ranks on *S-18* and *S-26*. With the rank of lieutenant, he assumed command of *S-48* in 1939 and served as her skipper for two years. But when war commenced, his old boat was held for training duties on the East Coast.

Connaway then went into the prospective commanding officer pool and served as a PCO on board *Sunfish* during her successful fourth war patrol. After taking command of *Sculpin* in October 1943, he quickly sized up his wardroom. His executive officer was Lieutenant Nelson John "Butch" Allen, a 1939 Academy graduate who had made patrols on *S-41* and one prior patrol on *Sculpin*. Connaway's third officer was Lieutenant George Brown, a former Yale and New York University student who had proven his abilities during *Sculpin*'s four previous patrols. Lieutenant Joe Defrees, as *Sculpin*'s fourth officer, was an enthusiastic 1942 Academy graduate who had made two prior patrols. The son of an admiral, Defrees took his role as torpedo and gunnery officer with great pride, as his mother had christened *Sculpin* back in 1938. *Sculpin*'s wardroom was filled out with four other officers, three being unseasoned young ensigns. Connaway's boat would complete its October overhaul with a full one-third of the crew being new hands.

One of the new sailors most pleased to report to *Sculpin* on October 21 was seaman Ed Keller, who had served on board *Sailfish* for a short period during early 1943. His dreams of submarine service had been temporarily dashed when he was transferred to the sub base, where much of his time had since been spent mess cooking and filling in for crews on liberty. Noting both *Sculpin* and *Sailfish* wrapping up their refits together in the shipyard, Keller decided to try his luck at getting onto his old boat.[2]

"The heroes went to sea," Keller recalled. "The grunt stayed back mess cooking. I wanted to be a hero."[3]

He was informed by *Sailfish*'s wardroom that their roster was full, but one of the boat's officers, Dutch Wetmore, went to bat for Keller. After visiting *Sculpin*, Wetmore returned and told Keller to pack his bags. *Sculpin* could use an extra electrician's mate striker. "I was very, very happy. The hairs stood up on the back of my neck," Keller remembered. He ran to the base, scooped up his seabag and his meager belongings, and raced back to *Sculpin* to report for duty. On board his new boat, senior petty officer Duane White was assigned to look after him to make sure Keller did his job and learned the ship. Keller was further delighted to run into Tom Brown, his sub school buddy who had made it on board *Sculpin* months prior when the pair first arrived at Mare Island.[4]

Sculpin was completing her overhaul and at-sea training period. The work in Pearl shored up many of the minor issues within the boat, but *Sculpin*'s after battery hatch, which had been welded shut due to leaks in July, remained sealed. The crew could only hope that they would not have to use it. On the afternoon of November 5, Keller was eager with anticipation as his boat's diesels rumbled to life. Vice Admiral Lockwood and other dignitaries were on hand as the base band blared out familiar departure tunes. Fred Connaway was on the bridge as his officer of the deck conned *Sculpin* past Ford Island and toward the harbor entrance.

As assistant navigator, quartermaster Bill Cooper was topside as his boat departed on its ninth war patrol. With Chief Signalman Weldon "Dinty" Moore serving as chief of the boat, the quartermaster gang had three rated enlisted men to serve four-hour shifts on the helm and to maintain the quartermaster's logbook for each twelve-hour rotation. In addition to Cooper, there were two fellow third class signalmen from Texas to split the shifts: newly reported Elmon Murray and Dowdy Shirley, a former striker recently promoted from seaman first class. To help fill the watch schedule, Cooper, Shirley, and Murray had another nonrated striker, seaman Bill Welsh, learning the ropes.

As *Sculpin* stood out to sea from Hawaii with her escort vessel, Cooper was well aware that another senior officer was present on the bridge. It was a man Cooper had come to know from his *Greenling* days, Captain John Philip Cromwell. The forty-two-year-old submarine division commander, a 1920 Academy graduate from Illinois, was under special orders from Charlie Lockwood. Cromwell had directions to form a wolf pack while at sea, if conditions warranted doing so, with either or both of two other subs that would be operating in the same vicinity, *Searaven* and *Apogon*. As a base commander, Cromwell was intimately familiar with the classified Ultra program for directing submarines toward key shipping. He was also familiar with Operation Galvanic, the invasion of the Gilbert Islands—considered to be the first stepping stone in the mid-Pacific island-hopping road to Japan.[5]

Just prior to *Sculpin*'s departure, Lockwood had fully briefed Cromwell on the Galvanic operation. He ordered his division commander to keep this knowledge to himself, in case the worst happened. If the boat was lost and any crewmen were taken prisoners, it was in their best interest that no one be able to disclose any details of the Gilberts invasion.[6]

As skipper, Commander Connaway had full control over his boat and his crew. But with Connaway on board, Bill Cooper realized this patrol had the potential to be special if a wolf pack was formed.

★ ★ ★

Outbound from Pearl Harbor, *Sculpin* made a brief stop at Johnston Atoll to refuel. Her patrol destination was 3,500 miles farther southwest, in the vicinity of Truk Atoll, the Japanese equivalent of Pearl Harbor. Key Japanese warships operated routinely from Truk, with carrier groups known by U.S. intelligence to sortie frequently between the Japanese home islands and the advance base. *Sculpin*, *Apogon*, and *Searaven* were thus under directive to operate within two hundred miles of the northern approaches to Truk, with the hope that the loosely connected subs could alert one another to make coordinated attacks when key target groups were sighted.

Cromwell and Connaway simply informed their crew that *Sculpin* would be operating in potentially rich waters. Although the crew was not privy to the exact patrol area, those in the know were quick to consult with the quartermaster gang on which particular charts were of most interest to the officers. New hand Ed Keller soon learned from others that Truk Atoll, a vital Japanese advance naval base, was the key area for operation. "Morale was very high," recalled Keller. "We knew the greatest hunting was near Truk. You had visions of coming back having sunk a carrier or a battleship."[7]

Arriving on station on November 16, *Sculpin* spent the first two days largely submerged during the daylight hours, her watch officers sweeping the seas with their radar and periscopes in search of Japanese vessels. It was not until 0300 on November 19 that the anticipated word was passed over the 1MC.

"Radar contact!"

Two new SJ operators, RT2c Edgar Beidleman and RM3c John Parr, studied their PPI screen in the conning tower. Their report was electrifying to the topside watch as their boat ran on the surface. Skipper Connaway and pack commander Cromwell, topside with their three lookouts, scanned the horizon for the distant ships. Lieutenant Joe Defrees, the officer of the deck, scurried topside to take over as Cromwell headed below to the conning tower to let the boat's regular personnel make the attack decisions. He did not wish to be in the way of Connaway's command.

Radar showed the target ship, still invisible to binoculars, to be heading north at 14 knots. Connaway ordered full speed, calculating that at his faster rate *Sculpin* could pull ahead of the ship and reach attack position around daybreak. During this end-around procedure, radar operators Beidleman and Parr kept up a steady report on the range to target. Slowly, their SJ set began showing additional, smaller pips, which were believed to be escort vessels. Due to the slower speed of the largest pip, Connaway presumed it to be a merchant vessel. The convoy he was attempting to head off was later determined to be centered around two prime targets—the 5,160-ton submarine tender *Chogei* and the 6,280-ton light cruiser *Kashima*. The warships had departed Truk for Japan at 0556 on November 18, and were cruising in company with two destroyers, *Wakatsuki* and *Yamagumo* (meaning "clouds on the mountain"), and the transport ship *Gokoku Maru*.[8]

As dawn was beginning to break, Connaway reached a satisfactory position ahead of the Japanese convoy. Ready for the attack, he had Defrees sound the diving alarm to take *Sculpin* down. Throughout the boat, electrically generated bell-like notes—frequently called the Bells of St. Mary's by submariners—chimed the call for the crew to assume their battle stations. Remaining at radar depth, Connaway coolly observed the approaching ships. He could now clearly make out a Japanese cruiser, a large merchant ship, and what appeared to be destroyers. In the conning tower and the control room, *Sculpin*'s attack team and plotting parties were in position. Quartermaster Bill Cooper was in his regular position as the battle stations helmsman in the conning tower.

George Brown handled the duties of diving officer in the control room. A veteran of four prior patrols on *Sculpin* and previous duty on the old *S-40*, the lieutenant was a solid leader. Raised in New York, he had joined the Navy in 1940, first serving on the cruiser *Chester* before volunteering for submarine school. Brown now kept tabs on his planesmen, ensuring that they kept the boat level as *Sculpin* made the final approach to fire her torpedoes.

Connaway, standing ready in the conning tower, raised the periscope around 0630 to take a final look to obtain his firing bearings. But what he saw changed everything. The Japanese convoy had made a sudden zig and was now charging straight toward his position at close range.

"Down scope!" shouted Connaway. "Take her down, emergency, two hundred feet!"

Diving officer Brown opened the negative buoyancy tank to take *Sculpin* down quickly, a procedure that created additional noise. "I believe this outfit heard the *Sculpin* or were alerted, for the whole convoy speeded up," Brown recalled. "However, they did not drop any depth charges at this time."[9]

As *Sculpin* ran silently for the next half hour, pack commander Cromwell and skipper Connaway discussed the situation. They decided their target merchant ship must have been very important to be traveling with so many escorting warships. It was imperative that *Sculpin* return to the surface as quickly as possible to attempt another attack. Helmsman Cooper, having turned over his duty to another quartermaster, headed aft to eat breakfast while his boat remained low to avoid a potential depth charge attack. He was just shoveling his first forkful of eggs down when a duty messenger approached him.

"We're going to surface," the sailor told Cooper. "Lieutenant Allen wants you in the conning tower."[10]

Cooper left his meal and hurried forward and climbed the ladder in the control room. He quickly consulted with the ship's XO, Butch Allen. Diving officer Brown was already in the process of steadily bringing *Sculpin* toward the surface. It was 0730.

"The skipper wants us to go up on deck and check things out," Allen explained. "We're going to surface and take out after them. You take the after lookout, and I'll take the forward."

As the battle stations surface quartermaster, Cooper was always the first through the hatch and the last man down. Standing atop the rungs of the steel ladder, he spun the wheel to undog the hatch as his boat broke surface. Cool water cascaded down onto his shoulders as he sprang through the open hatch onto the bridge, followed closely by Captain Connaway, Lieutenant Allen, and several lookouts. Racing aft, Cooper raised his binoculars and scanned the surface in his assigned direction.

"All clear," he called.

But the exec had a ship in sight. Calling to his quartermaster, he said, "What does that look like to you?"

Cooper swung his binoculars forward and replied, "That's a crow's nest right in front of us!"

Allen and Cooper studied the vessel for another minute. It was just over the horizon, about six thousand yards away, but the upper works of its mast and crow's nest were clearly visible. Unable to determine what type of ship it was, Allen decided it was best to sound the diving alarm and duck down to periscope depth to further assess the situation.

"Clear the bridge! Dive! Dive!"

Two raucous blasts of the diving alarm sent the topside lookouts tumbling down the ladder, followed by Allen. Cooper was last down the hatch, and he quickly dogged it down before assuming his station at the helm in the conning tower. Skipper Connaway was already running up the scope to fully sweep the horizon. He stiffened as the scope trained aft.

"It looks like they left a sleeper up there," he said. "Now he's on our tail!"[11]

Lookouts on the destroyer *Yamagumo* had spotted *Sculpin* as she surfaced at 0740. Lieutenant Commander Ono Shiro's destroyer had been lying back in a "sleeper" position, waiting for just such an opportunity to surprise an unsuspecting American submarine. Displacing 2,370 tons, *Yamagumo* was 388 feet in length and capable of 35 knots. She was also heavily armed with more than four dozen depth charges, eight topside torpedo tubes, six 5-inch deck guns, and numerous smaller-caliber antiaircraft guns. Shiro ordered *Yamagumo* straight toward *Sculpin*'s periscope as his men readied their depth charges aft.[12]

For Fred Connaway, there was no desire to try a risky down-the-throat shot to put a torpedo into the charging destroyer. He preferred to dodge the enemy counterattack, resurface as quickly as possible, and attempt to regain attack position on the key transport ship or the cruiser.

"Take her deep!" he shouted down to diving officer Brown.

Sculpin's planesmen put the boat in a hard dive, taking her down to three hundred feet, which was considered very deep submergence for an older *Sargo*-class submarine. The boat's best sound operator, Radioman 3c Grover Marcus, announced that the Japanese destroyer was approaching fast as *Sculpin* reached her prescribed depth. Seconds later, other men throughout the boat could hear the angry swishing of approaching screws far above, even without the assistance of listening gear and headphones.

Throughout the boat, men braced themselves for the worst. In the enlisted men's quarters in the after battery compartment, seaman Ed Keller was manning the sound-powered battle phones. Only a handful of other sailors was present, including ship's cook Edward "Andy" Anderson, who had been a chef in San Francisco prior to enlisting. There was also Keller's sub school buddy, Tom Brown, another seaman striking for his electrician's rating. Having gone from the maneuvering room to the galley to get coffee, Brown remained with Keller as *Sculpin* went into her crash dive to avoid the charging destroyer.[13]

To Keller, the destroyer's screws sounded as loud as a freight train roaring through a tunnel. It was his first such experience. Glancing nervously about the compartment, he noted his buddy Brown fall to his knees and begin blessing himself. Unlike Keller, Brown had two prior war patrols under his belt, and he fully expected the worst from this attack. "Tom knew that the screws were going fast, so he knew they were making a depth charge run," Keller recalled.[14]

Yamagumo roared above *Sculpin*, and the Japanese sonar operators clearly had their quarry located with their pinging. From the fantail, sailors began releasing lethal six-hundred-pound depth charges, each set to explode at deep depth. On his sound gear, Marcus heard the splashes and silently waited for the results. They were not long in arriving. Each explosion was immediately preceded by a light clicking sound.

Click—*wham*! Click—*wham*!

Erupting in thirty-second intervals, a string of charges exploded above *Sculpin* with tremendous force. Chunks of cork insulation were blown into the air like confetti throughout the boat, and light bulbs shattered from the intensive shock waves that tossed men from their feet. In the after engine room, the motor machinist's mates had a sudden emergency to contend with. The blasts from these depth charges were close enough to rupture an exhaust valve. Farther aft, packing around the starboard propeller shaft was blown loose. "Several sea valves were jarred off their seats and could not be made tight," Brown recalled.[15]

Yamagumo's first string of depth charges had battered *Sculpin*, but Lieutenant Commander Shiro's destroyer was far from through with her assault on the American submarine.

★ ★ ★

George Rocek sprang into action as soon as the blasts ruptured valves in his boat. Rated a first class motor machinist's mate, Rocek was the senior man in *Sculpin*'s forward engine room. Having made all eight prior war patrols, the tall, athletically built twenty-three-year-old knew the inner workings of his submarine intimately. He also knew that this depth charge attack was a good one, and *Sculpin* would not fare well with another round of explosions that close.

Rocek and others quietly worked to locate the source of the leaks as water sprayed into the engine rooms. Truth be told, he was just as scared as any other man as *Yamagumo* raced overhead to deliver her first load of charges. "The only thing was with us old-timers, you couldn't afford to let the fear show on your face," Rocek recalled. "Although we were young kids ourself, we had younger ones. They watched us. You couldn't afford to show them fear."[16]

The first charges had exploded close enough that Rocek heard the clicks of the detonators almost simultaneously with the resounding blasts of the detonations. Lockers burst open, light bulbs shattered, and insulation rained down. But most concerning to Rocek was the water spraying in from various pipes. He knew that the flexing of the sub's hull had loosened various flanges, but the incoming spray of water from so many sources looked to Rocek as if some unseen hand had loosened every nut in the engine room by a quarter inch. Steeling his nerves to show courage outwardly to his younger enginemen, he reported the leaks to the control room and led his men in tightening things down to reduce the spray of water.

George Rocek looked the part of a submariner. He had grown a heavy black beard during the past months. His appearance now was a sharp contrast to the grinning boyish face Rocek had sported when he first reported on board *Sculpin* on December 21, 1940. As a kid, he had grown up in Cicero, Illinois, a Chicago suburb that had been the headquarters of gangster Al Capone in the 1920s. George's father, James Rocek, had never been involved with the mob, but his humble tailor shop was located only a few doors down the street from Cicero's gambling parlor, which Capone's thugs often frequented.

When George was six years old, his own "gang" of buddies had given him the nickname of "Moon." Each summer, his mother shaved all the hair off her sons. As George and his pals were sitting on a curb one evening beneath a streetlamp, his buddy Dixie noted the light shining off Rocek's bare head. "It looks like a moon shining there!" he laughed. From that night forward, George's pals and even his family always called him Moon.[17]

By age sixteen, Rocek was bored with his Depression-era routine. "I was looking for excitement and I had a bit of the wanderlust," he recalled. He and a buddy left home in the winter, riding freight trains toward California, but made it only as far as Colorado. Out of money, out of food, and forced to swallow their pride, the buddies begged for food and work until they could hop trains back to Cicero.

Rocek spent the next couple of years working at a local gas station that was also located near Cicero's gambling hall. "A lot of those hoodlums came over to get their cars serviced," Rocek recalled. "We would deliver the cars to the hoodlums, and they'd give you a good tip. You could deliver one car and it would pay for the whole darn week in wages."[18]

After high school, Rocek tried to enlist in the Navy but was turned down because of dental problems. He continued working at the Cicero service station until a dentist could repair his teeth. Accepted by the Navy in June 1940, he completed boot camp at the Naval Station Great Lakes and then noticed a bulletin requesting volunteers to sign up for submarine service. Rocek had no idea what was involved, but to him, it sounded like another exciting adventure. By year's end, he had completed his submarine schooling and been assigned to *Sculpin.*

Once on *Sculpin*, Rocek requested to work with the engineering department, commonly known to submariners as the "black gang" for the greasy conditions they labored in. "As a kid at the gas station, I learned a lot about working on engines," Rocek recalled. "I kinda liked that, and that's the reason I put in for it." When the war broke out for America, *Sculpin* was stationed with the Asiatic Fleet in Manila. During the year that followed, Rocek saw his fair share of action, from Borneo to Australia to war patrols in the Pacific Theater.

As fate would have it, his old nickname of Moon returned on *Sculpin* in ironic fashion. Returning from liberty late one night, he stripped down and crawled into his bunk in the hot, stuffy after torpedo room. One of the electrician's mates, Arthur Clark, returned to the boat even later that night from a long evening of drinking ashore. As he entered the torpedo room, the blue night-light illuminated Rocek's naked body in his bunk. "It was shining on my rear end," he recalled. "He told the guys the next day when he opened the [door], all he saw was these cheeks. He said it looked like a moon coming over a mountain."

"You know, Clark," Moon said. "You wouldn't believe this, but I've had that nickname from the time I was six years old."

When one of the warrant officers refused to believe the claim, Rocek said, "I'll tell you what. The very next letter I get, I'll let you open it."

In the next mailbag delivered to *Sculpin*, Rocek received a letter from home from his sister Sylvia, who frequently wrote to him. "Sure enough, when he opened it, it said, 'Dear Moon,'" Rocek recalled. "So, then he believed me."

The Moon nickname for Rocek soon became permanent on *Sculpin*.

When *Sculpin* returned Stateside in January 1943 for an overhaul at Mare Island, all of the crew were able to take liberty to visit their homes. Rocek returned to Chicago on a troop train and later caught a cab to his home, which was adjacent to his father's Cicero tailor shop. He strolled in and said hello to his father. James Rocek did not recognize the bearded sailor. "Pa, it's me!" he said. "George!"[19]

Rocek saw tears welling in his father's eyes. Soon his father was sobbing and hugging the son he had not seen for two years. The Rocek family enjoyed a reunion that included both sons home from the war on leave. The local paper published photos of George and his older brother, Rudy, together. Rudy was photographed in his Marine uniform, poking fun at George's beard before it was shaved off with a straight razor. When the time came for him to return to California, Moon's mother, Christina Rocek, was in tears, wondering if she would see her boy again.

Eight months removed from this reunion, Rocek had survived two more *Sculpin* patrols. His current dilemma was more troubling than prior depth charge attacks. The motormacs scrambled to tighten nuts and shore up the leaks spewing from their engine rooms. Above, the screws from the Japanese destroyer could be heard coming in for another run.

This guy is not giving up, thought Rocek.

* * *

Lieutenant Commander Shiro made two initial depth charge runs over *Sculpin* at 0703, Japanese time. *Yamagumo*'s sailors could not discern any effects from their first six drops, so Shiro had his men reserve their weapons for a more solid lock on the enemy submarine.[20]

Yamagumo's sonar operators commenced echo-ranging efforts as their destroyer crisscrossed the ocean in an attempt to make a lock on their prey. At 0743, one of Shiro's operators reported that he had a solid echo off *Yamagumo*'s bow at 2,400 meters—one and a half miles distant. Sonar remained locked on *Sculpin*, and Shiro ordered his men to prepare another ten depth charges for deep-depth settings. *Yamagumo* charged toward the location of the submerged American vessel at high speed. At 0752, the ash cans began rolling off her stern.

In *Sculpin*'s radio shack, Grover Marcus had been calling off the bearings of the enemy destroyer's screws as *Yamagumo* swept the area during the previous quarter hour. As the echo ranging locked onto *Sculpin*, Marcus announced, "He has turned toward us. He's coming in!" Seaman Ed Keller, listening to the radioman's dialogue over his headset in the after battery compartment, no longer needed to know the bearings from Marcus. The angry *swish, swish, swish* of fast-moving screws was growing louder by the second, far above. "At that point, I got scared," Keller later admitted.[21]

"The weather conditions were perfect for a destroyer, sound and echo ranging highly effective," George Brown wrote. "There was a straight line on the bathythermograph down to 300 feet. Our evasion tactics were next to useless." The depth charges dropped by *Yamagumo* on this run were right on the money. At his diving station, Brown was stunned to see the hands of the depth gauge near him fall off as *Sculpin* was slammed by the concussions. "The pressure gauges near the diving station commenced flooding, and there was other minor damage about the ship," Brown recalled.[22]

The Japanese destroyer remained above, pinging away with its echo-ranging gear, trying to lock onto the submarine again. Brown took the chance to ease back to the galley, where Ed Keller sat alone with his headset beside cook Andy Anderson.

"When do we lose these bastards?" Keller asked the lieutenant.

Brown's answer shook the new sailor to his core. "We're not going to lose them. They have us."

"You've got to be kidding," Keller stammered. "If they hadn't gotten us on the past two runs, how're they going to get us?"[23]

Brown returned to his post. All hands nervously sweated out the constant pinging from the destroyer high above them. Men not needed for any specific duty crawled into their bunks to conserve oxygen as the air in the boat became increasingly foul. Around 0930, *Yamagumo*'s screws could be heard swishing closer again as she made another run.

The next set of blasts was close enough to cause new leaks. Brown found that these explosions created further damage, but that his planesmen were still able to maintain control of the boat at their maximum depth of around four hundred feet. *Sculpin* was heavy in the stern, due to the flooding that was filling the aft bilges. "In spite of the large up-angle (13 degrees or more) and much weight in the boat," diving officer Brown could keep his ship somewhat under control. But it was now requiring a hundred to a hundred ten turns of the propellers per minute to prevent her from sinking past crush depth.[24]

Although things were looking bleak, sonar operator Marcus made a sudden announcement that brought encouragement to those near him in the control room. Through his headset, he could hear a rain squall in the distance. Commander Connaway immediately coached helmsman Bill Cooper to steer toward it. *Sculpin* soon eased under the surface storm, which effectively shielded the boat from detection from *Yamagumo*'s efficient sound operators. Connaway ran with the storm for more than a half hour, and he used the protective cover to his full advantage.

Diving officer Brown ordered his men to begin pumping out the flooded bilges to help regain proper diving trim of the boat. But he soon found that neither the drain nor the trim pump would take suction. Frustrated, Connaway ordered Brown to make a tour of the boat to inspect the various levels of damage and flooding throughout *Sculpin*. As he departed the control room, Brown assigned his new assistant diving officer—Ensign Max Fiedler, a young reservist making his first war patrol—to temporarily take over his duties.

Heading aft, Brown found that the after engine room was heavily flooded. He had hoped to use the manifold to blow an air bubble into the No. 4 main ballast tank to help bring the trim under control. He instead decided this to be unwise, as the rush of water forward might short out the electrical leads to his main motors. "We decided to bail the water forward to another compartment until we could trim the ship without endangering main motors," Brown recalled.[25]

This process required the use of all spare engineers to form a human bucket brigade. The heat in the engine rooms was already intense, having climbed to about 115 degrees. For Moon Rocek and his fellow machinists, the task of passing heavy buckets of water caused them to sweat profusely in the thick, balmy air. As the men labored to pass the excess water forward, skipper Connaway decided it was high time to ease *Sculpin* up for a periscope observation. With any luck, the Japanese destroyer might have given up on them in the rain squall.

Although normally a routine procedure, it proved to be anything but for temporary diving officer Fiedler. He began blowing the ballast tanks at two hundred feet, and the expelled water quickly caused *Sculpin* to become more buoyant. As she swam upward, the depth gauge moved to a hundred eighty feet, and then to a hundred seventy. But the damaged gauge remained stuck, and Fiedler simply did not notice. "Normally, you'd tap the gauge, and it would free up," Rocek recalled.[26]

Oblivious to the gauge, Fiedler began blowing more air, unaware that his boat was shallower than the setting showed. *Sculpin*'s ascent increased, and her tail-heavy stern caused the bow to rise even faster. A moment later, Ed Keller was stunned to hear an alarmed sailor in the forward torpedo room scream, "What are we doing on the surface? The bow is out of the water!"[27]

Under the strain of the situation, the rookie diving officer had done the unthinkable. The forced blasts of compressed air had made *Sculpin* so positively buoyant that her bow burst through the waves, broached like a surfacing whale, and then slammed back down.

It was 1109. Lieutenant Commander Shiro's destroyer was still lurking nearby. His lookouts immediately began shouting as the American submarine burst to the surface, only a thousand yards off *Yamagumo*'s starboard bow. Shiro shouted orders to his helmsman. *Yamagumo* wheeled hard to starboard and charged forward, ready to finish off the floundering enemy submarine.[28]

* * *

George Brown turned to race for the control room to assist Ensign Fiedler with the emergency. But Commander Connaway was already shouting orders. "Take her deep! All ahead full!"

All flood vents were opened, and *Sculpin* started down fast. With her nose pointed down, her crash dive quickly accelerated, aided by all the excess water aft. Bucket brigade men dropped their pails and grabbed for anything to right themselves as the down angle increased at an alarming rate. A minute later, Ed Keller heard shouts over his headset from the forward torpedo room that *Sculpin* was passing her test depth, and yet she continued to plunge.

For an older *Sargo*-class boat like *Sculpin*, her official test depth was two hundred fifty feet. This was often exceeded in the course of escaping depth charge attacks, but four hundred fifty feet was considered the point at which her hull might begin to collapse from the immense pressures of the sea at that depth. Hull plates and the superstructure creaked as *Sculpin* continued to plunge. Lieutenant Brown arrived in time to blast air into the bow buoyancy tank, which proved to be just enough to check the submarine's uncontrolled dive. "We momentarily lost depth control and were down over 500 feet before regaining control," Brown later wrote.[29]

Brown began easing the submarine back up to safer depths. "The heat in the boat was terrific, having made a full power run the previous night," he recalled. "All the engine heat had been sealed in the boat with us." The previous depth charge blasts had damaged *Sculpin*'s steering mechanism to the extent that it was nearly impossible for exhausted helmsman Cooper to operate the wheel by hand power. "At this point, our evasion tactics were about at a standstill," Brown remembered.

As *Sculpin* returned to safer depths, *Yamagumo* roared overhead at 1125 and unleashed four more depth charges. The explosions were frightening, slamming the boat heavily and causing more extensive damage. Light bulbs shattered again, and the radio transmitter was torn from the bulkhead, smashing the receiver. In both torpedo rooms, the concussion caused severe damage to the outboard tube vents. Damage control reports began filtering into the control room from all areas of the boat. Six minutes later, at 1131, *Yamagumo* made another run, dropping three more depth charges that further shook the wounded submarine.[30]

The situation in the boat had become dire. Because *Sculpin* had so many leaks and the negative tanks had been vented several times, the air pressure in the sub exceeded five inches—twice the normal pressure. Far above, Lieutenant Commander Shiro was intent on finishing off his crippled target. The *Chogei* task group had steamed away by this time, but *Yamagumo*'s sonar operators continued with their diligent pinging against the submarine. At 1143, sonar indicated their target to be off *Yamagumo*'s port beam at 1,850 meters. Shiro charged his destroyer in again and had his sailors roll another ten depth charges over the side.

This latest round of explosions further worked against the mental stability of the dispirited submariners. In the forward engine room, Moon Rocek was alarmed by the fresh leaks. The bilges were already full, and water now sloshed about his feet. Working alongside him was Fireman 1c Joe Baker, a New York teenager who was making only his second patrol on *Sculpin*. To Baker, the constant barrages from the Japanese destroyer were severe.

Having made one patrol under former skipper Lu Chappell, Baker could not help but wonder if Fred Connaway was prepared for the challenge *Sculpin* now faced. In his stress and anxiety, Baker realized that the date was November 19, 1943. *What a hell of a way to spend my nineteenth birthday!* he thought.[31]

Despite the foul air condition in the boat and the severity of the leaks, Commander Connaway conferred with Captain Cromwell. They decided to keep *Sculpin* down and to ride out the next string of depth charges in hopes that the Japanese destroyer had about expended its load. By the count being kept in the quartermaster log, *Sculpin* had survived forty depth charges thus far.

At 1243, one hour after the last ten charges had rocked *Sculpin*, the sound of the enemy destroyer could be heard once again. *Yamagumo* had locked onto the American submarine. Skipper Shiro ordered another ten ash cans rolled off the stern, bringing the total number to fifty that *Yamagumo* had expended in her hours of assault. Shiro's men were right on the mark this time.[32]

The damage was extensive. "The forward and after torpedo rooms reported cracks around the torpedo tubes," Lieutenant Brown recalled. "The sound heads were driven up into the boat, shearing the holding-down clamps. Thus, we were without 'ears.'" *Sculpin* could no longer track the Japanese destroyer by sound. Brown was able to keep the boat from sinking deeper only by increasing the speed of the propellers to a hundred seventy turns, which made her easier to detect.[33]

From the forward torpedo room, word was relayed to battle talker Del Schroeder by torpedoman Herb Thomas that the forward hull was under immense pressure. The batteries that provided power to *Sculpin*'s crews were nearly drained, and it was still about six hours until sunset.

"Things were looking damned rugged for the *Sculpin*," engineer Joe Baker recalled. It was obvious to him that a drastic decision must be made quickly.[34]

Sculpin simply could not remain submerged any longer.

FIVE

Battle Surface!

Bill Cooper had a front-row seat for the most heated discussions ever held on board *Sculpin*. Since the Japanese convoy had first been sighted nearly ten hours prior, Cooper had almost constantly been on the helm in the conning tower or on the bridge as duty quartermaster. None of the conversations taking place in the control room or the conning tower sounded good to him.[1]

Wolf pack commander John Cromwell and skipper Fred Connaway were at odds with each other on what course to take.

"We'll have to surface while we can still bring her up," Connaway said.

"No," said Cromwell. "Keep her down! Keep her down!"

Cromwell reasoned that the destroyer simply could not have very many depth charges, if any, remaining. *Sculpin* should remain submerged and try to make it a little longer. Connaway argued that his boat would not survive another string of depth charges. "We're going to battle surface and give the men a chance," he said.

Sculpin's pharmacist's mate, Paul "Doc" Todd, on duty in the control room near the two officers, appreciated Connaway's compassion. "Captain of *Sculpin* wanted as many men as possible to escape," Todd recalled.[2]

Connaway, as the skipper of the boat, had the final call, even over his senior officer. Cromwell's protests were in vain.

"No, we're going to battle surface!" he firmly stated.

Talker Del Schroeder relayed the order over the 1MC to all hands. "Prepare for battle surface!"

Throughout the boat, there was a sudden banging of lockers as the men assigned to *Sculpin*'s topside guns raced to prepare for combat. More than a dozen additional men gathered in the control room as Lieutenant George Brown began blowing tanks to bring their submarine back toward the surface. Before Cooper darted up the ladder toward the hatch to prepare to undog, he heard one more troubling exchange.

Chief of the boat Dinty Moore served as the pointer for the 3-inch gun during battle surface actions. He was prepared to fight it out against the Japanese destroyer, but he expected that Captain Connaway would at least fire a parting salvo of torpedoes at their opponent.

"Don't you want to make ready the tubes?" Moore asked.

"No," said Connaway. "Just battle surface."

Cooper felt his skipper was simply giving up. *If we had the torpedo tubes ready to fire, all we would have to do is aim the boat at that Jap destroyer,* he thought. *We could fire all the tubes with a slight spread, and we would have a good chance of hitting him.*[3]

As Connaway started up toward the conning tower, he turned to diving officer Brown. "He ordered me to make sure *Sculpin* was scuttled, in case we lost the one-side engagement with the destroyer." Brown found that Connaway maintained a "calm, collected, courageous manner."[4]

Bill Cooper was standing atop the steel ladder to the bridge hatch as Connaway climbed into the control room. *Sculpin* had already burst to the surface, but the senior quartermaster was following standard protocol.

"Skipper, permission to open the hatch?" Cooper called.

Some of the gunners standing near the base of the hatch were irritated that Cooper had even paused. "Give us a chance!" shouted torpedoman James Harper, who was part of the 20mm bridge gun crew. "Open the hatch!"

Salt spray splashed over his shirt as Cooper cracked the hatch and rushed out onto the bridge. Commander Connaway and several lookouts followed him up. *Sculpin*'s gunnery officer, Lieutenant Joe Defrees, took position on the after portion of the bridge to direct the fire of his men. On the main deck, men hurried to man the 3-inch deck gun. On the bridge, *Sculpin* had a pair of 20mm antiaircraft guns, one fore and one aft of the conning tower. In addition, sailors hauled up a pair of .50-caliber machine guns to fire.

It was 1256 when Lieutenant Commander Shiro's lookouts spotted *Sculpin* bursting from the depths in a froth of white foam. Her conning tower showed signs of pressure damage and both periscopes were clearly bent. He called *Yamagumo*'s gun crews to their battle stations at 1300, but held off on opening fire on the enemy submarine.[5]

The delay on *Yamagumo*'s part gave *Sculpin*'s crew time to load their guns. With his skipper on the bridge, executive officer Butch Allen took station in the conning tower. From this vantage point, he planned to relay Connaway's key orders to the helmsman and other personnel in the control room. Standing nearby him, Lieutenant (jg) George Embury and his radar operators manned the SJ radar, ready to feed radar-range data to the gun crews above.

Below them, in the control room, George Brown held vigil as diving officer. Although ordered to sink his own boat if necessary to prevent her capture, he was not ready to give up the fight. "There were some men in the control room who asked what they might do," he recalled. "I ordered them to the torpedo rooms to make ready the tubes." Brown was not even sure the damaged tubes could be opened, but it was worth a try.[6]

The men belowdecks could only pray that the gun teams might pull off a miracle and allow *Sculpin* to escape.

★ ★ ★

When the call for battle stations, surface, was issued, Joe Baker grabbed a life jacket, waved to senior motormac Moon Rocek, and raced for the control room. Never in his wildest dreams had he envisioned his nineteenth birthday being celebrated in a hopeless gun battle with a Japanese destroyer.

Because Baker was the first loader for the 3-inch deck gun, it was his job to ram each shell into the chamber and slam the breech closed. It was now time for all his previous gunnery practice drills to pay off. Chief Signalman Dinty Moore dropped into the deck gun's left seat, where he would manually train the weapon. Across from him, torpedoman Herb Thomas dropped into the right seat to serve as setter. Raised in northeastern Iowa, twenty-four-year-old Thomas had quit school in 1938 to join the Navy.[7]

The day was bright and clear, but the wind had whipped up the seas, making whitecaps break across the deck. Baker would receive the shells from four other topside shell handlers—torpedoman Warren Berry and three engineers: Duane White, Edward Ricketts, and Harry Milbourn. The eighth member of the main deck gun crew was

Gunner's Mate 2c Bob Wyatt. Through his headset, he would take coaching from gunnery officer Defrees on the bridge and SJ ranges called from radar officer Embury in the conning tower.

The .50-caliber machine guns and two 20mm antiaircraft guns on *Sculpin*'s bridge were under direction of another gunner's mate, GM2c John Rourke. A twenty-two-year-old who hailed from New Haven, Connecticut, Rourke recalled, "I was trouble-shooter on the guns in case there was any stoppage or misfire." Rourke's bridge gun crews consisted of six other men: James Harper, Eugene Arnath, Charles Pitser, William Partin, Charles Coleman, and Alexander Guillot.[8]

The scramble to man all of *Sculpin*'s guns had taken only a moment. Connaway and Defrees passed the word for their men to commence firing, hoping to land some lucky shots before the Japanese destroyer decided to fire. Wyatt's deck gun roared to life as Chief Moore pulled the trigger to send the first shell on its way. Joe Baker saw that his crew's first shot sailed high over the Japanese destroyer. Baker was already ramming in his second shell as Moore and Thomas worked to lower the elevation on their gun.[9]

In the bobbing seas and in the course of making frenzied adjustments, Baker saw their second 3-inch shell burst in the ocean short of *Yamagumo*. Wyatt's team prepared their third shot, noting that the destroyer was maneuvering to avoid their fire. By this point, the other weapons on *Sculpin*'s bridge had joined the fight. The .50-caliber machine guns chattered away. The two Oerlikon 20mm cannons barked angrily as they chewed clips of shells in mere seconds.

Bill Cooper, surveying the action from his post on the cigarette deck aft, saw that torpedoman Harper, manning the aft 20mm, was struggling to feed his gun. His assistant had not made it to the bridge.[10]

"Can I help you?" Cooper yelled.

"Yeah!" said Harper.

Cooper grabbed a clip of 20mm shells and helped Harper begin loading his gun. They were firing at the Japanese destroyer when it suddenly began returning *Sculpin*'s fire.

It was 1301—five minutes after his lookouts had first spotted the American submarine bursting to the surface—when Captain Shiro ordered his 5-inch gun crews to commence firing.[11]

Yamagumo's first volley was dead-on. One of the shells slammed into *Sculpin*'s conning tower with a blast of flame and a flash of red-hot shrapnel. The blast demolished the submarine's main air induction system, which was necessary for diving, and cut down four officers. On the bridge, skipper Fred Connaway and gunnery officer Joe Defrees crumpled to the deck. In the conning tower, radar officer George Embury and Exec Butch Allen also perished, and other men near them were wounded.

Another *Yamagumo* shell exploded into *Sculpin*'s conning tower seconds later, further adding to the casualties. On the after end of the bridge, Bill Cooper had been helping Jim Harper with his jammed 20mm. The explosion knocked Cooper off his feet and severed Harper's arm at the shoulder.[12]

Shrapnel also tore through the exposed 3-inch gun crew down on the after section of the deck. First loader Joe Baker saw the conning tower explode, and felt a heat wave of metal shards ripping through his team. "I got hit in the leg with shrapnel, but we kept firing," Baker recalled. Above his position, Baker could see Fireman 1c Alex Guillot helping to fire a .50-caliber machine gun at the moment of impact. One of the first two shells exploded near Guillot's gun, wounding him severely. "I still remember how he looked, with blood streaming from great rips in his chest, passing ammunition until he fell over the side," remembered Ed Ricketts, third loader on the deck gun.[13]

Ricketts, also hit in the legs by shrapnel, glanced toward the bridge. He saw torpedoman Harper still at his 20mm mount, his left arm severed, as 5-inch shells and lighter-caliber bullets slammed into *Sculpin*'s upper works. As the first two heavy shells ripped apart the bridge, gunner's mate John Rourke jumped overboard wearing his life jacket. Cooper quickly followed suit, jumping from the wrecked bridge in company with another seriously wounded 20mm gunner, Charles Pitser, both without life vests.[14]

Yamagumo's main guns were joined by her 25mm antiaircraft batteries. During the next few minutes, they scored numerous hits, wrecking *Sculpin*'s upper works and puncturing her pressure hull with more explosions. Despite having a number of his crew wounded, gunner's mate Bob Wyatt continued to direct *Sculpin*'s 3-inch gun in firing on the Japanese destroyer. Joe Baker, shot through the leg above his left ankle, continued ramming in shells. By his count, Ricketts noted that *Sculpin*'s deck gun was able to fire eight rounds in the opening minutes of the duel, although none were seen to strike their opponent.

Dead and wounded men lay sprawled about *Sculpin*'s deck and atop her conning tower. Her hull pierced by 5-inch shells, there was no escape from *Yamagumo*. Those capable of functioning were still fighting, but the Japanese destroyer had the range, and she closed in to finish off her victim.

* * *

Seaman Ed Keller felt helpless. As the battle surface commenced, he was still manning his headset in the after battery compartment. Near him, enlisted men hoisted shells topside from the ready ammunition lockers, while singing "Praise the Lord and Pass the Ammunition."[15]

A minute later, he heard the booming of the deck gun. Then Keller felt and heard a terrible explosion in *Sculpin*, somewhere up above.

Over his headset, he heard someone cry, "The conning tower has been hit!"

In the control room, diving officer George Brown was informed that four of his fellow officers had been killed, including skipper Connaway and Exec Butch Allen. He was now acting commander of the boat. "At this time, I considered it unwise to wait longer for scuttling operations, because the next shell might damage the hydraulic system, thus making it impossible to operate the vents," Brown recalled.[16]

He called back to the maneuvering room, where electrician's mate Laroy Smith was running the boards. Brown rang up emergency speed, preparing to send *Sculpin* to the bottom at full speed to rob the Japanese of any possibility of salvaging their boat. He turned to the ship's talker, yeoman Del Schroeder, and said, "Pass the word to abandon ship."

Months earlier, Schroeder had turned down the chance to be assigned to *Sculpin*'s sister sub, *Sailfish*, as he had considered it to be an "ill fated boat." His relief crew friend Bud Pike had taken the *Sailfish* assignment, but Schroeder now had reason to question that decision.

Among the others crowded about the control room were three chief petty officers from the engineering gang—Richard Hemphill, Bill Haverland, and Phil Gabrunas. Brown ordered Haverland and Hemphill to spread the word throughout the boat manually, in case the damage had destroyed the 1MC speaker system in any compartment. He promised to wait for their return before scuttling the boat. Hemphill raced toward the forward torpedo room, while Haverland ran aft—through the galley, the crew's berthing compartment, and the engine rooms, and to the after torpedo room.

The call to abandon ship set about a mass exodus from the boat. In the after battery compartment, Ed Keller was stunned to hear

Lieutenant Brown's final words over his headset: "Abandon ship, and God have mercy on your souls."[17]

Seconds later, yeoman Schroeder raced through the mess hall past Keller. He was in tears, clearly distraught.

"What's the matter?" Keller called in his booming voice.

"I can't find my life jacket, and I can't swim!" Schroeder cried.[18]

Keller stripped off his own jacket and handed it to Schroeder, who donned it and raced aft for the hatch leading topside. *Sculpin*'s crew had only three choices for exiting the boat: the mangled conning tower, the hatch near the forward torpedo room, or the forward engine room hatch. The hatch just behind the conning tower from the crew's after battery compartment had ceased to be an option in July, when the boat was at Midway.

Keller could hear the explosions above and the sound of enemy shells erupting close alongside *Sculpin*. It was time for him to go. He raced aft, forgetting in his own panic to even remove his headset. As the cord pulled tight, Keller was yanked from his feet and slammed to the deck. Tossing the headphones aside, he scrambled to his feet and raced aft after Schroeder toward the hatch.

He was surprised to find that the men trying to make their way topside displayed no panic. There was no pushing and shoving. Keller lined up, watching as a young sailor scrambled up the steel rungs toward the upper deck. But as that man emerged through the open hatch, a Japanese shell struck him in the head, killing him instantly. Others caught his body as the sailor tumbled back down, and they set the lifeless man beside the engines.

Another sailor, Seaman 1c George Goorabian, glanced over at Keller before he started up the ladder. Noting that Keller was without a life jacket, Goorabian said, "I'll wait for you on deck and we'll go over together."

"For God's sake, don't wait for me!" Keller shouted.[19]

Keller grabbed the rungs to the ladder, scrambled up the hatch, and headed topside behind Goorabian. "As I got almost to the top, Goorabian was hit and half his body was blown off," Keller recalled. In almost the same instant, another shell slammed into *Sculpin*'s hull. The force of the violent blast ejected Keller up through the hatch and ripped away half of his clothing.

His body riddled with shrapnel, Keller landed in the ocean. "My trousers had been blown halfway off, down to my ankles," he recalled. Dazed, he calmly noted the beautiful clear water and the bright blue skies above. Gathering his senses, Keller kicked off his pants and began swimming as *Sculpin* zipped away, entering her final dive.[20]

★ ★ ★

Moon Rocek had remained at his post in the forward engine room until the bitter end. After hearing Lieutenant Brown's call for emergency speed, his throttleman had opened their diesels wide open. There was nothing more he could do at this point.

Earlier in the day, during the depth charge attacks, he had shuffled back aft to the maneuvering room to chat with his friend electrician Laroy Smith. "Some of the men were crapped out from the heat exhaustion, just laying there on the deck," Rocek recalled. Now, as the word to abandon ship was passed, he wanted to make sure his comrades knew what was happening.[21]

Rocek raced back to the maneuvering room and found Smith. "They passed the word to abandon ship!" he called. "We'd better get out of here."

"Okay," said Smith. "I'll be coming."

He never saw Smith again. Rocek turned and raced forward to the hatch in the forward engine room. By this point, Schroeder, Goorabian,

Keller, and others had already exited, or attempted to exit, the boat. Rocek saw one sailor's body lying near the ladder in a pool of blood. He headed up the hatch, stunned to see shells exploding all around *Sculpin* and the body of Goorabian topside near the hatch. "There was a guy sprawled out," Rocek recalled. "He was a mass of blood."

Terrified, Rocek dropped back down the ladder into the forward engine room. After waiting for a few seconds, he steeled his nerves, knowing that climbing the ladder again offered him his only chance of survival. Rocek stumbled out on deck. A short distance away, he could see the Japanese destroyer firing all of its guns on *Sculpin*.

Not knowing what else to do, he raced forward across the deck, past the battered 3-inch gun crew. Rocek reached the after end of the conning tower and pressed himself against its steel surface. In an instant, he realized his foolish position. He was facing the Japanese destroyer "and a belch of fire" was coming from the warship. Rocek decided to take cover in the doghouse, an opening in the lower aft end that ran side to side through the base of the conning tower.

"I got about halfway through, and they got a direct hit into the conning tower," Rocek recalled. The blast knocked him down and stunned him. His body ached, and his leg was bloodied from small pieces of shrapnel. He quickly took stock of himself. *I've got my arms. I've got my head. It's time to go over the side.*

Rocek stumbled out of the steel compartment and jumped into the ocean.

★ ★ ★

In the control room, George Brown waited anxiously for his two chief engineers to return. Standing beside him to help man the dive vents was Chief Motor Machinist's Mate Phil Gabrunas, a good friend of Moon Rocek. Gabrunas, one of the nine *Sculpin* veterans who had made all eight prior war patrols, would not normally have been standing duty at the Christmas Tree panel. But chief of the boat Dinty Moore was topside, manning the 3-inch deck gun, so Gabrunas had volunteered to stay behind with the engineering officer to help scuttle the boat.

Captain Philip Cromwell, the wolf pack commander on board *Sculpin*, stood near Brown and Gabrunas during the final minutes. Brown had informed him of his orders and urged the captain to head topside to save himself.

"I'm not coming with you," said Cromwell. "I know too much."

There was nothing Brown could say to change his mind. "He told me to go ahead, that he could not come with us for he was afraid the information he possessed might be injurious to his shipmates at sea if the Japanese made him reveal it by torture," Brown recalled.[22]

A moment later, chiefs Hemphill and Haverland raced back into the control room. They had successfully covered the boat fore and aft, making sure every man knew they must abandon ship immediately. Most crewmen were in the process of doing so, but Hemphill reported that at least two were opting to stay on board.

As Hemphill passed the wardroom, he found Ensign Max Fiedler seated at the table with a deck of cards, playing a hand of solitaire. With him was one of *Sculpin*'s two Filipino mess attendants, first class officers' cook Eugenio Apostol. Fiedler, the young temporary diving officer who had inadvertently caused the boat to broach in sight of the Japanese destroyer, was apparently grief-stricken.

"Come on, let's go!" Hemphill said. "We're scuttling the boat!"

"We do not choose to go with you," replied the ensign. "We prefer death to capture by the Japanese."

When the chiefs returned, Brown waited one additional minute, watching the clock in the control room. At that point, those who wanted to leave had been given as much time as the diving officer could spare. Hemphill and Haverland had already scrambled up the ladder toward the bridge, although Haverland would not be seen again after exiting the boat.

"Open the vents," Brown said to Gabrunas. All of *Sculpin*'s buoyancy tanks were opened to the sea. Racing forward at 17 knots, the boat would be under the waves in less than a minute, taking anyone still on board to the bottom of the ocean. Gabrunas raced up the ladder toward the bridge, followed by the lieutenant. As Brown struggled through the conning tower, the water was already waist-deep. "I am certain no one left the ship after me," Brown later stated.[23]

Although Chief Gabrunas had been seen to climb up through the conning tower, Brown never saw him again. "He either became fouled in wreckage or was killed by machine gun fire," he recalled.

By the time Brown made it onto the bridge, *Sculpin*'s decks were already plowing under the waves. His submarine had fought her last fight. The lieutenant jumped over the side and watched the conning tower disappear from sight.

★ ★ ★

Fireman Joe Baker and the 3-inch gun crew had done their part. During *Sculpin*'s final minute, he and his wounded comrades had continued firing shells toward *Yamagumo* while their shipmates abandoned ship.

Torpedoman Harry Toney and electrician's mate Eldon Wright were among the sailors caught topside in the final minutes. Toney, who had been in the mess hall helping to pass ammunition to Baker's gun crew, ran toward the conning tower when the call came to abandon ship. But someone shouted that the conning tower had been hit, so Toney continued aft, where he climbed to the deck through the forward engine room hatch. Topside, he took a quick look at the Japanese destroyer blasting away at *Sculpin* and joined others in diving over the side. Wright was running toward the conning tower when another shell hit and exploded. Like Toney, he opted to dive over the side.[24]

Baker and Dinty Moore remained at the deck gun until *Sculpin*'s nose started to plow under the waves. "We heard the vents being pulled, so into the ocean we dove," recalled Baker. Sight setter Herb Thomas saw bodies of shipmates sprawled out on the deck as he finally abandoned the gun. He wondered if his torpedo room buddies had made it out. Only later would he find that his boss, Chief Torpedoman Claiborne Weade, was among the sailors who were never seen again.[25]

By 1310, less than fifteen minutes after surfacing, *Sculpin* was gone. "Her last dive was a really nice one," recalled Ed Ricketts, who had dived over the side at the last moment. "The last I saw was the radar mast going under," remembered shell handler Toney.[26]

It had been five years and 115 days since *Sculpin* had slid down the ways in Portsmouth, New Hampshire. Her struggling survivors were perhaps a half mile away when a large waterspout erupted, followed by a heavy concussion that rippled through the waves. Somewhere along her five-mile plunge toward the ocean floor, *Sculpin*'s 252 storage batteries had likely shorted out and exploded, a final gasp from the proud submarine.[27]

Moon Rocek, treading water a short distance away from the waterspout, was rocked by the concussion. "You could feel it in your spine," he recalled. "You were supposed to float on your back, and then any explosions in the water wouldn't affect your spine. But they never told us."[28]

Ed Keller, wounded and naked, saw the Japanese destroyer racing past him so close that he had to look upward to see her decks. As

Yamagumo sliced past him, he became aware of the sound of machine-gun fire. Keller dived as deep below the surface as he could, and in that instant, *Sculpin* exploded underwater. He bobbed back to the surface with his ears ringing. *Yamagumo*'s aft gunners were raking the floundering survivors even after *Sculpin* disappeared from the surface.[29]

He then heard shouting from another sailor. He looked around and spotted radioman Julius Peterson, a nineteen-year-old from Idaho who had joined the boat with Keller only one month ago. Peterson, wearing a life jacket, shouted for him to come join him, gunner Bob Wyatt, and yeoman Del Schroeder.[30]

Keller grabbed onto the life vests of Wyatt and Schroeder to support himself in the water. As he did, he saw that Schroeder was already dead, his mouth open and his chest ripped by at least two machine-gun bullets.

A short distance away, senior surviving officer George Brown tried to rally the survivors. He shouted out to his men, working to collect all the survivors into one large group. He later cited chief of the boat Weldon Moore and Ensigns Charles Smith and Worth Gamel for selflessly helping to save others. "Those of us who were strong swimmers aided the wounded and weak swimmers," Brown related.[31]

There were a number of seriously wounded men in the ocean. As many as a dozen *Sculpin* sailors had been killed by *Yamagumo*'s 5-inch shells during the gun duel. At least three men had opted to go down with the ship versus being captured, including Captain Cromwell. More than two dozen others from the eighty-four-man crew had been killed. Some died while exiting the hatches, some injured men were dragged down with the ship, and others were machine-gunned in the ocean.

Yamagumo's gunners had taken care of business, so Lieutenant Commander Shiro called for a cease-fire once *Sculpin* was gone. His destroyer had not taken any large-caliber hits, so Shiro decided to recover some American survivors for their value to interrogators. At 1317, *Yamagumo* slowed and lowered her whaleboats to begin picking up some of the submariners.[32]

Bill Cooper was only semiconscious as *Yamagumo* slowed to lower boats. When *Sculpin* disappeared and her batteries exploded at great depth, the force of the concussion had knocked him out briefly. Cooper opened his eyes and kicked toward the surface, wearing only shorts and a pair of sandals. He became aware of a terrific pain in his back, and later believed that the explosion had slammed an iron bar into his back.[33]

He kicked off his sandals and began swimming toward the enemy destroyer. *It's my only hope for being saved,* he thought. En route, he passed the bodies of shipmates who had perished in the brief machine-gunning. Cooper caught up to Chief Moore and another sailor, and together they stroked for *Yamagumo*.

Herb Thomas encountered gunner John Rourke in the ocean. Rourke had been knocked unconscious by the force of the explosions, but his life jacket had offered just enough support to keep him from drowning. Thomas helped to support Rourke, and then removed his own life belt to offer to another young sailor, Seaman 1c Bill Welsh. The young man, who had been striking to earn his quartermaster rating under Bill Cooper, was badly wounded from one of the explosions.[34]

"Though wounded, Welsh talked to me while in the water," Rourke recalled. The trio treaded water and struggled to swim toward the Japanese destroyer. By the time it slowed to begin picking up survivors, Welsh was losing strength and the will to survive. Thomas slapped him about the face and shouted, "Open your eyes! There's a ship, and we're going to go on it!"[35]

Others were too far gone. Joe Baker, suffering from a gunshot through his leg and shrapnel wounds incurred during the gun battle, did his best to support another shipmate who was gravely wounded. "I tried to help him stay afloat, but it was too much," remembered Baker, who was left to fight for his own survival as his comrade passed away.[36]

Yamagumo's sailors pulled some of the Americans into their small boats and motored back alongside the destroyer. Other submariners grabbed lines that were tossed from above, and were hauled up the slick sides. Among them was seventeen-year-old Seaman 2c Mike Gorman. Back in October 1942 in California, he had begged his parents to sign his enlistment forms so he could join the Navy. Fresh from torpedo school, he had been the youngest new hand to join the *Sculpin* crew on October 21. Now he knew that he would have to rely on his strong faith for whatever was in store for him on the afternoon of November 19. Peering up from the water toward the destroyer deck high above him, Gorman saw only Japanese faces staring back at him.[37]

Skipper Shiro allowed his destroyer to remain idle for only a short while. Once his sailors retrieved their whaleboats, *Yamagumo* picked up steam and headed for Truk. His warship had collected forty-two American survivors. One half of *Sculpin*'s crew was gone. The bloodied and terrified men retrieved by *Yamagumo* were left to wonder what fate had in store for them now.

SIX

"A Living Hell"

Ed Keller nervously looked up at the destroyer's deck, pitching in the waves high above him. He and gunner Bob Wyatt had reached *Yamagumo*'s hull, where Japanese sailors in white uniforms pushed them toward a ladder lowered over the side. Enemy sailors grabbed Wyatt, and he began climbing. Viewing it as his only choice for survival, Keller released his grip on the life jacket of the dead yeoman he had been clinging to and followed suit.[1]

On the warship's main deck, they were brutally herded toward the bow by rifle-bearing sailors. Days earlier, Keller had watched a movie being shown in *Sculpin*'s forward torpedo room. It was *Black Swan*, a film in which a sailing ship had been overtaken by the British, who suspected that the vessel had been carrying illegal slaves. During the pursuit, the suspect ship had tied the slaves to anchors and dropped them overboard to hide the evidence.[2]

Oh, my God! thought Keller. *They want to tie us to the anchor and drop us overboard!*

Yamagumo's crew had no such intentions. Joe Baker, also herded to the bow, had his hands and feet securely bound with lines. Seated on the warm steel deck, he watched other *Sculpin* shipmates being dragged forward. Many of them had shrapnel and bullet wounds. Some were in serious condition. Among the worst was quartermaster striker Bill Welsh.[3]

Electrician Eldon Wright, hauled on board at the same time, saw that Welsh was so weak from loss of blood that he fainted upon reaching *Yamagumo*'s deck. "He had a triangular chest wound, and as he breathed, that triangular piece of flesh wavered in and out," recalled Herb Thomas. He had helped Welsh in the water and onto the ship, where he carefully stretched the young seaman out on the deck. Blood from Welsh's chest and shoulder wounds ran down his legs. Japanese sailors soon began talking excitedly, pointing toward Welsh's bloodied legs.[4]

Thomas noted a senior officer whom he believed to be *Yamagumo*'s skipper walking among the survivors as they were pulled onto the deck. Quartermaster Bill Cooper saw the Japanese pointing at his young striker and feared for Welsh. Cooper called for assistance, and Ensign Charles Smith rushed forward to help. "Smitty" had taken a bunk near Cooper in the forward torpedo room, since *Sculpin*'s wardroom was at capacity on her ninth run. "I got acquainted with him pretty good," recalled Cooper. "We were the only two on the boat from Tennessee."[5]

Cooper grabbed Welsh around the chest, and Smith grabbed his legs. They began hauling him toward the bow, but made it only halfway before a Japanese officer forced them to halt. Through shouts and gestures, he ordered them to lay the bloodied sailor on the deck. Cooper, Smith, and others watched in horror as a pair of Japanese sailors grabbed Welsh, hauled him to the side, and flung him back into the ocean. Pharmacist's mate Paul Todd, who believed Welsh could have been saved, felt the Japanese simply did not want to tend to his severe wounds.

Gunner's mate John Rourke then found himself in the same dilemma. A shipmate had helped him onto *Yamagumo*'s deck, where he lay bleeding from lacerations in his feet and back and vomiting from the salt water he had swallowed. After tossing Welsh over the side, the Japanese sailors approached Rourke, picked him up off the deck, and carried him back to the quarterdeck. "They proceeded to swing me, with the intention of throwing me over the side," Rourke recalled. "On the third swing, I kicked loose."[6]

Fighting free, Rourke lashed back at the Japanese sailors as they tried to grasp him again. Deciding that he was more spirited and apparently well enough to preserve, they began beating him severely. Only when Rourke's body was limp from the pounding did his captors drag him to the bow. They tied his hands and legs before dumping him in a pile alongside his fellow *Sculpin* captives.

Lieutenant George Brown, like others, was forced to strip off any excess clothing he wore, including any jewelry and personal items. He was herded forward through two rows of Japanese enlisted men bearing clubs, sticks, and small paddles. Brown was beaten in the body, legs, and head until he reached the prisoner circle on the bow, where he was bound and made to face forward.[7]

"The Japanese officials took one of my enlisted men around a gun turret and worked him over to get information about the submarine, and about our destination and home port," Brown later testified. When the battered enlisted man was returned, the Japanese hauled Brown to his feet and took him for interrogation. They were displeased to find that the sailor had given them information other than what Brown had offered when he was brought on deck.

Japanese sailors beat Brown with a small club and their fists for offering false information on the name of his ship, the skipper, and its tonnage. Then they began asking the lieutenant about the date of *Sculpin*'s sailing and its destination. The Japanese clearly knew *Sculpin*'s name, but the lieutenant was reluctant to give them any more. "When I refused to answer, they again beat me with their fists and told me the answers they received from the enlisted man," Brown remembered.

During this time, Ed Keller glanced about his surroundings in a daze. He saw blood running freely over the deck from his wounded comrades. The sailor next to him finally whispered, asking Keller how badly he had been hit.

"I'm not injured," he replied.[8]

But as he looked down at his own bare chest, he saw dried blood smeared over his body. He had been unaware that the blast that propelled him over the side of *Sculpin* had peppered him with shrapnel in the chest and in his leg. Now, in his state of shock, Keller wondered if he might die.

Yamagumo made high speed back toward Truk—roughly two hundred miles west from the site of *Sculpin*'s sinking—where Lieutenant Commander Shiro intended to deposit his captives for proper interrogation. When Lieutenant Brown was returned to the other *Sculpin* men, he was tied up and lay panting, recovering from his severe beating. He had time to think about how Captain Cromwell had implored skipper Fred Connaway to ride out just one more attack from the Japanese destroyer. Cromwell had insisted that the warship must be nearly out of depth charges. Some of the survivors noticed as they were hauled onto *Yamagumo*'s deck that only three more ash cans remained in her racks.[9]

* * *

Yamagumo steamed through the evening of November 19, en route to Truk. During that time, the forty-one *Sculpin* survivors were offered only bare sustenance. That night, several Japanese sailors came forward to offer a few eight-ounce cans of warm and foul-tasting water for the Americans to share, along with a few hard crackers.

Joe Baker was suffering from a bullet wound and shrapnel injuries, but some of his shipmates were in far worse shape. Blood ran freely across the deck as men writhed in agony. "Our hands and feet were tied, with only a piece of tarpaulin stretched over all 41 of us for protection in a hard rainstorm against a raging sea," Baker recalled.[10]

Motor machinist's mate George Rocek, being a former water polo player, had endured the ocean well enough. As he sat tied on the destroyer's bow, he looked over the wounds in his legs, where tiny pieces of metal had become embedded from the explosion that wrecked *Sculpin*'s doghouse compartment. During any opportunity when his hands were briefly untied, he took the chance to pick out small shards of metal. Some resembled old watch springs.[11]

Yamagumo entered the Truk Atoll anchorage before dawn on November 20. Skipper Shiro docked his destroyer at the busy seaplane and submarine base at Dublon Island, the Japanese equivalent to Pearl Harbor's Ford Island. En route to base, he had transmitted a report to Truk that was picked up by American intelligence code breakers. "At 1304, sank enemy submarine with gunfire. Have 41 prisoners. Will send action summary later." Further Japanese reports from Truk's harbor director were intercepted on November 20. One indicated that *Yamagumo*'s prisoners would be turned over to the base force commander at Truk, and that the destroyer would commence refueling.[12]

At Pearl Harbor, Vice Admiral Charlie Lockwood now knew the true fate of *Sculpin*. In order to maintain his classified Ultra intelligence team, this dreadful information would remain in the know only among a small number of senior U.S. Navy officials for the time being. Officially, when *Sculpin* failed to return from her war patrol, she would be designated as "overdue and presumed lost."

Soon after *Yamagumo* docked at Dublon Island, there was a flurry of commotion among the American prisoners on her deck. Each man's feet were untied, but Japanese sailors placed blindfolds over their captives' eyes and kept their wrists securely bound by lines. Herded to his feet, Joe Baker found moving without stumbling to be "complicated as all hell. This is where some of us received our first slugging, because we were curious and tried to see from beneath our blindfolds."[13]

The *Sculpin* sailors were prodded down to a little harbor launch that would ferry them to their final destination. Within Truk's vast lagoon, numerous warships were present, including the Japanese super battleship *Musashi*. When the launch reached shore, the blindfolded prisoners were pushed and prodded toward a waiting army transport truck. George Brown had been fortunate to at least retain his tattered pair of undershorts, but he was blindfolded and barefoot as Japanese guards prodded him and his shipmates with rifle butts.[14]

Some of the *Sculpin* men had great difficulty walking on the coral sands and rocks. With their hands bound, their falls were even more painful. Torpedoman Charles Pitser's arm had been nearly severed at the shoulder by one of the shell explosions. Radioman Jerome Baglien was even more challenged: He was still bleeding heavily from wounds in his thighs, and one of his calves had nearly been severed from his leg. Their captors showed no sympathy, beating and prodding anyone who lingered or stumbled.

Once on board the military truck, the prisoners were bounced along on a crushed-gravel road. Naked, ashamed, and blindfolded, Ed Keller could see enough under the corner of his blindfold to tell that they passed through a little village where they were exposed to public view from the locals. "We could hear women and children laughing along the sides of the streets," Keller remembered.[15]

The Japanese moved them to a detention compound on the far end of Dublon Island. Lying at the base of a 1,500-foot peak, the little compound—surrounded by a twelve-foot wooden fence—did not appear large enough to properly house forty-one captured U.S. submariners. Inside the facility, the *Sculpin* men were taken to a wooden prisoner structure, an area roughly thirty feet square, that was subdivided into three small prisoner cells on one side.

Japanese soldiers divided the Americans into three groups and began shoving them into the cells. With their hands still bound, each man was pushed into one of the small rooms and knocked to the floor. Fireman Cecil Baker, a young man from Indiana who had been on *Sculpin* since July, was shoved into the first cell on the left side of the compound along with a dozen other shipmates. They included Ed Keller, radioman Peterson, gunner Bob Wyatt, motormac Ed Ricketts, torpedoman Harry Toney, Tom Brown, seaman Mike Gorman, and several men Baker had not known well on the boat. "There wasn't even anything to sit on," Baker recalled. "We had to sit on our haunches with our hands tied."[16]

During the Americans' first day of incarceration, the Japanese guards offered no food or water. In the cramped confines, the space was stifling. Near the top of each cell, ventilation came from a three-foot-by-one-foot window and a larger, shuttered opening near the cell door. The only toilet facility was a hole in the floor in one end of the room that was swarming with flies at all times. Space was so tight that some men had to sleep around the toilet hole just to make enough room for everyone to bring their elbows down beside them. The men conversed among one another, but such talk drew the ire of the guards. One of the Japanese ended any conversation by reaching through the window slats to beat the prisoners with a wooden bat. Keller, struck in the head and shoulders numerous times, quickly learned to put his bound hands over his head for protection.[17]

Cries for help resulted in further beatings. Near Keller, Joe Baker occasionally cried out, "I need water! I need water." Each time Baker begged, the bat would be extended into their cell and the inmates were beaten.

Things were no better in the center cell. Engineman Moon Rocek found himself confined with another dozen shipmates, including junior officer Charles Smith and enlisted men John Rourke, John Parr, Robert Carter, Warren Berry, Herb Thomas, Leo Eskildsen, and Duane White. The final three men crammed into Rocek's central cell were the three most severely wounded.

Fireman Henry Elliott, a veteran of six patrols on *Sculpin*, hailed from rural Jasper, Alabama, in the Deep South, and was known to his buddies as "Rebel." During the surface battle with *Yamagumo*, Elliott had endured a high-caliber-shell wound that punched a hole the size of a half-dollar through his hand. Rocek saw that radioman Jerome Baglien had .50-caliber wounds in his upper legs that left a portion of his flesh hanging in shards. Torpedoman Charles Pitser—a stocky man of about 235 pounds who stood six foot two—had long black hair and heavily tattooed forearms. Once a man to be reckoned with, Pitser now lay in agony, clutching the remains of his dangling arm, which had been nearly severed in the gun battle.[18]

The Japanese offered no medical attention to these seriously wounded men. "We took turns standing to allow more room for them,"

Rocek recalled. "When we would stand up, the Japanese proceeded to work our heads over with a stick a little bit bigger than a two-by-four," said gunner Rourke, who was suffering from his own serious wounds.[19]

The third cell was slightly smaller, and only ten *Sculpin* survivors were pushed into it. They included Lieutenant George Brown, Ensign Worth Gamel, chief of the boat Dinty Moore, Doc Todd, fireman Paul Murphy, electrician Eldon Wright, and four others. The final four *Sculpin* prisoners, including ship's cook Andy Anderson and quartermaster Bill Cooper, were confined in a small, closetlike structure near the three main brigs.

Cooper was wounded and suffering from severe dehydration. "I had been on the wheel for eight of our last hours, hand steering the boat," he recalled. Because he had lacked hydraulic power, any order from full left rudder to full right rudder had required a hundred turns of his large steel wheel. The exertion had left Cooper quite parched long before he had raced topside to assist the 20mm gunners during his boat's ill-fated final battle surface. From his little closet, Cooper now begged for water. "They just laughed at me," he recalled.[20]

* * *

George Brown was only in his cell for about ten minutes before his hell started. As the most senior officer captured, he was the first to be interrogated at Truk. Led blindfolded from his cell and across the hot coral beach, he was halted before a small table set up in the compound yard.

Seated before the *Sculpin* lieutenant were a Japanese rear admiral and a half dozen other ranking Imperial Japanese Navy officers. An English-speaking interpreter began quizzing Brown about his boat, other U.S. submarines, their operating bases, what codes they used, and other communications information. Brown offered vague answers, and the Japanese were unimpressed. Each time the admiral disliked his answers, he nodded to two burly Japanese enlisted men standing nearby.[21]

Using long clubs, they struck the lieutenant with four or five smacks to his back and legs. At one point, the force of their blows knocked Brown off his feet and sent him sprawling across the table into the Japanese admiral. "I was then dragged off and severely beaten for daring to attack a Japanese admiral," Brown recalled.

At length, the Japanese finally decided the lieutenant was not willing to offer them any useful information. Brown was dragged to a pillbox, where he was forced to stand at attention around the clock for two full days. His only respite during this ordeal was occasional intervals of more questioning and beatings. "At any time I relaxed from a position of rigid attention, the guard would drop his rifle on my bare feet, or kick me in the shins and beat me over the head with his rifle butt," said Brown.[22]

On the morning of his third day on Truk, Brown was brought back to his rancid cell, where he collapsed from exhaustion. During his ordeal, the other *Sculpin* men had been hauled out for their own interrogations. Gunner John Rourke, also questioned during his first day on the island, was beaten repeatedly by the guards. He failed to understand their demands for him to come to attention. When the interpreter finally told Rourke what they were saying, the beatings ceased for a moment. One of the guards then removed Rourke's blindfold and asked the location of his submarine's operating base. When he professed ignorance, he was beaten again until the Japanese finally returned him to his cell, apparently deciding that he was a worthless source.[23]

Another sailor taken from Rourke's cell on the first day was fireman Leo Eskildsen, a man of Norwegian ancestry. His interpreter, who spoke only broken English, seemed skeptical that the submariner was truly a native American. "Some of these questions pertained to the

Sculpin and our operations, but most pertained to my family, and especially my nationality," recalled Eskildsen. He insisted that he was an American, the son of immigrants, but the Japanese did not believe him. His interrogator gave an order in Japanese, whereupon the guard beat Eskildsen on the back and rear end with a long club.[24]

After multiple rounds of beatings, Eskildsen was finally knocked down and could not rise. The guard then hoisted him to his feet so the session could continue. Only when the engineman was barely conscious and could no longer maintain his footing was he carried back and dumped into his cell. The process was repeated throughout the day for one *Sculpin* survivor after another. By the second day at Truk, every man had been hauled before the interrogation committee at least once.

Torpedoman Herb Thomas used deception in his answers, but soon found that the Japanese carefully compared notes after each session. He told them that American subs used a secret base between the Gilberts and Truk to refuel while on patrol. The Japanese soon produced a wrinkled brown chart from the 1800s and demanded that Thomas show where the island base was located. When he could not locate the mystery island, Thomas was severely beaten and hauled back to his cell, where he whispered about his ruse to his comrades. "We repeated the story," recalled shipmate Ed Ricketts.[25]

Others attempted delaying tactics. Moon Rocek stalled for time by saying he could not understand the interpreter's questions. "I was able to get away with it sometimes," he recalled. Eventually, the quiz kid would nod his head, and the bat-wielding Japanese guards worked Rocek over. Many of their blows rained down on his rear end, but some of their swings were particularly painful when they struck higher, against his tailbone.[26]

Ed Keller, still naked since the sinking of his ship, returned from his quiz sessions with cuts and bruises from all the beatings. But the most painful clubbings were made against his exposed testicles, to the amusement of his Japanese guards. "One day, while awaiting for Jap intelligence to question me, I was struck so hard by a Jap guard that I was forced to double up and vomit from the pain," Keller recalled.[27]

Some, like Joe Baker, were questioned and beaten as many as three different times over their first day of imprisonment on Truk. Although he and his enlisted comrades suffered greatly, Baker felt that *Sculpin*'s three officers—Brown, Worth Gamel, and Charles Smith—were more severely brutalized during their quiz sessions. Peering through the window of his cell, Baker saw Brown return from his multiday ordeal "black and blue from head to foot."[28]

Brown made great efforts to conceal any information on *Sculpin*'s radar gear, which was of great interest to the Japanese. Two members of the boat's radio gang had been lost with the boat, but four had been taken prisoner—John Parr, Julius Peterson, Cliff Taylor, and Jerome Baglien. Of them, only Parr, a new hand received just prior to *Sculpin*'s final run, had stood regular radar watches. "The officers informed all of us he was to be considered a gunner, not a radar man," recalled Ed Keller.[29]

But the Japanese beatings finally yielded the fact that Parr was the only radar operator among their captives. One afternoon, guards appeared at his cell and called him out by name and rank. Parr was taken before a group of officers beneath a tree and quizzed heavily on the secrets of American radar. When he was returned to his central cell hours later, Keller saw that Parr had been beaten severely about his shoulders and arms.

Over the next two days, Parr was frequently singled out for more quiz sessions. "They would keep him out for a half hour, put him back, and an hour later take him out again," recalled John Rourke. After multiple rounds of abuse, the radar man appeared punch-drunk and only semiconscious. On *Sculpin*, he had been carefree and something of a jokester. After days on Truk, Rourke found Parr to be reclusive and groggy from frequent beatings.[30]

Two other *Sculpin* survivors received special attention from their Japanese guards. One was motor machinist's mate Ed Ricketts, who showed signs of resentment when one of his captors began referring to him as "Monkey." Ricketts was removed from his cell and pounded by three guards, who used their fists, small clubs, and longer bats. According to cellmate Joe Baker, Ricketts was finally dumped back in their cell after the guards had worked him over "from head to foot, but hitting him mostly on his spine, his back, shoulders, and face, until he was unconscious."[31]

Another who received brutal beatings that exceeded the normal treatment was Ensign Charles Smith. His trouble started when he became too mouthy with one of the guards during the brief "recreation" periods, when the *Sculpin* men were allowed out of their cells. Smith became irritated with the abuse that occurred even during their exercise periods. Men like Paul Murphy could barely stand after days of lying motionless in cramped cells. In the compound yard, Murphy and others were ordered to assume squatting positions, with their knees partially bent and their hands over their heads. "Some of the fellows fell over from the intense heat, and were beaten until they got up again," Murphy recalled. Some guards offered water to the men, but forced them to kneel and look up. "They poured water down our throat and nose out of a bottle," said Cecil Baker. When the men began choking, the guards were greatly amused.[32]

These and other incidents of abuse in the compound yard did not sit well with Smitty. One of the guards who spoke some English enjoyed telling the ensign that Japanese planes would soon be bombing the United States. Smith replied that the Japanese would never get that far, and that American warplanes would instead bomb Japan. Enraged, the guard beat the ensign severely in front of his shipmates.[33]

On another occasion, Lieutenant Brown complained to the interpreter that his class ring had been stolen. The guard whom Brown accused was called forward to be searched, but he had already slipped the ring into the pocket of Smitty, who was also standing at attention before the interrogation table. "The guard himself searched Ensign Smith, and finding the ring he himself placed there, showed it to the interpreter," recalled John Rourke. The interpreter sentenced Smitty to a beating, whereupon guards forced him to stand back up each time he was knocked to the ground.[34]

After days of such treatment, few *Sculpin* survivors held much hope that they could last for a week on Truk.

* * *

George Rocek was becoming weaker, both mentally and physically. The quiz sessions, and the beatings that went with them, had drained his body. Only after the first forty-eight hours on Truk were the men offered any type of rations. Rocek found that this consisted of one salty rice ball, about the size of a man's fist, per day and a few ounces of water.

During the rare times when water rations were provided, each man had to struggle to receive some. "If it ran out before you got your share, it was your bad luck," stated Ed Keller. "To ask for more, as so many men in fever did at night, resulted in an unmerciful beating about the head and shoulders with a light club often as large as an indoor baseball bat."[35]

In the center cell, Rocek and others were beaten for standing to allow the most severely wounded men a place to lie down. During one such session, guards pushed long bamboo poles through the window to jab at torpedoman Charles Pitser. With one arm nearly severed, the husky, tattooed sailor simply could not defend himself. Shipmate Joe Baker stepped in, attempting to fend off the jabs to protect Pitser. Guards then removed Baker from the cell and beat him unconscious with clubs and their fists.[36]

By the third day, Pitser, Baglien, and Rebel Elliott had received no medical attention for their serious bullet and shrapnel wounds. Their wounds were beginning to stink as gangrene set in. With little to no clothing at all, the men suffered more as maggots, ants, and biting mosquitoes crawled through their sores. There was nothing anyone could do to alleviate their suffering, as the heat and stench from the unemptied toilet holes rose.

After several days of confinement, the men were finally allowed by the Japanese to use pails of water to scrub the floors of their cells to remove some of the blood, filth, and human waste. Some of the men—including John Rourke, Warren Berry, Duane White, Ed Keller, and Jerome Baglien—attempted to drink some of the cleaning water when they thought their guards were not looking. The men suspected of drinking from the pail were gathered for special punishment. Per Keller, the Japanese used clubs to "beat us until we collapsed from the pain in our legs and back."[37]

Torpedoman Herb Thomas came to dread a Japanese punch he and his shipmates dubbed "the haymaker." The guards swung with great speed. "It was like being slapped across the face with a closed fist," recalled Thomas. "They could hit you with haymakers and cause great pain. If they would have just kept punching us straight on in the face repeatedly, they would have killed us."[38]

On the fifth day, November 24, a group of well-dressed Japanese officers visited the prisoner compound. They were appalled by the condition of some of the Americans. "They could smell the gangrene," Keller remembered.[39]

The senior officer asked the Americans who was in charge. Lieutenant Brown announced himself as the senior officer among the prisoners and began answering questions from the Japanese officials.

"Who are the wounded?" he was asked.

"Just about everyone," said Brown.

When he informed them that not one man had received even an aspirin for their severe wounds, the senior officer became enraged. Turning to another officer, he began harshly reprimanding the man. "To punctuate the comments, he punched him in the face and knocked him backwards," Keller recalled.

After this visit, the amount of food and water improved for the submariners. Hours later, a Japanese Navy medical corpsman arrived with a supply bag to check over the *Sculpin* men. But Joe Baker felt that his techniques were crude and limited at best. The medic wiped off dried bloodstains with liquid from a green bottle that he poured onto a filthy rag. "No attempt was made to take out the bullet which I had in my leg," Baker remembered.[40]

Following the corpsman's visit, eight *Sculpin* sailors with the most serious wounds were ordered from their cells. Blindfolded, the men were made to march with a line around their waists that led to the next man. The group included Jerome Baglien, Moon Rocek, John Rourke, Rebel Elliott, Ed Keller, Ed Ricketts, Robert Carter, and Charles Pitser. En route, Baglien stumbled and fell, pulling the next man in the tie line, Rourke, down with him. "He had fifty-caliber wounds in both legs in his thighs, which crippled him to a degree that he could hardly walk," said Rourke. As the wounded men tried to regain their footing, guards pounded them with bat-sized clubs.[41]

Rocek found the treatment upon reaching the medical office to be little better. One of the medics used fish oil and bandages to clean some of the shrapnel wounds in his legs, but he was not offered any medicine. Rourke's blindfold was removed as the Truk doctor worked on his back wounds and the deep lacerations in his toes. One of the medics used a wirelike metal instrument to painfully probe into Rourke's open wounds. When he cried out in pain, the medical staff laughed heartily.[42]

After several hours of this rough treatment, Rourke, Keller, Ricketts, Carter, and Rocek were escorted back to the prisoner compound. The medics had done little for a deep laceration on Keller's foot that he had suffered after stepping on broken glass while trying to abandon ship. One doctor probed Keller's hip where shrapnel had entered his body, but he decided nothing further was needed other than some gauze stuffed into the open wound. Ricketts and Rocek, each sporting deep shrapnel wounds in their legs, were in no better shape after seeing the Truk doctors.[43]

The three most severe cases—Elliott, Baglien, and Pitser—were detained for further attention. Bridge gunner Pitser's arm had been nearly severed by the explosion of one of *Yamagumo*'s heavy shells. Japanese medics restrained him and amputated the arm without offering him any anesthesia.

Moving on to Rebel Elliott, they proceeded to cut his hand off at the wrist. Although he had a massive hole through his hand, Elliott had retained movement of his fingers. Pharmacist's mate Paul Todd felt that his hand could have been saved with proper surgery. The medics also removed a portion of one leg from radioman Baglien, who had had a chunk of one of his calves ripped nearly clean from the bone. Days later, Rocek would encounter these men and learn of their horrific treatment. "They told me that all the time they were doing this amputation, it was without any anesthetic, and they were plying them with questions about submarines," Rocek remembered.[44]

The Japanese detained Elliott, Pitser, and Baglien in the medical office for days as they recovered from their amputations. Their shipmates who had been returned to their cells spread the word to others about their treatment and the beatings they had received while stumbling to and from the Truk medical facility. The *Sculpin* men had little interest in accepting any further offers of treatment. Cecil Baker, whose eardrum had been ruptured during beatings in his second interrogation, decided not to mention the pain he was suffering.[45]

Rourke, having had his wounds probed in the medical office, was through with accepting help and further humiliation. "The next time they asked for men who wished to obtain medical attention at the hospital, I didn't answer up."[46]

The next days passed with little change for the submariners. Few believed they would live much longer in their rancid cells. For fireman Joe Baker, life at Truk was "a living hell for everyone concerned."[47]

SEVEN

"Chance of a Lifetime"

The pungent smell of exhaust and fuel invaded the sweet tropical aroma of the Hawaiian Islands. Bill Dillon inhaled deeply as he glanced toward the dock. In a matter of hours, his boat would be submerged more often than surfaced, and foul human body odor from seven dozen other men working in close proximity would become more commonplace.

From the bridge, Dillon felt the diesel engines rumbling beneath his feet. He noted shipmates on deck below casting off the heavy lines that had tethered *Sailfish* to the dock. It was just after 1300 on November 17 when his submarine eased away from the Pearl Harbor Sub Base. A crowd was on hand and a Navy band played "Aloha" and "Sink 'Em All"—a new tradition put in place by ComSubPac Charlie Lockwood—as the boat prepared for its tenth patrol.

Before heading below, Dillon watched as *Sailfish* eased slowly past the towering cranes of the Navy yard and then cruised down the channel past Ford Island. The shattered hull of the battleship *Arizona* remained, and battlewagon *Oklahoma* was in the process of being refloated. The damage to the pride of the Pacific Fleet made Dillon recall America's day of infamy on December 7, 1941. He hoped his new skipper would aggressively seek out attacks on enemy shipping on this patrol.

Lieutenant Commander Bob Ward stood proudly on the bridge, supervising his officer of the deck as *Sailfish* steered past Hospital Point and Hickam Field, and then through the anti-submarine net toward the open water. It had been three and a half years since the old *Squalus* had been raised and recommissioned as USS *Sailfish*, and now Ward was taking her back to the war zone for his first command patrol, officially her tenth run. New hand Ray Bunt felt as excited as he had been before a race as a kid. Topside long enough on lookout duty to watch the lush Hawaiian Islands begin fading into the blue-green horizon, he recalled, "One could hardly believe that we were at war."[1]

Sailfish departed Hawaii in company with the submarine *Gunnel* and *PC-596,* a four-hundred-fifty-ton subchaser that served as protective escort for the outbound boats. In the forward engine room, John Good was on duty with senior motormac Freddie Wheeler. The deafening roar of the diesel engines made him proud to be heading to sea on his first war patrol. Once out to sea, Good was on the compartment's headphones as talker Bud Pike checked in with each compartment prior to diving. Good reported that everything was properly rigged. Wheeler then dismissed him toward the control room so Good could take his shift on the diving planes.[2]

Aside from routine trim dives, *Sailfish* and *Gunnel* both ran on the surface until after dark, when their patrol craft turned back for Oahu. At 2100, *Gunnel* parted ways and proceeded independently toward Midway and her assigned patrol area. Ward's boat had similar orders to proceed toward Japan, and his *Sailfish* would also make a brief stop at Midway Island to take on additional fuel for the long haul.

Sailfish was loaded with twenty new Mark 14-3A torpedoes that had been serviced by torpedo experts on the submarine tender *Holland*. Extensive testing by Admiral Lockwood's staff during the late summer and early fall of 1943 had revealed defects that skippers had long complained of: torpedoes running ten feet deeper than their settings, and the failure of contact exploders when targets were hit straight on. Experts on *Holland* devised a stronger, lighter mechanical firing pin, some built from scrap metal from Japanese aircraft propellers found on Hawaii. After twenty-three months of fighting utilizing faulty fish, Lockwood's U.S. submarine service was finally heading to war with improved torpedoes.[3]

Ward's boat also set sail with ample provisions to last his crew for more than two months at sea. New commissary officer Ed Berghausen and his staff had *Sailfish* stuffed with goods from stem to stern. Two of his cooks, Albert Johnson and Cyril Gleeson, were making their first war patrols on the boat. The third, Ship's Cook Second Class (SC2c) Tom Sargent, had come aboard *Sailfish* in 1942 as a seaman second class, striking for a torpedoman's rating. But along the way, Sargent had gained an interest in cooking and had taken a three-week course at Pearl Harbor, eventually earning himself a ship's cook rating.[4]

Bill Dillon considered Sargent to be terrific. "He got to know the entire crew and what each man liked and disliked," Dillon remembered. Most off-duty sailors could grab coffee and sandwiches in the galley at any hour, but Sargent was not opposed to climbing out of his bunk to cook up a special request, even at odd hours in the night. His efforts to keep the crew pleased with their food was one factor that contributed to new, enthusiastic morale on the boat.[5]

Every square inch of extra space had been loaded with food and supplies. Dillon, still recalling how *Sailfish* had run out of toilet paper on a previous patrol, was enthused that supplies seemed more bountiful. But the downside was that food had even been stashed in the crew's quarters, and mounds of potatoes, onions, and other vegetables filled their shower. "We rarely had the luxury of taking a shower while on war patrol," he recalled. "But at the start of the patrol, it was not even an option." Washing clothes was a true luxury, so Dillon had purchased additional skivvies and undershirts in Hawaii. As they became fouled during the course of the patrol, he and other shipmates simply crammed their most pungent garments under their bunks.

During her first full day at sea on November 18, *Sailfish* was approached twice by friendly aircraft. The first, sighted by lookouts at 0820, was flying on a parallel course at a distance of eight miles. Radar operators Dillon and Frank Dieterich saw no pip on their radar screen, and attributed this lack of detection to the plane's low altitude. Six hours later, lookouts spotted another aircraft approaching at equally low altitude from sixteen miles out. Again, this plane failed to produce a pip on the SD until the pilot closed to within eight miles, whereupon *Sailfish* signalman Troy Ray exchanged recognition signals to prove their friendly status.[6]

The next two days were uneventful, and on the morning of November 21, *Sailfish* made her approach to Midway Island. Ward was topside as his OOD conned the boat through the tricky shoals, up Midway's channel, and to her berth in a nest of submarines alongside the tender *Bushnell* at 1007. *Sailfish*'s stay would be brief, only long enough for *Bushnell*'s repair crews to tackle some minor work items while the engineering gang topped off her fuel tanks. This task was presided over by MoMM2c Henry "Robbie" Robertson, *Sailfish*'s "Oil King." Aside from his regular duties in the forward engine room,

Robertson was accountable for all fuel taken aboard his ship and in daily checkups to know when it was time to convert a depleted fuel tank to a ballast tank while on patrol.[7]

Fueling to capacity required an additional 15,180 gallons of diesel oil and several hours. During this time, Ward ordered two of his junior officers to take care of another challenge. *Sailfish*'s communications officer, Dutch Wetmore, had been struggling with a balky electric code machine (ECM) since departing from Pearl Harbor. While at sea, messages were routinely copied by senior radioman Bob Johnson and other members of his radio gang: Bill Dillon, Paul Kelly, Ben West, and other nonrated sailors who were striking to become rated as radiomen. From the submarine headquarters at Pearl Harbor, a system of serialized messages known as "Fox schedules" was broadcast at varying times on different frequencies from a network of relay stations in the United States, Hawaii, Australia, and other locations. The use of multiple stations and the rebroadcasting of key messages at fixed hours each day via various very low-frequency (VLF) signals helped prevent enemy jamming attempts. Johnson's radio gang dutifully copied such radio traffic each day, but never acknowledged the messages unless their boat was specifically directed to do so.[8]

Dillon and his comrades copied Morse code into groups of five letters that could be decoded only by the communications officer. The copied code was delivered to Lieutenant (jg) Wetmore in the control room, and he would crack the code with his ECM, a device that resembled an oversized typewriter. Slots in the top of the ECM held various decoding wheels that required an officer who knew which wheel was to be used on each particular day. Wetmore took the coded note, placed the correct wheel in the top slot, and typed out the code from Dillon. The ECM then spit out a paper tape that Wetmore glued to a message blank and carried to the skipper to read.[9]

But Wetmore complained to Ward that his ECM was not functioning properly, and the skipper directed him to get the classified device replaced. In company with new radar officer Bill Bruckart, Wetmore hauled the ECM down the pier and across the sandy beach toward Midway's communication hut. Both officers carried their sidearms, .45-caliber pistols, weapons that were never otherwise worn. "Back on the ship, my sidearm was stowed under my mattress for the duration of the patrol," Bruckart remembered.[10]

Fully refueled and with a functional ECM on board, Sailfish was underway at 1611 as her crew cast off the lines that held her to *Bushnell*. Ward twisted the boat through the channel, and soon Midway was fading away. Air escorts provided cover until sunset, and then *Sailfish* was on her own. The following day, timekeeping was reset on the boat to reflect having crossed the international date line—thereby advancing the date on board by one day. Upon recrossing the 180th meridian en route home, U.S. naval vessels would actually repeat a date to return to the proper time zone.

En route to station, Ward ran *Sailfish* on the surface at night to charge her batteries. During the day, the boat was often submerged to avoid detection from enemy aircraft. His fully qualified and more experienced officers—Pat Murphy, Stan Cowin, and Dutch Wetmore—rotated four-hour shifts as OOD. Newer junior officers Bruckart, Ed Berghausen, and Wayne Evans stood their watches as junior officer of the deck (JOOD) as they learned. Due to his role as XO and as the ship's navigator, Lieutenant Bud Richardson was the only junior officer exempt from such duty.

The enlisted men had their own routines of four hours on and eight hours off duty. New yeoman Bud Pike found that his "off" duty from clerical work always included shifts on lookout duty, radar watch, helmsman duty, and other tasks. During his off-duty hours, he spent time in the forward torpedo room, where he slept or worked on his qualification notebooks. Pike, like his buddy Bill Dillon, was not much for gambling. On payday, when disbursing officer Ed Berghausen handed out cash to the crew, the normal acey-deucey games quickly shifted to poker. "Those who were gamblers immediately turned our mess hall into a gambling den," Dillon recalled.

School of the boat was a normal routine, but with nearly one half of his crew unqualified, skipper Ward had made it a priority for new hands to work on earning their dolphins. John Good, another sailor making his first war patrol, was coached through the qualification process by senior enginemen Freddie Wheeler and Joe Ring. Wheeler disliked the whole teaching process, so Good turned to a more willing shipmate in his forward engine room, MoMM1c Paul Traxler. An Ohioan with five years in the Navy, Traxler sported a rosy complexion that matched his auburn hair and beard. He offered to help Good with his notebooks, walking him through every detail of the submarine's engineering plant. He led his young apprentice into the lower flats to show him the lube oil storage tanks, the necessary valves required to transfer oil, and the intricate maze of pipes, fuel lines, pumps, and engines that moved the lifeblood of *Sailfish*. Good was appreciative of the tutelage, and his spirits soared.[11]

Good found that submariners were a crafty lot, and he soon learned of a scheme that several shipmates had hatched to create their own homemade wine. From Wheeler, he heard of chief electrician Lester Bayles's plan to ferment excess fruit juices in a small olive keg, liberated from ship's cook Tom Sargent, to prepare in the engine room. To disperse all the olives, Sargent promised, "I'm gonna 'olive' you bastards to death on this run."[12]

After Bayles mixed ample extracts of pineapples, peaches, and pears with a hefty amount of sugar, the concoction was ready. Wheeler painted the olive keg red, and Good sewed up rags to form a cushion. "Most of the engineers were tipped off as to what had been done," Good remembered. "Very few of the other crew members learned the secret, but those that knew would cautiously enter the engine room in the days that followed and curiously smile at the cushioned seat that rested between the two engines against the rag locker in the middle of the room."

It would be weeks before the would-be winemakers would be able to sample the results of their ingenuity.

* * *

Captain Ward maintained a steady two-engine speed en route to his patrol station. He worked to indoctrinate his new sailors and inexperienced officers by conducting daily training dives, tracking exercises, and attack problems among the men who would serve on the battle stations tracking team. Such work would go a long way in preparing them for their first encounter with enemy shipping.

His second-in-command, Bud Richardson, doubled as the ship's navigator. As such, he was responsible for taking evenly spaced altitude readings of the sun when the boat was surfaced to help maintain the ship's position line or course. Richardson's assistant navigator was first class signalman Troy Ray from Denver; Ray had served on destroyers prewar before volunteering for sub duty. With three patrols on *Silversides* and two prior runs on *Sailfish*, Ray was the most seasoned member of the quartermaster gang.

At night, he and Richardson would employ celestial navigation by "shooting the stars"—using a handheld sextant to measure the altitude of a star, planet, or the moon to compare to tables of position to calculate a "line of position" for their vessel on the earth. Two or more such lines of position helped Richardson and Ray generally cross through their ship's location and provided a "fix" on their locale. When the skies were clear, star fixes were shot every morning before sunrise and every night before sunset.[13]

This task became more complex as *Sailfish* pushed closer toward Japan during her second week at sea. By November 29, the seas were increasing in intensity and the winds were growing stronger, creating cloudy skies that challenged traditional navigation. It was in the midst of these rising storms that Bob Ward began receiving important messages from ComSubPac's Pearl Harbor staff that would have dramatic effects on the course of his war patrol.

That evening, senior radioman Bob Johnson picked up a dispatch that proved to be an Ultra from Admiral Lockwood's staff. But he was not privy to its contents. His job was merely to jot down the coded character sets and pass them to the communications officer, Dutch Wetmore. Using the proper decoding keys of the day, he began typing out the code on the new ECM in the control room. The beginning of the message contained padding words like "peanuts" but also "Ultra."

An Ultra dispatch was highly classified, intended only to be read by the decoding officer and his skipper and executive officer. Wetmore's pulse increased as he read the details. A key Japanese fleet—consisting of the aircraft carriers *Zuiho*, *Unyo*, and *Chuyo*—was to depart Truk Island on November 30, in company with the heavy cruiser *Maya* and four destroyers. He quickly handed off the coded message to Bob Ward and Bud Richardson.

Wetmore returned to his ECM, as Johnson soon had a supplemental message from ComSubPac to report. It was also an Ultra, beginning with the phrase "chance of a lifetime." This one gave exact positioning details of where the enemy carrier force could be intercepted along its route toward Japan. In its entirety after decoding, the message read:[14]

> Chance of a lifetime X Ultra Serial 66V for action *Sawfish*, *Gunnel* and other subs in vicinity X 28 and 36 Peanuts X 2 auxiliary carriers and 4 destroyers X 0330 X 2nd X 23-30 North 148-56 East X Position at same time following day 30-08 North 146-15 East X Successive positions of this unit and time and date indicated are as follows: 2100 3rd 33-52 North 142-20 East and 6 hours later: 34-40 North 140-20 East X Avoid detection or radio transmissions in vicinity of track until after contact.

After reading the Ultra dispatches, Ward and Richardson called their officers to the wardroom. The fact that the intelligence group in Hawaii was routinely intercepting and decoding Japanese transmissions was classified. "The rest of us were told that another boat had made contact and reported a task force headed from Truk to the Empire," recalled Lieutenant Pat Murphy. "An estimated position, course, and speed were provided."[15]

Ward now had a chance in his first command to strike an enemy carrier fleet. The only problem now lay in the fact that his boat was battling the effects of a typhoon. Navigator Richardson's best estimated position was based on a few old star sights and dead reckoning. *Sailfish* had been patrolling off the Empire routes from Wake, Marcus, and Truk, but now Ward headed closer toward mainland Japan. The boat buzzed with excitement.

Ward was meticulous about the readiness of his ship. Every evening, it had become standard practice to "rig for red" when going on lookout duty. This meant that all areas adjacent to bridge access would be illuminated by red lights only to help reduce the time for eye adjustment as men climbed to the darkness of the bridge. "The Captain wore red goggles even during supper and leisure in the wardroom, so he could be ready for any call to the bridge," Bill Bruckart remembered.[16]

Ward's use of the red goggles had interesting side effects. While playing cards with his junior officers around the wardroom table, he was unable to see the numbers on the red cards' suits. "We made the most of it with misleading information," Bruckart recalled. During one meal, when steward R. D. Mosley served chocolate pudding for dessert, Lieutenant Pat Murphy teased Ward by saying, "Captain, how do you like the lime Jell-O?"

Ward continued to work his unqualified officers into the rotation, each mentored by seasoned officers Bud Richardson, Pat Murphy, or Stan Cowin. "En route and on station, I was given training as periscope observation watch officer and, between looks, as diving officer," Bill Bruckart remembered. "To put it in other words, I was 'Peeping Tom' and 'Elevator Boy.'"[17]

During one such rotation on periscope watch duty, Bruckart ran up the scope and made a shocking discovery. "I looked into the face of a Jap fisherman, sitting in a small boat on a rather placid sea!" Startled, he immediately called for "Down scope!" and summoned the skipper. Ward informed his junior officer that there was nothing directly to be done other than avoid further detection.

Ward's confidence in his wardroom increased each day. His unqualified junior officers were progressing well toward earning their dolphins and qualifying for solo watch privileges. The only real challenge he now faced was complaints about the hygiene of his assistant engineer, Warrant Electrician Wayne Evans.

A former enlisted man who relished the lifestyle of a pigboat sailor, Evans was six foot two and therefore nicknamed "Shorty." "Shorty never changed his socks," Ward recalled. As he passed by the wardroom, he often noted Evans sleeping on his lower bunk with his feet inevitably sticking out beyond the bunk. "Shorty was a damn good man, but I had a hell of a time getting him to wash his feet and change his socks."[18]

* * *

The stormy seas grew increasingly violent on November 30, the day after Ward received the Ultra dispatches. During the excitement of tracking the Japanese carrier fleet, a serious mishap occurred.

At 1500, in the after torpedo room, the crew was going through a routine check of their Mark 14 torpedoes. The senior torpedoman aft was TM2c Emmett Lucas, a twenty-four-year-old from Ohio who had made five prior war patrols. *Sailfish* was running submerged at ninety feet as the after tube nest was flooded with water in preparation for checking each torpedo's afterbody for tightness. Although the outer breech and muzzle doors to the tubes were closed, the torpedo in Tube No. 8 suddenly roared as its motor started running when the water level in that tube was approximately three-quarters of the way to the top. As the water level rose, the torpedo lurched forward due to the rough seas, and its trigger mechanism was activated, causing the torpedo engine to come to life. It propellers emitted a hair-raising whine and smoke entered the compartment.[19]

"Hot run in tube 8!"

The compartment talker's call over the 1MC was shocking. A live torpedo running in the tube could spell disaster. Captain Ward, torpedo officer Pat Murphy, and junior officer Bill Bruckart—whose normal battle station was the after torpedo room—raced aft to Lucas's compartment to assess the danger.

Although its propellers had run for only a matter of seconds, the torpedo had been pushed on down the tube out of sight of the torpedomen. In his patrol report, Ward noted that the condition of depth and gyro spindles "indicated that the torpedo was all the way gone or at least 5-6 feet down the tube. The outer door could not be opened and the indicator still read all the way closed." In order to activate the exploder in its warhead, the propellers had to turn for the equivalent of about five hundred yards. "We were fortunate that the hot run was in an after tube," Murphy later recalled. "Had it been forward, we would have had to lie dead in the water to prevent forward movement from arming the thing."[20]

Ward and Murphy now had to figure out what to do with a live torpedo partially ejected from an after tube. Ward ordered his boat to the surface around sunset to further assess the situation. Murphy and Bruckart made their way aft in the rough seas with a group of *Sailfish*'s senior torpedomen, including Chief Bill Blatti, TM1c Joe Mendel, Emmett Lucas, and others. Among these men was TM3c Ray Bunt, who had been rated as a master diver long before he enlisted in the Navy in 1942.

"Pat Murphy and the Captain agreed that, for safety, the exploder should be dropped from the warhead," recalled Bruckart. Murphy went forward with a wrench, hoping to remove the numerous bolts holding the exploder while Bruckart tended a line affixed to the torpedo officer and to a deck stanchion. With the ocean swelling up and down, this thought was quickly cast aside, as the tube openings were submerged most of the time.[21]

At 1730, Murphy decided an undersea inspection was in order. Former lifeguard captain Bunt donned his mask and went over the side with his torpedo officer. They returned to the surface to report that the torpedo was partially ejected from Tube No. 8, with about twelve feet of its length jutting out. In such a stormy ocean, there was no practical way for the crew to attempt to salvage the Mark 14 by forcing it back into the tube to close the outer door.

Ward opted to fire the tube using 375 pounds of impulse pressure. But the blast of high-pressure air failed to dislodge the warhead on the first attempt. Ward called for a second firing attempt, and this time Lucas and his after crew happily reported back that the torpedo had departed. The skipper was not completely satisfied until diver Bunt went over the side a second time to confirm that the war fish was indeed gone. Leery of problems with this tube, Ward ordered it secured for the remainder of the patrol. "After the torpedo was gone, the outer door could still not be closed but it could be operated through an arc of about 25-30 degrees," Ward logged.[22]

Sailfish was now down to only seven torpedo tubes if she were fortunate enough to find the Japanese carrier fleet. *Sailfish* patrolled across Wake, Marcus, and Truk on December 1 and 2, covering the traditional routes toward Japan. The weather had grown steadily worse as the effects of an approaching typhoon were felt. The barometer plunged, and strong winds brought gigantic swells. The boat pitched heavily, rolling from side to side, and blinding rains greeted those serving topside as lookouts. Below, loose gear and dishes had to be secured in lockers.

Running on the surface in the evenings became progressively more dangerous as the storm built. "Regular engine speed almost burned up the bearings and almost knocked out the alignment of the machinery with the vibrating shafts of the screws," recalled John Good. "The screws whirred in crazy speed in midair out of the sea and violently rent the sub with tearing tremors on every lunge. Engines shook as though they were about to burst from their foundations and go through the bulkhead." Ward ordered all main engines secured except a small auxiliary engine, known as a dinky, in the after engine room that supplied enough power to keep the screws slowly turning to maintain some propulsion. "When the boat went down one side of a wave, it was like being on a roller-coaster."[23]

Sailfish rolled heavily in the angry seas, and maintaining footing topside was nearly impossible. Tall waves slammed men against the railings and structures, leaving them clawing desperately at times to save themselves from being washed overboard. Yeoman Bud Pike endured his share of hours with binoculars on the periscope shears. He estimated the waves to reach as high as forty feet at times. "It was so rough that at first they lashed us to the shears," he recalled. For two days, *Sailfish* was slammed mercilessly as the black skies unleashed torrents of driving rain and winds that howled about the exposed conning tower. Pike and others eventually began to lose faith that their boat would find any Japanese convoys in the typhoon.[24]

Exec Bud Richardson had no ability to update his navigational fix. After three days of battling the effects of the storm, *Sailfish* was struggling. "At one time we were making full speed on all four main engines, with the dinky thrown in for good measure," Richardson recalled. Richardson was discouraged that even with the aid of the small auxiliary engine, his engineers could coax no more than 11 knots of speed out of their boat.[25]

The ocean became so treacherous that Ward finally ordered two of his lookouts below, leaving only himself, Richardson, quartermaster Harry Tonden, and one lookout, Ray Bunt, topside to withstand the effects of the weather. "Hope of finding the task group was diminishing as the weather deteriorated," recalled Good. "Our only hope left was to scan the area by radar."[26]

On December 3, *Sailfish* continued to battle severe elements. Ward kept his boat at radar depth to avoid losing a man overboard in the towering seas. In the conning tower, Dieterich, Dillon, and other sailors spent endless hours watching the PPI screen for any sign of the enemy. Its jagged green beam swung around and around, but nothing showed.

"We headed for an intercept at the best speed we could make in the heavy weather," recalled Pat Murphy, "with little hope of finding our target."[27]

EIGHT

Carrier Passage to Japan

November 29, 1943
Truk Atoll

George Rocek knew something was different. Although he had lost complete track of time, he and his shipmates had spent ten days of incarceration and abuse on Truk. The Japanese guards gathered the *Sculpin* survivors, marched them from their cells, and lined them up.

This day, there were no interrogations and no beatings. The guards called the prisoners forward, one by one, and shaved all of the hair off their heads. Each American prisoner was then issued Japanese Navy undress blues, the uniform of an enlisted sailor. For men like Joe Baker and Ed Keller, it was a great relief to put on even an enemy's uniform after spending more than a week naked under wretched conditions. Each POW was then issued a flat, square wooden block with Japanese writing on it to wear around his neck like a dog tag. Their captors announced that the prisoners were to be transported to Japan, where they would be kept until the end of the war.[1]

During the very early hours of November 30, that journey commenced. With their wrists tied, the *Sculpin* men were blindfolded and herded out to army trucks that drove them down to the harbor on Dublon Island. When the trucks halted, the prisoners were unloaded and their hands were untied. Each man had to walk with his hands resting on the shoulders of the man in front of him. Gunner John Rourke, suffering from shrapnel wounds to his back and two lacerated toes, struggled to walk fast enough. Anytime he stumbled or slowed, he was beaten with a club.[2]

At the harbor, the Americans were loaded onto two whaleboats that headed out into the lagoon. The natural tendency was to look up to see where they were going, but Rocek found that to avoid a beating, the only safe place to look was downward. Anyone who looked up was assaulted with a bat. Rourke, however, eased up his blindfold and saw that their launches were heading for Japanese aircraft carriers. He whispered the word to his shipmates.[3]

All forty-one survivors were loaded on board the carrier *Unyo*, but the Japanese soon sorted them into two large groups. Twenty-one of the *Sculpin* men—including Rocek, the sub's two junior officers, and eighteen other enlisted men—were then herded over onto another carrier, *Chuyo*. For the first time, Rocek was able to see the pitiful condition of the amputees. He was stunned and angered to hear Charles Pitser and Rebel Elliott describe how the Japanese medical staff had handled their amputations at Truk.[4]

Although the *Sculpin* prisoners were relieved to be past ten days of terror on Truk, none could guess what kind of hell lay in store for them if they ever reached the Japanese home islands. None had the slightest idea of the names of the carriers they were loaded into. Ironically, their vessels of transit were *Chuyo* and *Unyo*, the very same flattops that

Sculpin had fired torpedoes at just five months earlier. (See the second chart in Appendix A.)

★ ★ ★

The Japanese task force preparing to depart Truk was impressive.

It included Captain Hattori Katsuji's 11,200-ton light carrier *Zuiho*, which had participated in the Guadalcanal campaign in 1942 and suffered bomb damage at the carrier battle of Santa Cruz in October. The two larger carriers in the force were sister ships of the escort carrier *Taiyo* class. Both had been converted during 1942 from *Nitta Maru*–class cargo liners into auxiliary aircraft carriers to help boost the Japanese fleet. The former *Yawata Maru* emerged from the Kure Naval Arsenal on August 31, 1942, and was recommissioned as *Unyo* (translating in English to "cloud hawk"). At normal load, *Unyo* displaced 20,321 tons, with a length of 591 feet, a beam of seventy-three feet, and a draft of twenty-five feet. Her flight deck stretched 564 feet, leaving twenty-seven feet of her exposed bow pointing forward.

Unyo's sister ship *Chuyo* ("hawk that soars" or "heaven-bound hawk") had been recommissioned on the same date at Kure. Converted from the passenger liner *Nitta Maru*, *Chuyo* sported the same flush-decked configuration as *Unyo*. Both carriers were driven by two sets of geared steam turbines that could produce top speeds of 21.4 knots (24.6 mph). *Unyo* and *Chuyo* could travel about 8,500 nautical miles when fully fueled, and were capable of carrying up to thirty aircraft, including spares. Two elevators serviced a single hangar deck on each carrier. Their slow speed (compared to the 34 knots of Japanese fleet carriers) and lack of arresting gear prevented this class of carriers from being relevant to the main Japanese fleet offensives.

On July 29, 1942, *Unyo* had departed Yokosuka for Saipan, making the first of more than forty plane-ferrying and supply trips from outer bases such as Saipan, Palau, and Truk to mainland Japan. *Chuyo* entered similar service that year on December 12, and by November 21, 1943, she had made a dozen ferrying missions between Yokosuka and Truk. For most of these trips, *Chuyo* had been escorted by at least three destroyers, and occasionally was in company with another Japanese escort carrier or two.[5]

American intelligence agents were well aware of the regular voyages of Japanese carriers between the home islands and Truk during 1943. Traffic analysis, in the form of decrypts of JN-25 messages to various carriers and the Truk port director's arrival and departure messages, outlined that Imperial Japanese Navy flattops were ferrying reinforcement aircraft to Truk, from which location they could be flown on to Rabaul.[6]

These Japanese warships were highly desirable targets for American submariners. On April 9, an Ultra alert flashed to Lieutenant Commander John Scott's *Tunny* set her up to intercept three carriers. *Tunny* fired ten torpedoes at two carriers and Scott heard seven explosions at proper intervals, but Truk's port director reported the safe arrival of all three carriers the following day. *Tunny*'s crew would later learn that they had fallen victim to faulty American torpedoes that had evidently exploded prematurely. During the spring months, some Japanese ships had actually arrived in port with unexploded torpedoes embedded in their sides.[7]

Faulty American torpedoes allowed the Japanese carriers to escape damage on several occasions. On June 11, Lieutenant Commander Roy Benson's *Trigger* fired six torpedoes at the carrier *Hiyo* and heard four explosions. One was premature, and although others did rip *Hiyo*, she was able to limp back to Yokosuka for repairs. Frustrated by many reports of failures, Admiral Chester Nimitz ordered the deactivation of magnetic exploders on June 24 for all torpedoes used by ships and aircraft under his command. But sinkings did not increase dramatically during July and August of 1943. It was only during September—after much reworking of torpedoes to correct deep running and faulty exploders—that American submarine success rates began to climb.[8]

During this time, *Chuyo* and *Unyo* made several more trips between Yokosuka and Truk without suffering damage. Upon returning to Japan in late July 1943, *Chuyo* entered a dry dock in Yokosuka for a much-needed overhaul that would consume much of August. *Chuyo* resumed her voyages on September 7 in company with the carrier *Taiyo*, but their return trip was nearly fatal. South of Yokosuka on September 24, *Taiyo* was hit in the starboard quarter by a torpedo from the U.S. submarine *Cabrilla*. Due to damaged torpedo shafts, *Taiyo* was towed back to port by *Chuyo*. Although several American submarines had claimed to sink Japanese carriers—and in some cases been credited with doing so—all had failed to achieve that goal.[9]

During October and November, *Chuyo* had made five more voyages to ferry aircraft and supplies from Yokosuka to Truk. Her most recent transit had ended on November 21, 1943, when she arrived in Truk Lagoon in company with *Zuiho* and *Unyo*. The trio of flattops remained in port for the next nine days, during which time the *Sculpin* POWs were enduring their interrogation and torture. By this point in the war, American torpedo performance had improved markedly. During November 1943, U.S. submarines had had their best month of the war to date: forty-three ships totaling 285,820 tons were sunk, and another twenty-two were damaged for 143,323 tons, a total of 429,143 tons. Some hundred twenty Ultra messages were sent out during November, giving information on the movement of various convoys and warship forces.[10]

On November 29, the analysts picked up another key message from the Truk port director, sent to various ship and shore addresses and to warship fleets. When decrypted, it read: "Entries and departures, 30 November. Departing via North Channel: 0530, ZUIHO, CHUYO, UNYO, MAYA, destroyers AKEBONO, USHIO, SAZANAMI, URAKAZE, course 241. After 0840 course 000." The noon positions for this carrier fleet, bound for Yokosuka, were also relayed.[11]

From Pearl Harbor, Ultra alerts were sent out to American submarines patrolling the region between Truk and Japan. The first Ultra and two later amplifying ones were primarily addressed to *Skate*, on patrol near Truk. The fourth Ultra was sent from ComSubPac on November 29 to *Gunnel*, *Sawfish*, and other subs in the vicinity, including *Sailfish*. The message opened with the phrase "chance of a lifetime" and went on to describe the carriers and destroyers departing from Japan's advance base in the Pacific. The Ultra included precise locations of where the enemy fleet was expected to be positioned the following date.[12]

The first sub to find the three Japanese carriers was *Skate*, making her second war patrol. She had departed Midway on November 15 and was patrolling north of Truk when the Ultra was received on November 29. At 1053, Commander Gene McKinney sighted two destroyers and a converted carrier at a range of about fourteen thousand yards. Minutes later, he could see two more carriers astern of the first flattop, and two additional destroyers.

McKinney believed *Zuiho* to be a converted carrier, followed by two larger carriers. In reality, *Zuiho* was lighter, displacing only 11,200 tons when unloaded, versus the 17,830 tons displaced by *Unyo* and *Chuyo* without loads. Built on a former tender hull, *Zuiho* was actually twenty-five meters longer than the other two flattops and 4.5 meters narrower, making *Zuiho* look taller and plumper through a periscope than her two sister carriers.[13]

Numerous aircraft were guarding the fleet, and a charging destroyer forced *Skate* to ninety feet to evade. But McKinney returned to periscope depth at 1106 and made ready his stern tubes to fire on what he deemed to be the largest of the three carriers. "This ship had no upper works but did not look like any of the known type," he logged.[14]

"The two large carriers were overlapping as we fired," he wrote. His Mark 14-3As were set for ten-feet depth, and all were heard to run normal on sound. Tube No. 7 could not be equalized in time, so only three were fired. One minute and fifty seconds after firing, McKinney saw a large geyser of water rise just forward of the center of the nearest ship, which heeled to port. "The explosion was heard but there was no smoke," McKinney logged. Neither *Chuyo* nor *Unyo* was hit by this spread, so McKinney must have seen his target carrier turning sharply as one of his war fish exploded prematurely.[15]

Skate was forced down and received thirteen depth charges during the next quarter hour. McKinney pursued the convoy during the early-morning hours of December 1, and radar contact was established. But as dawn approached, he was forced down by Japanese aircraft and a charging destroyer. *Skate* would claim damage to only one of the carriers.

* * *

The American prisoners of war on the two carriers were well aware that they would be prime targets en route to Japan. On *Unyo*, fireman Joe Baker correctly believed that his ship was not long out of the harbor when the first action commenced. He could hear the distant explosions of depth charges as Japanese destroyers apparently worked over an American submarine.

"We really began to sweat, expecting to get hit with a fish at any moment," Baker recalled. He and his comrades had been locked in a hot hold three levels below the flight deck, roughly even with the waterline. Japanese guards had warned them that should their vessel be torpedoed and sunk during its voyage, the Americans would not be released from their hold. "We would be expected to go down with the boat," Baker remembered.[16]

The first attack by *Skate* was unsuccessful and did little to change the treatment of the POWs. Although the carrier force remained on high alert, and the men frequently heard the sounding of battle stations alarms, they considered their treatment to be fair. Pharmacist's mate Paul Todd requested medical attention, food, and tobacco for his shipmates, and was pleasantly surprised that some of each was actually offered by their captors.[17]

After ten days of cramped confinement in the Truk cells, the *Sculpin* prisoners now had enough room in their hold on the carrier to stretch out. Each man was issued a thin pad and a blanket, and the room included a head with a handle to pump waste from the toilet. Their food largely consisted of daily rice balls that tasted bitter and salty, with meager rations of water. Quartermaster Bill Cooper was not a fan of rice, but he decided that present circumstances dictated he was better off eating it than starving himself. His treatment thus far on *Unyo* had proven far more merciful than the horrors he had endured from Imperial Japanese Army soldiers on Truk.[18]

Seaman Ed Keller was pleased that Japanese intelligence officers visited the *Sculpin* prisoners daily in their hold on the carrier. They offered cigarettes and made efforts to teach the Americans key Japanese phrases that they would need to know during their duration as "guests" of Emperor Hirohito. "They taught us certain phrases, for instance, the words for attention, permission to go to the bathroom, and how to say thank you and good morning," Keller recalled.[19]

But living conditions and treatment were far different for the twenty-one *Sculpin* survivors being transported on the carrier *Chuyo*. Their compartment was small, with only a head in the corner with a three-foot steel toilet handle to manually pump refuse when it was used. Food was available, but the Japanese offered very little water, only a few ounces per man per day. "We asked for water and they just wouldn't give us the amount of water we wanted," Moon Rocek recalled.

The *Sculpin* men were kept in a compartment that had once been used on the passenger liner *Nitta Maru* to lock up passengers' valuables. It was crowded, and ventilation was nonexistent. *Chuyo*'s deck department officer had selected the former vault area as a convenient spot that could be locked and guarded. The carrier was not made to hold prisoners, so this space would have to do. The men slept on straw mats, and food was passed down through a small hatch near the ceiling.[20]

Hours ticked by like days for Rocek.

* * *

Following *Skate*'s first attack on the Japanese carrier force, Vice Admiral Lockwood's staff had all submarines in the vicinity on high alert. Next to spot the Japanese carrier group was *Gunnel*, patrolling off Chicha-jima. She had departed Pearl Harbor on November 17 in company with *Sailfish* and topped off at Midway on November 21 before heading toward her patrol area near Japan. Her radar operators made contact at 2200 on December 2 at the extreme range of twenty-five thousand yards. The skipper, Lieutenant Commander John Sidney McCain Jr., made out two auxiliary carriers of the *Zuiho* class and four destroyers. The convoy was making 18 knots and zigging 40 degrees every four minutes.[21]

McCain decided to concentrate on the first and nearest carrier. Operating at forty feet, *Gunnel* struggled to maintain depth as the carriers suddenly swung directly toward her. Dropping down to eighty feet and using a 4-degree spread, McCain fired four bow tubes at 2257 from the point-blank range of six hundred fifty yards. His shots missed *Zuiho,* and one of the destroyers moved in to deliver four depth charges. By the time *Gunnel* returned to the surface in the early hours of December 3, she was unable to chase down the convoy again. McCain sent a dispatch to ComSubPac at 0219 giving information on the attack.[22]

Zuiho, *Chuyo*, and *Unyo* had thus far escaped two direct submarine attacks, but the force was still far from port and not yet out of the woods. Shortly after 1000 on December 3, the periscope watch on *Sunfish* sighted an enemy convoy in the distance through the heavy swells. Lieutenant Commander Richard Peterson could see two aircraft carriers and at least two destroyers about ten miles distant, making an estimated 19 knots. Peterson commenced an approach, but at submerged speed he could close the distance to no less than twelve thousand yards. Frustrated at missing such a prime opportunity, he broke off the approach at 1030 and *Sunfish* sent a contact report after surfacing nine hours later.[23]

The carrier force had been making good time, but as they approached the waters east of Hachijo Island on December 3, an out-of-season typhoon was moving to the northeast. At 2100 on *Chuyo*, Lieutenant (jg) Takuji Azuchi took his place on the bridge as officer of the deck. Since reporting on board *Chuyo* in February 1942, Azuchi had served as her operations officer, or deck department head. In this billet, he also doubled as the carrier's damage control officer.

Azuchi supervised the pool of lookouts, many of them specially trained gunner's mates who were deemed to have excellent vision. At this stage in the war, the escort carrier crew had insufficient radar to rely upon, so powerful binoculars were used by sailors to scan the waves for enemy periscopes or torpedo wakes. But now the sea was raging with severe rainstorms and high waves that made visibility very challenging.[24]

Azuchi knew that, according to a seaman's common sense, when encountering a developing typhoon at sea, a ship should simply avoid steaming near its center and make a detoured course to minimize the effects from the storm. But Azuchi found that this was not the case this time. The senior officer of the convoy, and thereby convoy commander, was Captain Katoh Yoshiro, skipper of the heavy cruiser *Maya*. Despite the towering seas that lay ahead, his orders from *Maya* to the carrier commanders were to maintain a straight course without detouring.

Azuchi wondered if Captain Katoh had underestimated the power of the typhoon or if he was simply just being too obedient in sticking to their original schedule. By the end of Azuchi's watch, the storm had grown to such intensity that the convoy was unable to maintain its proper formation. Each carrier and its destroyer escorts increased their separation to avoid collisions in the colossal seas.

When *Chuyo* approached the center of the typhoon, OOD Azuchi received word from flagship *Maya* by blinker to decrease speed from 20 knots to 18 knots. Azuchi dutifully shared this word with his skipper, Captain Okura Tomasaborou, who was always on the bridge during the voyage.

At 2300, Azuchi was relieved on the bridge by *Chuyo*'s gunnery officer, Lieutenant Commander Hideo Sekine. Azuchi was tired after a long day and ducked down to his quarters to get some sleep. He kicked off his shoes and crawled into his bunk, opting to leave his fatigues on to be ready.

Azuchi worried that the carriers were going through the worst of a nasty typhoon and that they had ceased to zigzag in the punishing seas. But he drifted off to sleep, having little fear of any American submarine being able to attack in the midst of a typhoon.

NINE

First Strike

December 3, 1943
250 miles Southeast of Tokyo Bay

Sailfish surged to the surface at 1745. At three hundred ten feet in length, the submarine bobbed like a cork in the towering waves, plunging deeply into the troughs. As soon as the conning tower hatch was undogged, Bob Ward followed his exec, Bud Richardson, and officer of the deck Dutch Wetmore topside. *Sailfish* was still battling the typhoon, with driving rain and tremendous seas. Their eyeballs soon ached from squinting into winds that howled between 40 and 50 knots. Visibility ranged from zero to only as much as five hundred yards on brief occasions.

Ward would have preferred to keep his boat submerged, but the Ultra messages from ComSubPac had been precise. A Japanese carrier fleet was in the vicinity, and *Sailfish* lay right along their approach course. It was also imperative to run on the diesel engines as long as possible, allowing the electricians to jam juice into their depleted batteries. The two forward engine room diesels began the battery charging process while *Sailfish* surged forward into the heavy seas on her No. 3 and No. 4 main engines. She was able to make only 7 knots with one hundred revolutions per minute of her screws.

Two hours later, junior officer Bill Bruckart made his way to the conning tower. He was scheduled for the 2000 to 2400 shift as junior officer of the deck, under the supervision of OOD Stan Cowin for the first two hours, and Dutch Wetmore for the second half of his shift. In the driving rain, Bruckart found it impossible to even use his binoculars. "In addition to the blackness of the night, I remember waves so high that I looked almost straight up at them," he recalled.[1]

The seas rolled over *Sailfish* at such heights that water cascaded down into the air inductions. Senior engineman Montie Walkup had considerable amounts of seawater coming through these vents into his engine rooms. He ordered his men to run their drain pump continuously just to get the water out of their bilges.[2]

Sailfish had been given specific information via her Ultra directives. But all the analysts could do was relay the intercepted data from the Japanese port director at Truk. Follow-through on this Ultra meant that Bob Ward was left to run along the convoy's track for a full two days, hoping against the odds to make contact in the middle of a typhoon. "It was well worth the wait," Ward recalled.[3]

Just below the bridge, radarmen Frank Dieterich and Bill Dillon stood vigil over the PPI scope in the conning tower. For hours, its screen had remained blank after every sweep of the beam. Lieutenant (jg) Bruckart was nearing the end of his four-hour shift topside when the welcome call finally came at 2348 from the SJ operators below him.

"Radar contact! Bearing 114 True. Range 9,500 yards."

Ward immediately called his tracking party to the control room. His radar had an enemy ship roughly five and one-third miles away. He had drilled his fire control party thoroughly en route to station, and now everyone was prepared for the task at hand. Warrant Electrician Wayne Evans took up station around the small plotting table near the base of the conning tower ladder, where he would soon be joined by communications officer Wetmore, the latter still on the bridge as OOD. Together, they would track and plot all target data that was supplied to them either by topside lookouts, periscope observations, radar, or sonar. For the moment, there was nothing to see other than a fresh pip showing on the conning tower radar scope.

Within three minutes of the first pip appearing on the PPI, Wetmore and Evans received clarifying data that the target vessel was on an estimated course of 320 degrees True and was making about 18 knots. At 2352, a second ship contact was made. Dieterich announced that this one was a smaller ship, about nine hundred yards closer than the first contact. One minute later, a third ship contact was made on a vessel about the same size as the first contact. It was located a thousand yards beyond the first contact. At 2355, a fourth contact was made on another smaller vessel.[4]

When the first radar contact was announced, Lieutenant Commander Ward had ordered full speed ahead. Now, with four ship contacts being reported on his PPI scope, he knew he had a Japanese convoy—most likely the expected carrier group. But eight minutes after the first blip, *Sailfish* had managed to reach a surface speed of only 12 knots. With these targets at relatively close range, Ward abandoned any thoughts of racing ahead of the ships to lie in wait. "The seas are mountainous with a driving rain," he wrote in his report. "Can't see a thing but blackness and water with the water mostly in my face."[5]

Ward called for another radar bearing on the targets. Seconds passed, and Dieterich failed to respond. Anxious, the skipper asked, "What's wrong?"

"I think it's tuning," Dieterich replied. Ward was momentarily frustrated, but soon realized that his senior radarman was simply making fine adjustments on his SJ gear to offer the best possible solution. "He was so conscientious and so interested in maximum performance with the radar gear that he was always fiddling with it," Ward recalled.[6]

By this point, his crew was at battle stations. The announcement over the 1MC had been followed by Dutch Wetmore swinging down the handle for the general alarm. Throughout the boat, the Bells of St. Mary's sounded. All hands not already at their assigned duty station rolled out of their bunks. Cards, magazines, and books were abandoned in a flash in the mess room.

The battle stations helmsman, Harry Tonden, spun the large steel wheel to the left at 2358, as the skipper ordered a turn to port to 300 degrees. Ward wished to avoid one of the smaller pips, believing this closest ship contact to be a destroyer. Two minutes later, directly at midnight, this vessel was still miles distant but now on *Sailfish*'s starboard quarter. Ward and his officers were suddenly alarmed to see this destroyer switch on what appeared to be a large searchlight.

Through the raging typhoon, an eerie green-tinted light swung toward the direction of *Sailfish*. The enemy vessel appeared to be sending a signal to the other vessels in its convoy. "He could not have seen us, so assume he was signaling to someone else near us or he had a doubtful radar contact," Ward logged.[7]

Taking no chances, the skipper ordered, "Take her to radar depth."

Lieutenant Richardson ordered the bridge cleared and pulled the diving alarm. He waited for Ward and Bruckart to drop down the hatch before he did the same. His feet had scarcely hit the conning tower deck before senior signalman Troy Ray was dogging down the hatch. It was 0001 on December 4 as *Sailfish* was leveled off at forty feet, radar depth.

The conning tower was now packed with radar operators Dieterich and Dillon and those who had cleared the bridge. Nearby, torpedo officer Pat Murphy and his assistant, fire controlman Jim Woody, stood by their new Mark III TDC, which would direct the firing of *Sailfish*'s torpedoes. The Mark III consisted of a position keeper, used to track the target ship and predict its current position, and an angle solver that automatically took the target's predicted position from the position keeper. The TDC was the computational part of a submerged integrated fire control system that tracked an enemy target and continuously aimed torpedoes by setting their gyro angles—vital to helping ensure that the course of the launched torpedoes would intercept that of their target vessel.

Ward dropped into the control room below, where he could more easily maneuver his attack periscope to establish bearings on the target ships. "That was a useless exercise, as nothing could been seen through the scope," Bill Bruckart recalled. Upon clearing the bridge, Bruckart scurried aft to his assigned battle station in the after torpedo room.[8]

The control room became a hot spot of activity as Ward conned his boat toward the best attack position. Plotting officers Wetmore and Evans huddled over their small chart table, while Chief Yeoman Bill Crytser, a lean Californian of wiry build, stood ready to help identify any shipping targets should a visual confirmation ever be obtained. Each submarine carried a set of Office of Naval Intelligence books containing enemy ship silhouettes. One labeled ONI 208-J was an identification manual of Japanese merchant ships, while ONI 41-42 covered Japanese warships and ONI 220-J showed all known Japanese submarine silhouettes and data. But for this attack, Crytser had no visual descriptions to look up.

His junior yeoman, Bud Pike, had donned the battle stations headset to serve as Ward's battle talker to relay orders to the torpedo rooms or other compartments. Leading signalman Ray stood ready to assist the skipper with raising or lowering the periscope and in calling out bearings from its dials. Chief of the boat Bill Blatti stood sentry over the bank of hull indicator lights known as the Christmas Tree, still ever mindful of the main induction disaster that *Squalus* had suffered years before. In the dimly lit far corner of the control room, senior radioman Bob Johnson sat in his radio shack listening intently to the distant thump of propellers from the Japanese ships above.

The biggest challenge in making a torpedo approach at radar depth lay in the fact that *Sailfish* was battling the effects of a major typhoon. Ballast tanks of seawater could be blown with compressed air to bring the boat to the surface, and the same tanks were flooded with ocean water to cause the boat to dive. The battle stations diving officer, Lt. (jg) Stan Cowin, ordered minor necessary up or down angles on the boat by coaching two enlisted men on the bow and stern planes. Each man handled a large steel wheel that controlled their respective planes—essentially steel protrusions that helped force their submarine in either an upward or downward trajectory. Similar to a carpenter's level, an arc-shaped glass tube called an inclinometer that was positioned before the planesmen displayed *Sailfish*'s current angle on the boat. Cowin often advised his men to "keep a zero bubble," meaning that a perfectly balanced air bubble in the inclinometer kept the boat perfectly level. But keeping a zero bubble was nearly impossible in the violently rolling seas that rocked *Sailfish* even at forty feet of depth.

Minutes after diving, Bill Dillon was operating the SJ radar gear on the starboard side of the conning tower. Seated below him, Frank Dieterich continued to call out the changes he observed on the PPI's sweeping scope. Because Pat Murphy didn't have the ability to visually observe target data through the periscope, his TDC solutions relied this night solely on the data generated by radar. Dieterich announced that the nearest destroyer was only four hundred yards away. The other ships appeared to be maintaining a distance of roughly a thousand yards between them.

From the data being fed to him, skipper Ward surmised: "The picture looks as though we are on the left flank of a fast group of men of war, consisting of a destroyer, then possibly a cruiser, then a carrier or battleship, then another carrier or battleship with possibly something beyond that."[9]

Although he did not know exactly what the hell he was attacking, Ward knew that he must take a shot. An encounter with a group of Japanese warships was a rare opportunity, and it mattered little that he was firing blind in the midst of a typhoon. He simply selected the largest of the two nearest pips as his target.

"Open the forward doors," he ordered.

Battle talker Bud Pike relayed the word to the battle talker in the forward torpedo room. There, leading torpedoman Joe Mendel, standing sentry at the blow and vent manifold, issued orders to his men. They stood ready to operate the interlocks, which had to be aligned to open the outer torpedo tube doors and flood the tubes prior to firing. Only when the skipper was certain that an attack was imminent would he order his torpedomen to flood the tubes. If for some reason the torpedoes were not fired, Mendel and his men would face draining the tubes, removing inspection plates from their torpedoes, and thoroughly drying everything.

Once the doors were opened, another sailor operated the manual gyro setter, which would match the pointers from the conning tower's TDC solutions. In quick order, Mendel had the word relayed back to the skipper, "Forward tubes ready."

By 0009, radioman Johnson announced that the nearest destroyer was passing close aboard to starboard and ahead, the thumping of its screws plainly audible in his headset. "The destroyer kept coming over, so we went down to 60 feet and let them pass by at what we guessed as approximately 200 to 250 yards," recalled Lieutenant Richardson. For tense seconds, all hands waited for the violent blast of depth charges, but none were dropped. As soon as the tin can swept past, *Sailfish* eased back up to radar depth.[10]

Ward waited three minutes and took a final ping bearing from his radarmen. By radar setup, the nearest large pip on the scope showed to be 2,100 yards away. By his orders, the forward torpedoes had been set to run at depths of twelve feet, with gyro angles ranging from 53 degrees to 37 degrees right, with tracks varying from 108 degrees to 120 degrees to port. Each war fish would be fired with a spread of at least 1¾ degrees, helping to allow for any miscalculations in plot.

Dillon, making his third patrol, was surprised at the call of his new skipper in taking this long shot. *We've only closed the distance to 2,100 yards,* he thought. *That's a hell of a distance to fire torpedoes. And we don't even know what we're shooting at!*

But at 0012, Ward began barking the orders.

"Fire one!"

Standing beside torpedo officer Murphy, fire controlman Jim Woody hit the firing button as Pike repeated the order to Mendel's crew in the forward room. Upon hearing the order to fire, Mendel smacked the manual firing plunger on Tube No. 1 with the palm of his hand just to make sure. His compartment's talker then instantly called back to Pike in the conning tower, "Number one fired!"

A loud *kawoof!* announced the sound of the escaping Mark 14 torpedo, and *Sailfish* shuddered as she belched forth her first 2,800-pound missile into the angry seas. The torpedo's propellers were giving it propulsion forward even before the blast of compressed air had completely expelled it from the tube. At the same instant, another torpedoman opened a vent valve called the poppet valve and allowed the compressed air to be forced back into *Sailfish*—thereby preventing a large telltale bubble of air to escape to the surface. He then closed the poppet valve before an excessive amount of seawater could enter. But the amount of water that did enter the tube helped to compensate for the lost weight of the torpedo.

Thirteen seconds after firing his first torpedo, Ward ordered another one dispatched.

"Fire two!"

Sailfish shuddered again as Tube No. 2 spit forth another Mark 14-3A torpedo. Fifteen seconds later, Ward called, "Fire three!"

Mendel's torpedomen matched the setting on Pat Murphy's TDC and prepared their fourth warhead to be launched with a slight spread in the gyro angles. Fourteen seconds after firing its third fish—and less than three-quarters of a minute after launching the first Mark 14—*Sailfish*'s forward gang received another directive.

"Fire four!"

By launching such a spread of four torpedoes, Ward fully expected at least one of his torpedoes to hit, even if one or more missed. Standing by with the fire control party, signalman Ray counted down the seconds on his stopwatch. In the forward room, Mendel's torpedo gang also counted the seconds from the time of first firing until the moment of an expected impact. In the radio shack, Bob Johnson tracked the speeding warheads through his headset.

"All torpedoes running hot, straight, and normal."

Having fired all of his forward tubes, Ward ordered helmsman Tonden to swing his boat to port to bring his stern tubes to bear. He hoped to get off another salvo before any enemy counterattack commenced. In about a minute, the results of the forward nest were realized. Johnson reported distant explosions, their timing indicating direct hits from the first and fourth torpedoes. *Sailfish* had hit something, likely a capital warship. But there was little time to celebrate, as sonar operators Johnson and Paul Kelly announced a set of screws from an incoming ship, likely one of the Japanese destroyers, intent on hammering the convoy's attacker with depth charges.

"Take her deep," Ward ordered. "Rig for depth charge!"

With an enemy warship charging down upon his submarine, Ward had to at least temporarily abandon his hopes of firing his aft torpedo tubes. Bill Dillon instinctively slid down the steel ladder from the conning tower to the control room and sprinted forward. He bypassed the tiny ship's office, the CPO berthing quarters, officers' country, the wardroom, and the skipper's stateroom in his sprint to man the sonar gear in Mendel's torpedo room. Diving officer Cowin quickly flooded the ship's negative tank to allow seawater to rapidly increase *Sailfish*'s weight. As the negative tank vented inboard, working as a vacuum to rapidly suck ocean water into the midships tank, air howled through the control room. *Sailfish* achieved negative buoyancy quickly and began dropping like a rock.

Ward's crew responded to the rig-for-depth-charge order by immediately securing all hatches and any noisy equipment. Dillon had scarcely reached the forward room and donned his headset before the hatch to his compartment was dogged down. "Silent running" meant that all motors and air-conditioning equipment were shut down as the boat took a downward angle. *Sailfish* was still in her descent at 0016 when two depth charges exploded fairly close aboard. Newer sailors unaccustomed to such violence were tossed from their feet as the heavy concussions shook their vessel like a cat shaking a mouse. Light bulbs flickered and loose cork insulation drifted down.

A minute later, at 0017, another pair of depth charges erupted, these slightly more distant. John Good, making his first patrol in the forward engine room, later recalled, "The depth charges burst viciously and intermittently. First one burst ahead of us, then two quickies astern of us, but still not very close to the sub. They were randomly tossed charges, which indicated they had not located our position."[11]

During the next half hour, another seventeen depth charges were unleashed by the Japanese destroyer, bringing the total to twenty-one. Although the depth charges were alarming to the new hands on the *Sailfish*, her more seasoned veterans counted their blessings. None exploded close enough to cause any severe damage.

During this time, Joe Mendel, Ray Bunt, and the forward torpedo gang worked diligently to reload their tubes. Using block and tackle, the men gingerly swung spare three-thousand-pound torpedoes from their racks via ceiling-mounted pulleys into the empty tubes. A hook was rigged on a ring inside the tube before pushing and pulling each Mark 14 into its respective tube.

At 0158, less than two hours after firing torpedoes, Ward ordered his boat back to the surface. With officers of the deck Dutch Wetmore and Shorty Evans, plus three lookouts, he waited at the base of the ladder leading to the bridge. In the forward torpedo room, Bill Dillon passed off his headset to another sailor and raced forward to man the radar gear again in the conning tower. Other sailors were heading topside in foul-weather gear and carrying binoculars as Dillon took his position alongside Frank Dieterich.

Skipper Ward struggled to maintain his footing on *Sailfish*'s bridge. He and his lookouts still faced howling winds, driving rain, and colossal waves. But they were eager to discover just what kind of capital ship they had torpedoed.

TEN

Chuyo in Peril

Takuji Azuchi had been asleep for less than an hour. As *Sailfish*'s first torpedo erupted in his carrier, he felt the shock waves in his stomach and heard a tremendous explosion. The lieutenant sprang from his bunk and raced for his battle station on the bridge of *Chuyo*.[1]

Azuchi's path topside led through the damaged area. The torpedo had ripped open one of the forward passenger compartments, where fires raged and black smoke was billowing into the passageway. The area was in complete chaos. Several bodies lay crumpled in their final positions, while shipmates helped drag other wounded men from the area. Ocean water was pouring into the forward deck area from the jagged rupture in the hull. When Azuchi reached the bridge, he learned that *Chuyo* had been struck on her port side below the bridge.

Although the carrier's engines and steering gear were untouched, the bow section was heavily damaged and had taken a downward attitude. The increased drag forced Captain Tomasaborou to drastically slow the speed of his ship. He called for his communications officer,

Lieutenant Misao Yamaguchi, to get off an urgent message. Yamaguchi's message to Tokyo said: "At 0010, this ship incurred a torpedo hit. Fire broke out in the forward living quarters. However, this ship is able to steam."[2]

The *Sculpin* prisoners were near the area of the torpedo hit, which was just one or two decks below them in the passenger area. George Rocek and those seated on the deck were suddenly flung several feet into the air. Their compartment was locked from the outside, and shouts to get their guard to release them went unanswered.

They could hear the chattering of Japanese voices as damage controlmen went to work. In nearby compartments, there were sounds of hammering and pounding as men labored to shore up hull damage with timbers. For the time being at least, the Japanese guards showed no interest in letting the Americans out. They hoped the damage controlmen would do their job effectively.

Captain Katoh, the task force commander and skipper of *Maya*, decided that the rest of the convoy must push on. The typhoon conditions were still raging and it was imperative that the other carriers make it to port. Towering walls of ocean water battered the convoy. On *Zuiho*, a wooden cutter tied to the davits near the bridge on the port side had its lashings rip free, and the cutter was carried away by the seas.[3]

The *Sculpin* prisoners on *Unyo* were aware of the rough sea conditions due to the rolling of the ship. At the time of *Sailfish*'s torpedo attack, they heard a distant explosion. "It was loud enough that it sounded like it was on our ship," recalled Ed Keller. "We didn't know what had happened, and they never told us. We just heard the explosion. We knew nothing else." Moments later, Keller felt his carrier picking up speed.[4]

Katoh continued on with *Maya*, *Unyo*, *Zuiho*, and three of their escorting destroyers. He ordered the destroyer *Urakaze* to remain behind to help escort the crippled carrier back into port. On *Chuyo*, Captain Tomasaborou ordered all men to battle stations after the *Sailfish* torpedo hit. Once the torpedo damage below was partially shored up, Tomasaborou decided he could offer his crew at least some relief. He thus ordered the second alert condition set, which would allow the *Chuyo* crew to be split into two shifts. One group would be on duty while the other was on standby.

Urakaze moved back and made a depth charge attack on the American submarine, dropping twenty-one depth charges. In such heavy seas, *Urakaze*'s crew was unable to obtain a solid lock on *Sailfish*, and the attack delivered was less than effective. *Urakaze* returned and maintained guard on the damaged carrier, which was able to steam north at the reduced speed of only 4 knots.

On the bridge, Lieutenant (jg) Azuchi ordered his lookouts to be especially vigilant for any sign now of an American periscope or torpedoes. "Silence and gloomy air prevailed," Azuchi recalled.[5]

* * *

It was 0158 on December 4 when *Sailfish* returned to the surface. Bob Ward stood on the bridge, gripping a railing with one hand as colossal waves towered above his boat. It was less than two hours after he had fired four torpedoes at the Japanese warship convoy. Still unaware of what he had hit, the skipper was intent on running down the cripple and finishing it off.

The diesels roared to life and *Sailfish* charged in the direction in which the convoy had last been seen on radar. For the time being, the PPI scope in the conning tower presided over by Frank Dieterich and Bill Dillon was blank.

Ward ran up the enemy's track for half an hour. On the bridge, binoculars proved to be useless in the dark. Blinding rain soaked the men and howling winds made footing treacherous. "Unable to make much speed without shipping black water," Ward noted.[6]

At 0230, Dieterich announced, "Radar contact! Range eight thousand four hundred yards." The target pip showed a bearing of 310 degrees True, just 10 degrees off the course the convoy had been steering when first encountered hours earlier.

Ward called his tracking party back to the control room and urged his engineers to make their best speed toward the contact. Ten minutes later, Dieterich and Dillon noted that the target on their radar appeared to be circling. The pip was small, but Ward found it hard to believe that a small destroyer could be picked up four and three-quarter miles away in this kind of weather. *Sailfish* eased in closer as the radar pip was monitored intently. "At times the pip has an edge on it, giving a momentary indication of another target very close to the one we are tracking," Ward logged.[7]

Two hours passed as *Sailfish* steadily narrowed the range to the targets. Bud Richardson, as Ward's assistant approach officer, found the process of properly tracking the enemy ships to be "a peculiarly difficult" one. The Japanese ships presented erratic courses, and one destroyer moved about the group in circles, presenting a number of challenges. During that time, the contacts ceased circling and settled onto a northwesterly course. Their speed appeared to track at between 2 and 5 knots. "Radar pip now looks like we may have two targets very close together," Ward logged at 0430.[8]

By 0550, morning twilight began to improve the visibility. Although the rain had stopped, water was still spilling over the bridge from tall waves, some of it cascading down through the hatch. The targets being tracked were now down to 3,500 yards and their speed was varying between 1 and 3 knots. Ward felt he must fire soon, as the skies were growing lighter. He decided he would fire three bow tubes on the surface and then attack again by periscope, making a quick reload during the approach.

"Open the forward doors," Ward ordered. The word was quickly relayed to Mendel's forward room.

Pat Murphy's final TDC solution showed the target vessel to be making only 1 knot. With the range down to 3,200 yards, Ward ordered a slight spread on his fish, and settings at ten feet—two feet shallower than her original spread against the convoy. The gyros read 002 degrees, with an estimated track of 148 degrees starboard.

"Fire one!"

Bud Pike relayed the word to the forward room. Twelve seconds later, Tube No. 2 was fired, followed another twelve seconds later by Tube No. 3. The sea conditions were rough, but each Mark 14 was set to run on high speed. Signalman Troy Ray counted down the runs on his stopwatch, expecting intercepts in about two minutes.

At 0557, Ward observed and heard two torpedo hits. "First hit looked like a momentary puff of fire," he wrote. "Second hit looked like and sounded on the bridge like a battleship firing a broadside—even with the locomotive rumble so characteristic of sixteen-inch shells." Ward commenced swinging *Sailfish* to bring the stern tubes to bear. He and fellow officers Dutch Wetmore and Shorty Evans enjoyed "quite a thrill" in seeing their torpedoes explode against an enemy ship for the first time.[9]

In the engine room, John Good had been counting down the seconds until he and his companions heard a boom. "It was a solid hit!" he recalled. "We grinned in the knowledge that we had done our jobs well."[10]

Topside, things were becoming dangerous for the men on the bridge. Brilliant red star shells streaked skyward and streams of heavy antiaircraft tracers cut through the predawn scud. Ward estimated at least a dozen enemy guns were firing toward the direction from which they believed the torpedoes had been launched. Clearly the Japanese had no clear view of *Sailfish*. To him, his enemy "didn't seem to know where we were because the shooting was directed everyplace but towards us."

Chief Lester Bayles, a *Sailfish* plank owner, was standing duty in the control room near the air manifold. He was amazed at the boldness of his new captain. "I could see daylight coming down through the conning tower hatch. I had never seen that before in a surface attack," Bayles remembered. "I knew this skipper was different."[11]

For the first few minutes of firing, the bright shells were more of a visual hindrance than a hazard. The intense flashes ruined the vision of Ward and his topside comrades. A minute later, the situation changed. The destroyer had likely picked up *Sailfish* on radar, as red tracer shells began streaking toward her. By 0600, Ward found "plenty of them" zipping overhead dangerously close.

"They made quite a show of it," Ward recalled. "I believe that there was a major ship there that fired a full salvo broadside, because we got the terrific broadside salvo noise and flash, and the rumble of heavy shells in the air."[12]

In the potentially deadly situation, Ward found humor in the moment. As the heavy shells thundered overhead, Lieutenant (jg) Wetmore ducked behind the thin steel bridge railing to take cover. Out of pure instinct, the skipper crouched down behind Wetmore, a useless effort that provided many laughs later in the *Sailfish* wardroom.

It was time to play it safe and get below.

Ahoogah! Ahoogah!

Two raucous blasts of the diving Klaxon were followed immediately by Wetmore shouting, "Dive! Dive!" The three lookouts, skipper Ward, Wetmore, and Shorty Evans dropped through the conning tower hatch as *Sailfish* began to nose underwater.

In the forward torpedo room, Mendel's crew was already in the process of using their block and tackle to swing three more torpedoes into the empty tubes. Three minutes after diving, radioman Bob Johnson reported the first of four depth charges exploding. Thankfully, they were distant, as the enemy warships apparently had no lock on *Sailfish*.

"From veteran submariners, we learned that this depth-charging was a snap," motor machinist John Good remembered. The next half hour of silent running was still unnerving for some of his newer shipmates. In the forward engine room, Good noted that Chief Montie Walkup had in tow a green teenager who seemed to take comfort in remaining on the shirttails of this veteran engineer. "Fear plays strangely upon the emotions of man," Good later wrote. "Another fellow busied himself eating anything and everything he could get in the mess hall during the depth-charge attacks."[13]

Ward remained at periscope depth and continued driving in toward the convoy. The pace was agonizingly slow, but visibility improved as daybreak began affording some illumination. With the rain abating, he hoped to soon get a glimpse of his targets.

* * *

It was about 0500 Japanese time (0600 on *Sailfish*) when *Chuyo* was struck by *Sailfish*'s second torpedo attack. It was devastating.

Lieutenant (jg) Azuchi had been on the bridge since his carrier had taken her first torpedo hit shortly after midnight. *Chuyo* had since been able to manage only 4 knots' speed in the pounding seas, in company with destroyer *Urakaze*. It was nearly dawn when disaster struck a second time. One or possibly two torpedoes exploded in *Chuyo*'s machinery spaces and boiler rooms.

Captain Tomasaborou's calls to his engineering officer, Lieutenant

Commander Kichitaro Fujitsu, went unanswered. His ship was already coasting to a halt when an officer attached to Fujitsu's command reached the bridge, gasping for air.[14]

"All men on duty in the Engineering Department are dead, sir!" he said.

The news hung like a dark cloud over *Chuyo*'s bridge. Azuchi found that a "pathetic air prevailed among the people who were on the bridge, including Commanding Officer Okura." There was no means of communication between the bridge and the engineering department except a sound-powered speaking tube. Without power, all telephone and radio circuits throughout *Chuyo* were nonfunctioning.

As the carrier went dead in the water, Captain Tomasaborou had his men spread the word verbally that every man should be at his battle station—a seemingly obvious order under the circumstances. With daybreak approaching, all efforts now turned to saving the carrier. Strict vigilance was maintained by extra lookouts. If anything looked like a submarine periscope in the rough ocean, men were ordered to fire warning shots toward it to attract the attention of others.

Tomasaborou hoped his ship could be saved. News of the damage from the second torpedo attack was sent by *Urakaze*'s skipper to the rest of the task force. Captain Katoh decided his heavy cruiser might be able to tow the stricken carrier into port. He ordered the carriers *Zuiho* and *Unyo* to proceed on to Yokosuka, in company with the destroyer *Ushio*. Katoh turned *Maya* back toward the last reported position of *Chuyo* in company with the destroyer *Sazanami*, while another destroyer, *Akebono*, raced ahead at full speed.

In the meantime, Tomasaborou ordered his men to begin building rafts. In order to abandon ship in the cold weather and rough seas, he knew that numerous rafts would be necessary to offer his crew any chance of survival. Each division began constructing rafts with the buoyancy materials they had on hand, and they made ready to don life jackets if their carrier appeared to be in imminent danger of rolling over.

★ ★ ★

Far below *Chuyo*'s bridge, George Rocek and twenty of his *Sculpin* companions were still locked in the former passenger ship's valuables vault when *Sailfish*'s second torpedo attack took place.

It had been hours since the first torpedo explosion had tossed them about their compartment. The sounds of shouting Japanese sailors and the pounding of damage control parties shoring up wrecked compartments below had ceased for some time. Rocek wondered if the American submarine had given up or been driven away by escort warships. The effects of the typhoon were still evident from the staggering movements of the ship, along with the fact that their carrier was now moving forward at a greatly reduced speed.

Perhaps five or more hours after the initial torpedo explosion, Rocek was startled to hear and feel the concussion of one or more explosions. These appeared to be a good distance aft of his compartment. *Must be secondary explosions triggered by that torpedo hit,* Rocek thought.[15]

Whatever the source of the explosions, the prisoners realized they were now in serious trouble. The power suddenly flickered and then went out, throwing their already gloomy hold into pitch-blackness. The deck beneath their feet no longer vibrated, an indication to any good sailor that their vessel was now dead in the water. Rocek was further troubled to hear breaking-up sounds in other compartments. *The force of the typhoon and these secondary explosions are snapping the timbers the Japs used to shore up those bulkheads,* he thought.

Two new sources of danger caused great fear in the *Sculpin* men. Smoke began seeping into their compartment, and then water began to slowly creep into their hold. Their carrier was obviously on fire and taking on water. It was now imperative that they escape from this compartment. Loud voices could be heard in the passageways, as could the sounds of numerous men racing to tackle fresh damage control concerns.

Chief of the boat Dinty Moore talked with his fellow POWs. Although two young ensigns were among the twenty-one men sharing the *Chuyo* compartment, Moore was respected by all due to his years of experience. Should they escape their cell and be confronted by any Japanese officers, they would simply state that some of the damage control parties had set them free. The submariners were all wearing Japanese sailor undress blues, so they might not be as obvious in the current state of affairs on their carrier.

But the hatch to their compartment was locked, and efforts to shout at the guards went without results. Water was now sloshing over their feet as the deck pitched and rolled in the storm.

They've abandoned us! Rocek thought.

Panic set in. "We yelled and pounded on the locked hatch," Rocek recalled. Splashing through the water and coughing from the acrid smoke, they undogged the hatch door from the inside. It moved enough to see that the door was locked from the outside. Rocek and others broke off the steel pump handle from the head's flushing mechanism. Using some of the larger men to pull on the hatch, other *Sculpin* men were able to jam the three-foot-long metal rod through the tiny opening.

"Okay," Moore said. "On the count of three, everyone push on the crowbar and the others pull on the door!"

Moore then shouted, "One, two, three, pull!"

Sailors swore as they put their weight into the crowbar. The lock and its flimsy latches creaked, but the hatch held fast.

"Again!" said Moore. "One, two, three!"

This time, the efforts of the *Sculpin* men were enough to bust the hatch door right off its hinges.

If this was an American ship, these hatches would be a lot stronger, Rocek thought. *We would have never broken out of that hold!*

With the hatch open, the men were faced with a darkened and unfamiliar vessel full of smoke. Chief Moore hurriedly organized his shipmates for their journey topside. Many of the men were relatively new to him: enlisted men Jerome Baglien, Maximo Barrera, Bill Brannum, Robert Carter, John Kennon, and John Parr had reported on board *Sculpin* only in late October prior to the ninth patrol. The majority of the *Sculpin* men had had no prior service on a U.S. warship or had previously served only on submarines.

But two men—torpedoman Warren Berry and motormac Harold Laman—had had prior experience on surface ships. Berry, who hailed from Dallas, had spent two years on the destroyer *Talbot*. Laman, who had been on *Sculpin* since January 1942, had served on the battleships *Arizona* and *Tennessee* prior to the start of the war. Deciding that Laman had the best chance of navigating through a darkened capital warship, Moore tapped him to lead the group.

The men held hands to prevent themselves from becoming separated in the dark. Special effort was made to assist the amputees—Baglien, Rebel Elliott, and Charles Pitser. In the smoky passageways, the men were forced to backtrack more than once after reaching dead ends or damage that halted their progress.

Rocek feared what would happen if they did reach the flight deck. Surely, the Japanese sailors would not act kindly to American submariners after another U.S. submarine had crippled their carrier.

ELEVEN

Third Strike of the *Sailfish*

December 4, 1943
0730

Bob Ward was finally beginning to see the true picture. It was 0730 as he slowly swung *Sailfish*'s periscope through the waves. The rains had ceased for the moment. The stormy skies had lightened. It was just enough to offer the skipper a little visibility as he stalked his wounded quarry.

Radar insisted a large pip was still there, and now motionless. But it was not until 0748 that Lieutenant Commander Ward took in an immensely satisfying sight. His wounded ship was suddenly visible at ten thousand yards—more than five and a half miles away. But the profile confirmed what he had been hoping to see. She was a large ship, with a distinctive, flat upper deck that was void of any large island superstructure.

"It's an aircraft carrier!" Ward announced to scope jockey Troy Ray, assistant approach officer Richardson, and everyone else around him.

In his patrol report, Ward would write "aircraft carrier" and underline the two words for added emphasis for anyone who read them.[1]

Lieutenant (jg) Bill Bruckart, manning the sound-powered headset in the after torpedo room, heard his skipper enthusiastically comment, "Well, look at what Santa Claus left us!"[2]

Best of all, the Japanese carrier was dead in the water. Three weeks before Christmas, it was the wildest gift for any sub skipper. As *Sailfish* continued to press toward the crippled warship, talker Bud Pike relayed disturbing news from both torpedo rooms. The gyro pots of one aft Mark 14 and one forward room torpedo were found to be flooded during precautionary checks of the war fish. Ward passed the word to both torpedo room gangs to pull these torpedoes and replace them. There was no time for maintenance during an attack approach.

Bud Richardson recalled that Ward, "like the rest of us, became very excited" about the wounded flattop in their grasp. But the submarine commander remained calm enough to carefully listen to the opinions of other key members of his torpedo-attack team. "These were the things at times like that that helped make us all feel that he was a part of us and not just our skipper," Richardson remembered.[3]

Frank Dieterich and Bill Dillon continued to call out ranges and bearings on the enemy ship as their boat narrowed the distance during the next hour. At 0912, Ward momentarily sighted the upper works of a destroyer standing by the carrier. "The picture now indicates that we have a badly damaged carrier plus one destroyer," he noted in his report. For the moment at least, there were no other Japanese warships to worry about. "If there were a cruiser here with 85-foot tower and 125-foot mast, he'd show up like a sore thumb compared to the carrier's 60-foot flight deck," wrote Ward.[4]

Diving officer Stan Cowin was severely challenged with maintaining periscope depth. The mountainous seas caused the boat to roll heavily. At sixty feet, Ward could see nothing through the attack scope but green waves, with his lens looking into an approaching wave or being under a wave almost all the time. He called for Cowin to bring her up another five feet to improve his view, but it did little good. "At 55 feet, we damn near broach and still can only see about twenty percent of the time," Ward wrote.[5]

Ward cautiously surveyed the stricken carrier. He remained surprised at his luck in that only a single destroyer was in sight. No other screws could be heard on sonar. Ward continued calling off details to his tracking party, hoping to identify his target carrier. One of his men made a rough sketch that would be included in the patrol report. Chief Bill Crytser busily thumbed through the ONI 41-42 warship silhouette book, hoping to find the right ship, while Dutch Wetmore and Shorty Evans dutifully maintained their plot on the control room table. Crytser had no way of knowing that their target vessel, converted to a carrier during the war, was not one that he would find in the recognition books.

Sailfish passed down the carrier's port side, from aft toward her bow, sliding by to view the ship from a distance of 1,500 yards. "He has many planes on deck forward and enough people on deck aft to populate a fair size village. The only visible evidence of previous hits is a small list to port and a small drag down by the stern," Ward logged. "The number of people on deck indicates they are preparing to abandon ship—a reassuring picture."

At 0937, *Sailfish* was abeam of the carrier and nothing else was in sight. Ward eased his submarine around into position, setting up to take a kill shot with his stern tubes. This time, he had the luxury of using the periscope, adding additional data to the radar reports. Within moments, Pat Murphy's TDC had generated a range to the carrier of 1,700 yards away.

It was time to seal the deal.

At 0940, Ward began giving the orders.

"Fire one!"

* * *

George Rocek and the *Sculpin* survivors were still making their way topside.

As Harold Laman led them to the next deck, they found the carrier sailors to be in a frenzied state. With the power out, fires in the engineering compartments, and the ship taking on water in multiple compartments, the *Sculpin* POWs were able to maneuver around the damage control parties with little issue. "We had already made up a story that if anybody wanted to know how we got out, we would say that the damage controlmen let us out," Rocek recalled.[6]

During their efforts to find their way topside, they encountered plenty of Japanese sailors. "They paid no attention to us," Rocek later stated. "They had their hands full with problems."

The twenty-one Americans held hands as they groped their way through the blackened, smoky passageways. They made their way up one steel ladder to a higher deck, likely the hangar deck. As they passed one compartment on this deck, someone noticed hundreds of life jackets hanging on the bulkhead. They appeared to be old passenger ship jackets that had been used when the vessel was the former liner *Nitta Maru*. Rocek, Chief Dinty Moore, and their able-bodied comrades helped strap jackets around the amputees after donning their own life jackets. If the carrier went down, everyone now at least had a shot of surviving in the ocean.

Moving aft in search of a ladder to the flight deck, the *Sculpin* survivors stumbled into another compartment that resembled a galley. Among various food items, some of the men found crates packed full of Japanese soda. After days of receiving barely enough water to sustain one person, the men gobbled food to replenish their malnourished bodies and chugged bottle after bottle. "We drank the hell out of that soda!" remembered Rocek.

Refreshed, they finally joined a line of terrified Japanese sailors who were pushing their way toward a ladder leading up to *Chuyo*'s flight deck. But a Japanese officer noticed the prisoners among his enlisted men and began shouting orders.

The *Sculpin* men were led to an area below the flight deck where long pine logs had been lashed underneath the deck above. Rocek and his comrades struggled to release the heavy logs and pass them in a human chain to a ladder where they were hauled up onto the flight deck, one by one. The process took some time. "When we got them all topside, then they brought us topside and put us in a circle on the top of the flight deck," Rocek remembered.

He saw Japanese sailors using the long pine logs to construct makeshift rafts that would be used if the carrier went down. One excited Japanese officer began shouting at the Americans and pointing to their life jackets. These were quickly removed, most given to other Japanese sailors or carried away. Another Japanese sailor appeared with a long strand of line, which was used to begin tying the prisoners of war together. "They tied about twelve of us together with a half-inch line, and then they ran out of rope," Rocek recalled.

Seated on the carrier's flight deck with his arms bound behind his back, Rocek could do little more than take in the scene around him. Most of the Japanese enlisted men on the flight deck wore no life preservers, although hundreds of the *Nitta Maru* jackets were available just a deck below. *Maybe they figure they won't get sunk,* he wondered. The officers he could see were treating the situation in an entirely different manner. Rocek saw several wearing long coats due to the cool weather; over them they had attached life jackets. Some even wore their ceremonial swords on their sides. *They're not about to part with those swords,* Rocek thought. *I guess it's like a family heirloom to them.*

The *Sculpin* men remained seated in the center of the flight deck for more than an hour. Few paid them much attention, but one Japanese officer did offer some words of encouragement at one point. "He came over to us and tried to tell us that there was help coming," Rocek recalled. "They had radioed in for help." The officer, in broken English and hand gestures, indicated to the Americans that another ship was en route and it would tow their carrier into port.[7]

The seas were still very heavy, causing the lifeless carrier to roll in the swells. Rocek continued to stare out to seaward, straining to see anything. The horizon had cleared slightly as the rain slackened. Some time later, he noticed others pointing toward a speck on the horizon. As it approached, he decided it must have been either a cruiser or a destroyer coming to tow *Chuyo* back to port.

★ ★ ★

On *Chuyo*'s bridge, Captain Tomasaborou and his executive officer, Commander Toshiyuki Eto, continued to monitor the efforts of their crew. Aside from the structural damage, the two torpedo attacks had caused serious loss of life and injured men, both in the passenger area and in the engineering spaces. Lieutenant Commander Midori Fukushima, the senior medical officer and surgeon on board, had more injuries than his limited medical staff could properly handle.

It was now a little after daybreak, and the vicious typhoon had died down somewhat. Visibility had improved, and the seas were a little less severe. Lieutenant (jg) Azuchi had been making the rounds through the ship, keeping tabs on the damage control efforts of his men. Eto, unable to leave the bridge, sent a messenger down to Azuchi with a specific request. Eto asked that Azuchi stop by the XO's cabin on his next trip belowdecks and retrieve his ceremonial samurai sword. Azuchi was very familiar with the sword, which was inscribed with the words *Shikai Nami Sizuka* ("water on all sides, waves are calm"). Eto was particularly proud of this sword, and he had boasted to his fellow *Chuyo* officers that, according to legend, as long as the sword was in Eto's possession, he would be safe.[8]

Azuchi proceeded down to officers' country but was alarmed to find the passage already filled with water. He struggled to force open the door to Eto's quarters, where he found the XO's treasured sword. Azuchi then pushed his way into the adjacent quarters of the skipper, but did not find the sword for Captain Tomasaborou. He decided his skipper must already have been carrying his sword on the bridge. Starting back toward the bridge, Azuchi found a carton of cigarettes and tucked them under his arm.

By the time he reached the flight deck, he found the *Sculpin* prisoners of war seated on the wooden deck. He assumed the torpedo blasts must have freed them from their lower valuables locker, but he saw no reason why American prisoners needed to have life jackets that could save Japanese lives. Azuchi ordered them to remove their jackets, and he carried several of them to the bridge with him.

Handing Commander Eto his sword, Azuchi then asked Captain Tomasaborou to put on one of the life jackets. Tomasaborou refused, leaving his junior officers to decide that he had no intention of leaving his command ship alive, should she finally succumb to her torpedo damage.[9]

Visibility was much improved for the lookouts on *Chuyo*'s bridge. It was around 0930 (0830 Japanese time), when Lieutenant (jg) Azuchi heard a lookout shout, "I've sighted a mast!"

"Are you sure it's not an enemy sub's periscope?" the lookout captain shouted back at him. "Recheck it!"

The same lookout quickly replied, "No mistake! It's a mast, sir."

Azuchi immediately reported this to Captain Tomasaborou, and both stared in the direction of the sighting. Azuchi looked through the towering waves and soon made out the top of a mast coming over the horizon, visible only in between each monstrous crest. *Sure enough!* he thought. *It is the mast of a destroyer coming to our rescue.*

A signalman climbed high atop *Chuyo*'s signal station and began blinking toward the approaching ship. Due to the high waves, his signals swung up and then down, and then left and then right. In response, the destroyer began signaling back: "This is *Akebono*. This is *Akebono*." Captain Tomasaborou knew that *Maya*'s skipper had sent at least one ship back to help tow his carrier.

"The atmosphere on the bridge completely changed in a moment, and life revived," recalled Azuchi. The officers and men had reason to rejoice. *Akebono* had returned, and word was that *Maya* was also on her way to help save their drifting carrier.

The approaching mast of *Akebono* had garnered the attention of most men who were topside, including the American prisoners who were seated on the flight deck. There were no warning bursts from topside guns nor any alarms that sounded before Azuchi felt a terrific explosion rock *Chuyo*.

He caught a fleeting glimpse of the Japanese sailor who had climbed atop the signal station to communicate with *Akebono*. That man had been blown high into the air, his body landing far out in the ocean. Azuchi instantly realized that his luckless carrier had been struck for the third time by an American submarine attack.

urvivors from the sunken submarine *Squalus* are helped onto USS *Falcon* (ASR-2) from the McCann rescue chamber. *Naval History and Heritage Command, NH 97292*

Lieutenant Oliver Naquin, the *Squalus* skipper, stands hatless with his hands in his pockets on May 25, 1939, on a coast guard vessel en route to port. | *Naval History and Heritage Command, NH 85832*

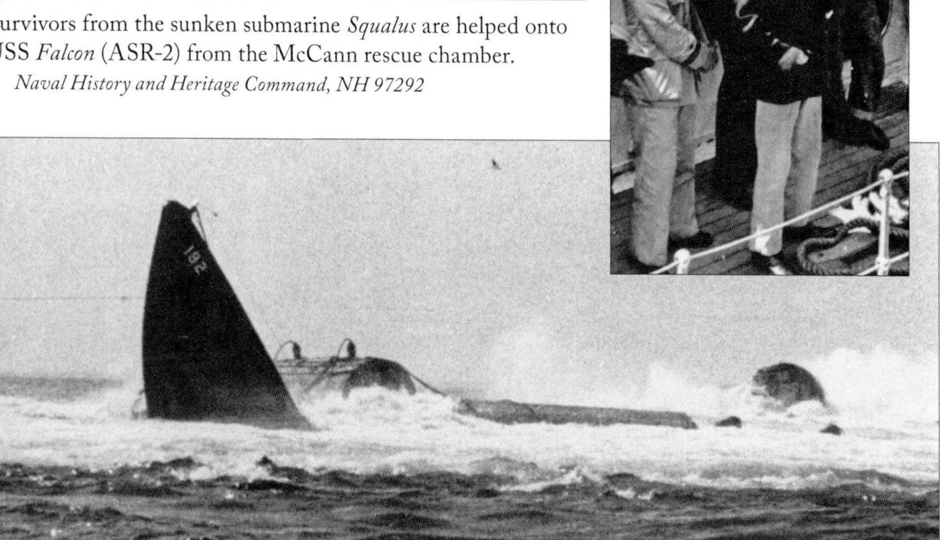

ooking like a surfacing sailfish, the bow of *Squalus* breaks the surface on uly 13, 1939, during the first attempt to salvage the boat. | *USN 1149026*

USS *Sailfish* under way, seen off the Mare Island Naval Shipyard in California, April 13, 1943. | *Naval History and Heritage Command, 19-N-43269*

Sailfish's skipper, Lieutenant Commander Bob Ward (*left*), is seen with his executive officer, George "Bud" Richardson, in July 1944, holding their boat's Presidential Unit Citation (PUC) flag. | *David Pike*

Sailfish radar operator Bi "Skip" Dillon (*left*) with hi infantryman brother Bob an a local in Hawaii on liberty i late June 1943. | *Bill Dillo*

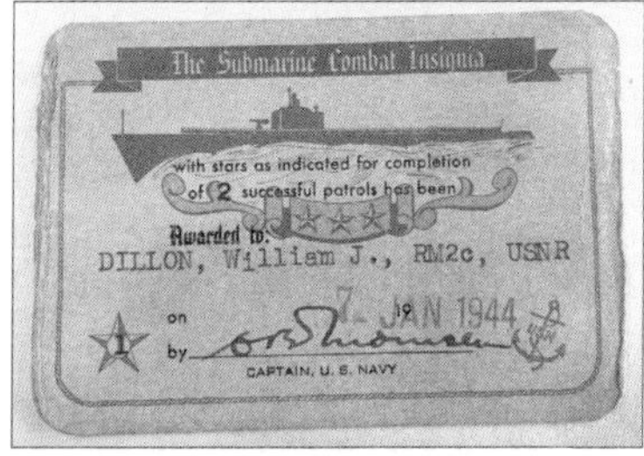

The Submarine Combat Insignia
with stars as indicated for completion of 2 successful patrols has been
Awarded to:
DILLON, William J., RM2c, USNR
on 7 JAN 1944
by
CAPTAIN, U. S. NAVY

Dillon received this card, along with his combat pin, for *Sailfish*'s tenth war patrol. It indicates he was also eligible for the submarine combat insignia for the boat's eighth war patrol. | *Bill Dillon*

Sailfish yeoman Luverne "Bud" Pike (*left*); his wife, Evelyn; and best man Bob Kempf at their January 30, 1944, wedding, shortly after *Sailfish*'s tenth patrol. | *David Pike*

Gunner's mate Lewis McCarty (*left*) made eleven patrols on *Sailfish* He is seen on liberty in Hawaii in late 1943 with buddy Joe Mende who was in charg of the forward torpedo room. | *Bill Dillon*

USS *Sculpin* (SS-191), seen leaving Mare Island Naval Shipyard in May 1943, helped effect the rescue of crewmembers of her sister sub *Squalus* in 1939. | *US Navy*

Commander Fred Connaway, skipper of *Sculpin*, was killed in action on her bridge on November 17, 1943. | *US Navy*

Captain John Philip Cromwell was a wolf pack commander on board *Sculpin* for her final patrol. | *US Navy*

Sculpin chief of the boat Weldon Edward "Dinty" Moore (*far right*) and shipmates in 1943 with the *Sculpin* battle flag he designed. | *Carl LaVO*

The 2,400-ton Japanese destroyer *Yamagumo*, seen here in 1939, made repeated and accurate depth charge attacks on the submarine *Sculpin* on November 19, 1943. *Yamagumo* then finished off *Sculpin* in a one-sided surface gunnery duel. | *Kure Maritime Museum, Japanese Naval Warship Photo Album: Destroyers*

Motor machinist's mate George "Moon" Rocek was the only man to survive the sinking of both *Sculpin* and the Japanese carrier *Chuyo* in 1943. He is seen months earlier during his last visit to his father's tailor shop in Cicero, Illinois, having fun with his hometown's newspaper reporters. George (*right*) is about to have his beard shaved by his older Marine brother, Rudy Rocek, who was also home on leave. | *Christine Moody*

Edwin Karl Frederick Kell was a seaman first class at t time of *Sculpin*'s loss. Keller w the only *Sculpin* POW who h also previously served on boa *Sailfish*. | *John Kel*

Lieutenant George Brown, the senior surviving officer, gave the orders to scuttle *Sculpin*. | *Carl LaVO*

Sculpin, viewed at Mare Island, California, on May 1, 1943, just months before her loss. This 3-inch, .50-caliber deck gun is where her crew fought its last surface battle against *Yamagumo.* | *Naval History and Heritage Command, NH 97305*

Torpedoman First Class Warren Berry served as a loader on *Sculpin*'s 3-inch gun. | *Charles Hinman, www.oneternalpatrol.com*

Torpedoman First Class Herb Thomas served as the gun's setter. | *Herbert Thomas*

Chief Motor Machinist's Mate Phil Gabrunas was lost while helping to scuttle *Sculpin*. | *Carl LaVO*

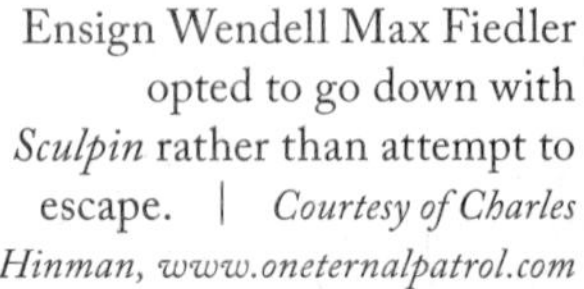

Ensign Wendell Max Fiedler opted to go down with *Sculpin* rather than attempt to escape. | *Courtesy of Charles Hinman, www.oneternalpatrol.com*

Wolf pack commander John Cromwell stayed in *Sculpin*'s control room and went down with the ship to prevent the Japanese from torturing classified intelligence from him. For his gallantry, Cromwell was posthumously awarded the Medal of Honor. | *Painting by Fred Freeman, copyright 1949*

Three wounded *Sculpin* survivors operated on at Truk were Radioman Third Class Jerome Baglien (*left*), Fireman First Class Henry "Rebel" Elliott (*center*), and Torpedoman Second Class Charles Pitser (*right*). None of these three survived the sinking of the carrier *Chuyo*. | *Charles Hinman, www.oneternalpatrol.com, and William Brown*

The 20,000-ton Japanese carrier *Chuyo*, seen at anchor in Truk Lagoon in May 1943. *Chuyo* was carrying twenty-one *Sculpin* survivors when *Sailfish* made repeated torpedo attacks against her on December 4, 1943. | *Sakai City Maritime History Science Museum Collection*

Former battleship sailor Harold Laman helped lead *Sculpin* survivors to *Chuyo*'s flight deck after she was torpedoed. | *Charles Hinman, www.oneternalpatrol.com, and Jerry Redman*

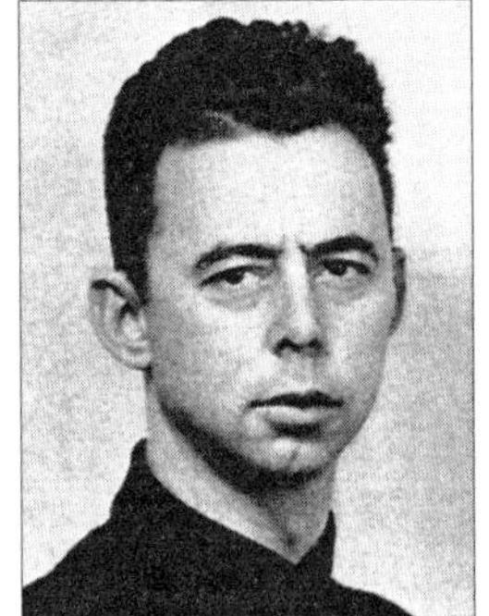

Ensign Charles Smith (*left*) and officer's cook Maximo Barrera (*right*) clung to a life raft for hours with George Rocek after the sinking of *Chuyo*. Neither Smith nor Barrera was rescued. | *Charles Hinman, www.oneternalpatrol.com*

The Japanese carrier *Unyo,* a sister ship to *Chuyo,* carried twenty *Sculpin* survivors back to mainland Japan. *Unyo is* seen limping back to Yokosuka in reverse on February 5, 1944, after torpedo damage has destroyed her bow. | *Anthony Tully*

Quartermaster Second Class Bill Cooper, on *Sculpin*'s bridge during her final fight, was one of the POWs transported to Japan on board *Unyo.* | *Bill Cooper*

Motor Machinist's Mate Joe Baker was wounded in action while fighting with *Sculpin*'s deck gun crew against *Yamagumo* during the surface battle. He is seen receiving the Bronze Star Medal in May 1947 from Admiral Chester Nimitz. | *Joe Baker*

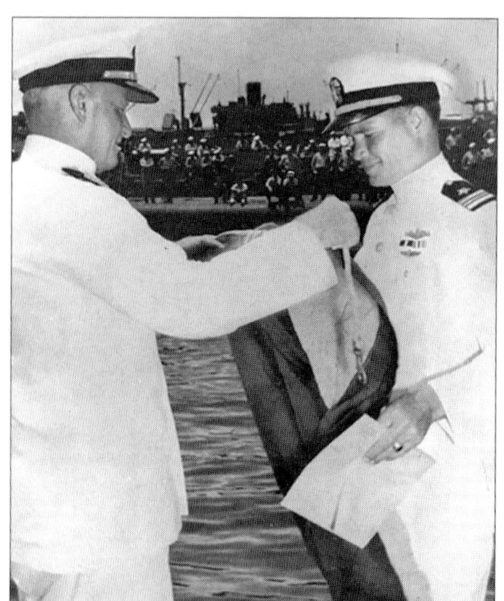

Lieutenant Commander Bob Ward, skipper of *Sailfish*, received a Navy Cross for sinking the carrier *Chuyo* and two other ships on *Sailfish*'s tenth war patrol. Ward (*right*) is being presented with a PUC flag on July 8, 1944, in Pearl Harbor by Admiral Chester Nimitz. | *US Navy photo, Tracy Griffin*

Sailfish crew on deck after the tenth war patrol. Starting at far left, the officers seen are: Lieutenant (jg) Bill Bruckart (*arms folded over knees*), Lieutenant (jg) Dutch Wetmore, Lieutenant Pat Murphy, Warrant Electrician Wayne Evans (*partially obscured behind Murphy*), skipper Bob Ward, Ensign Ed Berghausen (*directly behind Ward*), Lieutenant Bud Richardson, and Lieutenant (jg) Stan Cowin. The white arrow points to radar operator Bill Dillon. | *Bill Dillon*

Chief Torpedoman Willard Blatti (*right*), seen receiving the Bronze Star from Rear Admiral Wilhelm Friedell in San Diego in November 1944. Blatti was *Sailfish*'s chief of the boat on her tenth patrol. | *US Navy*

Sailfish chief petty officers pose with the PUC flag, July 1944. *Left to right*: Chief Electrician's Mate Lester Bayles, Chief Yeoman Bill Crytser, Chief Motor Machinist's Mates Montie Walkup and Bill Lyon, and Chief Radioman Bob Johnson (who made all twelve patrols on *Sailfish*). | *Rita Mendel*

During her twelfth war patrol, *Sailfish* and her crew effected the rescue of a dozen US naval aviators on October 12–13, 1944, who had been shot down off Japanese-held Formosa. *Sailfish* resident cartoonist Bob Kempf made this sketch for the ship's newsletter. | *Bill Dillon*

A rescue party of *Sailfish* officers and men worked to quickly pull downed aviators onto their boat from their yellow life rafts. During such lifeguard missions, US subs would recover more than 500 aviators in World War II. This image is of USS *Tang* sailors helping downed naval aviators on board near Truk Island in April 1944. | *Naval History and Heritage Command, 80-G-227989*

This Bob Kempf cartoon depicts *Sailfish* skipper Bob Ward yelling at a quartermaster who dumped a bucket of water down on him by mistake. The prank was meant to scare some of the newly rescued naval aviators on board *Sailfish*. | *Bill Dillon*

Sailfish officers seen around December 1944 after the twelfth war patrol. Front row (*left to right*): Lieutenant (jg) Ed Berghausen, Lieutenant Joe Sahaj, Lieutenant Stan Cowin, and Lieutenant (jg) Tom Smith. Standing (*left to right*): Lieutenant Pat Murphy, Lieutenant Dave Gaston, Commander Bob Ward, Ensign Craig Hertsgaard, and Lieutenant (jg) Wayne Evans. | *David Pike*

Twenty of the *Sculpin* POWs who survived their voyages on the carriers *Unyo* and *Chuyo* were sent to work this copper mine and nearby foundry in Ashio, Japan. | *Carl LaVO*

The Ashio prisoner-of-war camp, officially Ashio Camp 9-B, seen postwar in a view taken from the camp's entrance gate. More than three dozen captured US submariners would live and work from this compound in 1944 and 1945. | *Carl LaVO*

Sculpin's only surviving officer, Lieutenant George Brown (*far right*), is seen on September 6, 1945, having just been released from Mitsubishi Prison Camp No. 2. | *Carl LaVO*

Sailfish crew on deck with their battle flag after their twelfth and final patrol in late 1944. Front row, officers (*left to right*): Lieutenant (jg) Wayne Evans, Lieutenant (jg) Tom Smith, Lieutenant Dave Gaston, Lieutenant Pat Murphy, Commander Bob Ward, Lieutenant Stan Cowin, Lieutenant (jg) Joe Sahaj, Ensign Craig Hertsgaard, and Lieutenant (jg) Ed Berghausen. The white arrow points to Bill Dillon. To his left are John "Saul" Miller, Al Kasuga (*bearded*), and Bernie Williams. | *Bill Dillon*

USS *Sailfish* viewed bow on, under way off the Mare Island Naval Shipyard in California on April 13, 1943. | *Naval History and Heritage Command, NH 97307*

Stern view of *Sailfish* taken the same day. Note the open after torpedo room escape hatch and crew on deck. | *Naval History and Heritage Command, NH 97308*

Sailfish crewmen seen topside in late 1944. Radioman Bill Dillon stands on the lower cigarette deck to the left of the flag. At lower left, holding the shell of a turtle, is torpedoman Ray Bunt. The three men standing on the left side of the group are (*left to right*) Gail Lusk, Bob Kempf, and Troy Ray. | *Bill Dillon*

Sailfish illustration provided to the crew during the war by a Walt Disney cartoonist. | *Bill Dillon*

Survivors of *Squalus* and veterans who later served on *Sailfish* stand beneath the submarine's conning tower during the boat's final ceremony in September 2002 at the Portsmouth, New Hampshire, memorial. | *Bill Dillon*

Thousands of well-wishers line the pier at the New Hampshire shipyard as *Sailfish* makes her last dive on Navy Day, October 27, 1945, prior to the boat's being decommissioned. | *Milne Special Collections & Archives Division, Dimond Library, University of New Hampshire, Durham, NH*

Sailfish radar operator Bill "Skip" Dillon stands below his submarine's final scoreboard of enemy ships sunk on August 1, 1945. | *Bill Dillon*

Sculpin survivor George Rocek (*left*) was the only American survivor from the Japanese carrier *Chuyo* after she was torpedoed by *Sailfish*. Rocek is seen with *Sailfish* veteran Bill Dillon at a 1980s submarine reunion. | *Bill Dillon*

Five *Sculpin* veterans pose at a mid-1980s *Sculpin/Squalus/Sailfish* Association reunion. *Left to right*: Bill Cooper, George Brown, Ed Keller, George Rocek, and Julius Peterson. | *Sam Swisher*

The author with *Sailfish* veteran Bill Dillon in October 2021. | *Linda Musler*

USS *SAILFISH* TORPEDO ATTACKS AGAINST IJN CARRIER *CHUYO*

December 4, 1943

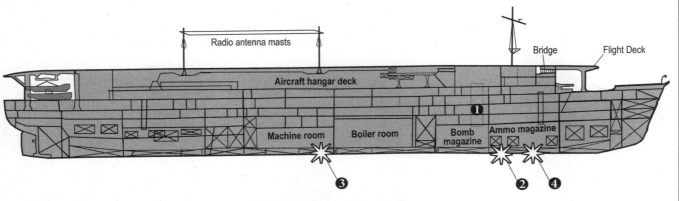

1. Approximate location of storeroom where George Rocek and twenty other *Sculpin* POWs were detained.
2. 0012: First *Sailfish* torpedo explodes below the No. 3 crew space, on portside.
3. 0557: Second attack; *Sailfish* torpedo hit in port engine room; *Chuyo* loses power.
4. 0942: Third attack; *Sailfish* torpedoes hit under bridge on port side. *Chuyo* sinks in about six minutes.

TWELVE

Carrier Down

"Fire one!"

Battle talker Bud Pike coolly relayed the captain's orders to Bill Bruckart, manning the phones in the aft torpedo room.

The time was 0940 as *Sailfish* commenced launching her third spread of torpedoes at the Japanese aircraft carrier. With Tube No. 8 secured after the previous week's hot-run mishap, the aft gang duly launched Mark 14s from Tubes 5, 6, and 7, using a spread of 0 degrees for the first, 2 degrees right on the next one, and 2 degrees to the left on the third war fish. Pat Murphy's TDC showed the range to be 1,700 yards on a target that was dead in the water. Bob Ward had little concern of completely missing, even if one torpedo might prove to be slightly off track. Each was set to run at twelve-foot depth.

Signalman Troy Ray counted down the seconds until the moment of expected impact. In the radio shack, Bob Johnson reported all three torpedoes to be running hot, straight, and normal. Two minutes later, at 0942, the unmistakable sounds of two more torpedo hits were heard through the submarine. This was followed by a very heavy swishing sound, then by exceptionally loud breaking-up noises heard not only by the sonar operators but also very clearly throughout the boat.[1]

Lieutenant Commander Ward did not have the satisfaction of actually seeing his torpedoes slam home. He had the scope up, anticipating just that pleasure. But maintaining depth control was nearly impossible in the violent seas above. At the moment of the explosions, *Sailfish* was at sixty feet. "All I could see when the scope was out of the waves was a sky full of tracers being shot up in the air from the carrier's bearing," Ward wrote.

His focus was now on bringing his bow tubes to bear.

"Right full rudder!" he called to Harry Tonden. "Take her to seventy feet."

As *Sailfish* swung to starboard, the skipper mentally chastised himself for underestimating his target's true range. It was immediately apparent, based on the timed length of runs to the explosions, that the enemy carrier had been lying a good thousand yards farther out than the 1,700 yards his team had computed from his periscope observations. "Can't figure out how I made the range error," Ward admitted in his patrol report. "Have been using a carrier flight deck height of 60 feet on the stadimeter."[2]

Just as his bow was swinging into position on the carrier's location, two depth charges exploded fairly close. By 0950, *Sailfish* had completed her swing, as Johnson continued to report breaking-up noises on sonar. One minute later, Ward brought her back up from seventy feet to fifty-five feet to take a look around. But on the generated bearing where the carrier should have been, the skipper found nothing in sight. When he moved his scope slightly left and then slightly right of this bearing, there was nothing. It had been roughly ten minutes since his torpedoes exploded, but there was no sight of the carrier anywhere! It had simply vanished.

Ward continued to swing the scope to find where the destroyer had gone. Instead of locating the carrier's former guardian warship, he was instead shocked to suddenly spot a Japanese heavy cruiser heading in his direction. In his zeal to finish off the crippled *Chuyo*, he had never taken notice of the approach of *Maya* some distance away. Ward now rapidly called out the details for his recognition team at the plotting table.

"She has three gun turrets forward, with a high bridge structure, two smokestacks, a tripod mast aft, and two large after gun turrets," he said. "Angle on the bow, forty starboard. Angle is decreasing rapidly! She's turning toward us, making high speed! Range four thousand yards."

With a separating distance of only two and a quarter miles, Ward would have to act fast if he wanted to take a shot. He shouted to quartermaster Harry Tonden to wheel his boat hard to port to bring the forward tubes to bear. Time was of the essence. As luck would have it, the heavy troughs of the typhoon-whipped seas were so deep that *Sailfish* suddenly began to broach. The Japanese lookouts knew exactly where the American submarine was now.

The range to *Maya* had dropped to less than 3,200 yards before *Sailfish*'s tubes could reach the right position for a daring down-the-throat shot. Ward shouted to diving officer Stan Cowin, "Take her to ninety feet! Rig for depth charge attack!"

Ward was very frustrated with himself. He had underestimated the range to the carrier by a thousand yards, and he had taken two close depth charges from a destroyer that he still had not been able to see. With his boat broaching and the surprise sighting of a Japanese cruiser charging down upon him, he was forced to dive and, he said, "thus threw away the chance of a lifetime."[3]

Officer of the deck Pat Murphy logged simply, "Unable to consummate attack." Escape for *Sailfish* now lay in Ward's conning of the boat. At ninety feet, he had no radar and no periscope info to utilize. His only input came from his sound operators. The incoming cruiser could clearly be heard on the QC sonar head. "Attempted to get a ping range on the QC head," Ward logged. "Took turn count on JK head of 220, indicating 18 knots. By the time data was obtained from sound to allow even a chance of a hit, he was astern and fading out fast."

Years later, he would admit, "It took me by surprise. My concentration was in keeping track of the escorts that might interfere, and keeping track of the carrier so we could sink her. What I should have done was make a complete trip around her, waiting for that kind of effort. But I didn't. I went ahead and sank the damn carrier. And then the cruiser went by close aboard, hell-bent for leather, without giving me a chance to line up on her."[4]

Ward was equally critical of himself in *Sailfish*'s patrol report. "The Monday morning quarterbacks can have a field day on this attack!" he wrote. "To top it all off, I have personally criticized the sinking of the *Soryu* [actually *Kaga*], where the towing cruiser could have been gotten first, then the carrier at leisure—yet I didn't go up ahead of the carrier and make absolutely certain that this wasn't a similar setup. This cruiser was undoubtedly on the off bow of the carrier."[5]

The heavy cruiser *Maya* rumbled right on past *Sailfish* as Ward dodged her, but a Japanese destroyer immediately took up the hunt. During the next ten minutes, Bob Johnson and Bill Dillon heard her screws fading in and out on their listening gear as she crisscrossed the scene in search of the American attackers. Seven depth charges exploded, none close enough to cause any serious concerns. Skipper Ward would forever lament the chance to hit the Japanese cruiser that had been lost. "If we had gotten him, it would have been a big day," he recalled.[6]

The sonar operators kept up a steady report on the destroyer's position, allowing Ward to keep his opponent abaft *Sailfish*'s beam. During this period of silent running, the forward and aft torpedomen worked as quietly as possible to prepare their tubes for the chance to fire again. By 1128, Joe Mendel's forward room reported that all four of their loaded Mark 14s had been checked for readiness, and Emmett Lucas's after room also reported their reloading to be complete.[7]

An hour later, all enemy counterattacks had ceased. During that time, Ward had eased *Sailfish* back to the estimated position where his aircraft carrier had taken her final torpedo hits. Johnson reported no enemy screws on sound at 1228.

"Bring her to periscope depth," Ward ordered.

But the Japanese had apparently been lying in wait, silently. As *Sailfish* approached a depth of sixty feet, another depth charge rocked the boat, alarmingly close.

"Take her deep!" Ward shouted.

Lieutenant Cowin's planesmen put the boat on hard dive and took her back down to safer depths. Ward coached his quartermaster to point *Sailfish* out to the west. She steadily crept at 2 to 3 knots submerged speed to a point about 3,500 yards west of the last torpedo-attack position. The skipper waited another hour before taking another chance to survey the situation.

At 1330, he returned *Sailfish* to periscope depth. It had been nearly four hours since his last torpedoes had been fired. At sixty feet, and then fifty-two feet, Ward carefully surveyed the ocean above for fifteen minutes. This time, there was no charging destroyer to force him down again. "If the cruiser (or carrier) were in the vicinity, they would have been seen," Ward logged. "I am convinced the carrier has been sunk and the cruiser has gotten clear."[8]

At 1400, Ward ordered his helmsman to proceed to her normal patrol area. The seas above remained clear of enemy vessels until sunset. The air in the boat had grown quite foul by the time *Sailfish* finally surfaced again at 1818 to start her diesels and charge her depleted batteries. During that time, Chief Pharmacist's Mate (CPhM) Emerial "Doc" McMurtrey from Salt Lake City had made the rounds to spread powdered carbon dioxide absorbent through the boat. McMurtrey was a veteran of four prior patrols on *Trigger*; his early service had been that of an operating room technician on the battleship *Tennessee*. Because McMurtrey was *Sailfish*'s only medical person, his work often involved tending to lacerations and ailments, but his task this day was for the good of all on board. The fresh air rushing through the compartments was invigorating.[9]

On the bridge with duty officers Dutch Wetmore and Shorty Evans and their lookouts, Lieutenant Commander Ward found no enemy warships in sight nor on radar. He proceeded with his war patrol, finding nothing during the next hours. The seas were much calmer by this point, with only a 20-knot estimated wind speed accompanying waves that swelled as high as twenty feet—still rough, but tame by comparison to what his boat had fought twenty-four hours prior. Visibility was also improving, aided by the silvery sliver of a first-quarter moon beginning to break through the cumulus clouds.

At 2040, the radar watch reported another ship contact at only 1,800 yards. It was evidently a small vessel, as Ward and his lookouts were unable to obtain a visual through their binoculars. He decided it must have been a nimble anti-submarine vessel, often called "spit kits" by submariners. "It has been a busy day since midnight and don't feel like playing with a spit kit we can't see at 1,800 yards in this visibility," Ward wrote.[10]

He steered clear of the small vessel and proceeded toward his assigned patrol station. Twenty-four hours had lapsed since *Sailfish*'s first assault on the Japanese carrier force, and most of the crew had been at battle stations for the majority of that period. All hands were exhausted. Proud skipper Bob Ward's final entry in his report for December 4 came at midnight.

"One full day's work completed."

* * *

The final demise of *Chuyo* was swift.

At 0942, the final two torpedoes to strike *Chuyo* exploded in her forward section. On the bridge, Lieutenant (jg) Azuchi saw men blown into the sea and noted that his carrier was beginning to sink quickly by her bow. *Sailfish*'s latest Mark 14s ripped open more compartments toward the bow, allowing vast quantities of ocean water to pour into the stricken vessel. More bulkheads collapsed as the sea rushed in, and the carrier began to nose downward.

"All hands, abandon ship!"

Captain Tomasaborou's last order came within a minute of *Sailfish*'s final torpedo hits. By impulse, Azuchi turned to his captain and tied the lifeline of a buoy he was holding to the belt of Tomasaborou's overcoat. "This was not prearranged," Azuchi related. From this moment forward, he would remain tethered to his commanding officer, and they would act as one.[11]

Below, on the flight deck, Azuchi witnessed unspeakable losses. "Some jumped into the sea, some held on to a raft, some seemed to be confused and did not know what to do," he recalled. "The POWs were also as confused as the crew members."

Captain Tomasaborou ordered his men to clear the bridge and make efforts to save themselves. On his way up one level to reach the flight deck, he passed through the Flag Deck, where he shouted, "Lower the ensign!"

Azuchi looked around, but *Chuyo*'s battle flag was nowhere to be seen. In the confusion, he assumed that the skipper mistakenly believed the ensign to still be flying on the mast. Attached to his skipper by a lifeline, Azuchi followed him out onto the flight deck. Many sailors were saluting one another and bidding their comrades farewell. *Chuyo* was rapidly standing on her nose, her stern section beginning to rise from the ocean as her bow slid under the waves.

"Those who were on the flight deck lost their footholds and fell down into the sea, as though they had been carried away by an avalanche," Azuchi recalled.

★ ★ ★

Sculpin motor machinist's mate George Rocek had been staring at the approaching Japanese destroyer *Akebono* when *Sailfish*'s final torpedoes struck *Chuyo*. He felt the shock waves of the explosions forward of his position and saw a large puff of black smoke curling up high above the flight deck within seconds.

Rocek and chief of the boat Dinty Moore grabbed a nearby searchlight to steady themselves. "They had one of these collapsible searchlights on the flight deck, maybe about twenty-five feet from the starboard side," he recalled. Most of his fellow *Sculpin* survivors had been seated nearby when the torpedo exploded. *Chuyo* was already listing to port, placing the POWs on the higher side of the flight deck.

As the carrier began sagging forward, Rocek and Moore continued to cling to their searchlight for support.[12]

They shouted toward their companions to come over to their searchlight to get away from the masses of Japanese sailors. As the carrier began nosing down rapidly, Rocek feared that his fellow prisoners of war would become trampled in the mass of humanity that was quickly losing its footing on the slanting flight deck. He was alarmed that the others seemed panic-stricken as the ship's nose slid downward under the ocean.

Chuyo's plunge increased in speed as the flight deck rose higher on the starboard side. Moore and Rocek struggled to maintain their grasp on the searchlight as men around them began tumbling down the flight deck into the ocean. *Chuyo*'s high side, once about sixty feet above the waves, rapidly rose to an estimated hundred feet as she sank. Rocek finally turned to his senior enlisted comrade and shouted, "Let's go, Dinty!"

Rocek released his bear hug on the searchlight and fell down the flight deck toward the water. His body skidded along the rough wooden planking, ripping out the back side of his blue Japanese Navy trousers; then seconds later he slammed into the ocean, flailing about in hopes of reaching the surface.

Chuyo was disappearing beneath the waves, creating a powerful downward-suction effect. Hundreds of men, including the twenty other *Sculpin* prisoners, were instantly clawing for survival as bodies slammed into bodies and were pulled down by the sinking ship. As a youngster in school, Rocek had been on his high school water polo team, and he considered himself to be a great swimmer. But this was unlike anything he had ever experienced.

He found himself unable to break the suction that tugged his body deeper into the water. For unspeakable seconds, he felt that he was experiencing the agony of drowning. Helpless, Rocek stared pitifully upward until he was finally forced to take a breath. Ocean water filled his lungs, and he panicked. *This is it!* he thought as he lost his battle to reach the surface.

And then, perhaps from the force of a mighty pocket of air being expelled from within *Chuyo*, Rocek suddenly felt the terrifying grip of the downward forces release him. His body was being pushed upward by some equally strong force, and he saw a brighter light. "I made one last attempt to break surface, and I did," he remembered.

Rocek coughed up salt water and breathed in fresh air in between his choking. Seconds later, he spotted a Japanese raft only about fifteen feet away from him. Gathering his remaining strength, he swam hard through the mighty waves until he was able to latch onto the side of the raft. Towering swells attempted to rip him away, so Rocek worked his hand and wrist through some of the lashings to secure himself to the bobbing raft.

After hacking out the last of the water from his lungs, he noted that the raft was filled with Japanese sailors. During the next few minutes, more survivors swam over and grabbed onto the raft until Rocek estimated there to be more than two dozen men hanging on. He was pleased to see that his little raft was soon joined by two other *Sculpin* survivors, mess attendant Maximo Barrera and Ensign Charles Smith.

Minutes turned to hours as the pitiful survivors bobbed in the towering seas, clinging to life and praying for rescue. For Rocek and his fellow *Sculpin* survivors, it was the second time in two weeks that they had survived a warship's sinking. But for the time being, their only hope of recovery lay in Japanese warships that were currently consumed with trying to destroy the American submarine that had created their misery.

* * *

Takuji Azuchi slid down the steeply slanting flight deck as *Chuyo* began her rapid bow-first plunge under the waves. Captain Tomasaborou tumbled and slid down into the ocean with him, the pair still connected by a life buoy line.

Lieutenant (jg) Azuchi struggled to keep his head above water as his ship went under. More than once, he found himself being dragged underwater by the powerful suction of a small whirlpool. The swirl pulled him under and pushed him back up several times, his body twirled like limp clothing in a washing machine. Azuchi swallowed salt water and began choking. In the next instant, he bobbed back to the surface a short distance away from the bubbling whirlpool.[13]

Looking around, he spotted a large piece of wood nearby and latched onto it. He had no desire to die. Several other *Chuyo* sailors were clutching onto the flotsam, which was near the limits of its buoyancy. Coughing up more ocean water, Azuchi was suddenly stricken by a harrowing realization. *Where is my commanding officer?*

During his desperate attempts to avoid drowning in the suction, he had pulled on the lifeline connecting him to Captain Tomasaborou. It was now limp, containing only a piece of the skipper's belt. Somewhere in the deadly vortex of downward suction, the forces of the sea and the sinking ship had snapped Tomasaborou's belt. Azuchi scanned the waves and called out for him, but *Chuyo*'s commander was simply gone.

He spotted other members of his damage control team clinging to pieces of wood. As time passed, someone suggested that they sing Japanese military songs to help boost morale so they could hold out for rescue. But Azuchi ordered them to stop. "It is important to preserve our energy and our spirits," he advised. And so the carrier men drifted and kicked in silence amid the forceful waves.[14]

The rising swells pulled at Azuchi and his comrades. It took all their strength just to maintain their grip on the chunks of wood. Further frustrating their efforts was the fact that vast quantities of oil had been spewed from *Chuyo* in her final demise, and it covered the waves in thick black slime. The pungent substance coated their bodies and faces, burning their eyes and creeping into their throats. Soon it was nearly impossible to tell one blackened man from another as they struggled to even breathe.

Another hour passed, and Azuchi grew weak from clutching the wooden flotsam. A short distance away, he spotted one of the handmade rafts, to which hummocks and other buoyancy objects had been lashed. Deciding it was stout, he struck out for it. In the hefty swells, his best attempts to swim seemed to help him make little progress. Looking back at the distant piece of wood he had abandoned, Azuchi questioned his choice. Using the last of his strength, he pushed forward until he reached the raft, and strained to pull his body atop it.

Several other Japanese sailors were atop the raft, and another ten men remained in the sea, clinging to its sides. Azuchi was relieved that he was not suffering from injuries, but his body was now spent after hours battling the cold weather and the dangerous ocean. He wished he could just go to sleep to alleviate his body's agony. Glancing across at a baby-faced young sailor, he saw that man's will to live also slipping away.

"Let's beat each other to get rid of our drowsiness," said Azuchi. "Do not ever fall asleep, no matter how sleepy you are. Let's beat each other and hold out, shall we?"

The sailor was shocked. "Sir, I cannot beat an officer," he stammered.

Azuchi was in no mood to be questioned. He began punching the *Chuyo* man about the face, raising the man's ire. Fearful the crazed officer might drown him, the teenager finally began fighting back, striking the lieutenant. The pair engaged in this back-and-forth striking for several rounds, until both were thoroughly exhausted.

Spent, Azuchi pulled out a pistol that had remained on his belt. He raised it to fire, but hours of submergence in the salt water had rendered it useless. It failed to fire, and he flung it into the sea in disgust. Azuchi then collapsed atop his raft and lost consciousness.

* * *

Drifting among the *Chuyo* survivors were a number of the former *Sculpin* prisoners of war. Now their fate was equally as insecure as that of their former captors. Americans and Japanese alike bobbed about in the thick, oily waves, trying to keep their mouths above the chilly water while praying for some form of rescue.

Moon Rocek had no idea how many of his *Sculpin* comrades were still alive. The raft he clung to contained only Japanese men, plus Ensign Smith and officers' cook Barrera from his former submarine. With his wrist jammed through lashings on one side of the raft, Rocek had endured hours floating in the rough, cold ocean. For the time being, the only destroyer in sight had no intention of helping the men. "She was afraid the submarine was going to get her, so she just kept circling and pinging," he recalled.[15]

During the first three hours following the sinking of *Chuyo*, her guardian destroyer, *Urakaze*, had dashed about the area in search of *Sailfish*. Commander Shooichi Yoshida's *Urakaze* (meaning "wind on the sea") was one of nineteen *Kagero*-class destroyers built for the Imperial Japanese Navy during the late 1930s. She was commissioned on December 15, 1940, and had escorted at least ten convoys between April and October 1943. *Urakaze*, flagship for the Destroyer Division 17 commander, Captain Toshio Miyazaki, had dropped a number of depth charges on December 4, and continued using echo ranging for several hours in search of the American attacker.[16]

It was well after noon before Commander Yoshida deemed it safe enough to begin rescuing some of the *Chuyo* sailors. The seas remained rough, but his sailors tossed lines to various survivors, who were then hauled through the swells to climb the slippery sides of the warship. *Urakaze*'s men also dropped a flexible hanging-rope ladder—known to sailors as a Jacob's ladder—over one side to allow other men to more easily clamber up to her deck.

Rocek and his two *Sculpin* companions were greatly relieved to finally see *Urakaze* approach their crude life raft several hours after the carrier's demise. Several Japanese survivors managed to climb up the ladder, and soon Rocek decided it was time to take his chances with rescue. He grabbed one of the lines and attempted to climb the destroyer's side. "Once she rolled, then all of your weight was on that wet line, and then you slid right back down," he recalled.

Rocek resumed his clutch on the side of the raft until *Urakaze* slid up close enough for him to reach for the Jacob's ladder. As luck would have it, another wave suddenly pushed his raft right up against the rope ladder. Rocek grasped it and began pulling his body over the raft. In the same instant, *Chuyo*'s executive officer, Commander Eto, pulled himself over the top of the raft, knocking other survivors out of his way. "A Jap officer stepped and crawled over me," Rocek remembered. "When he stepped on me, it broke my grasp on that ladder, and I went down."[17]

Rocek floundered back to the surface, frustrated. He was exhausted, but luck was with him. "Another wave pushed me back up against that ladder," he recalled. With no energy left to climb it, Rocek simply threw his left arm through one of the rungs of the Jacob's ladder. He grasped his left wrist with his right hand. *Urakaze* was rolling heavily in the swells, which alternately lifted his body from the sea and then plunged him back under the next wave. After several dunkings, his body suddenly began to ascend the side of the destroyer.

Japanese sailors on *Urakaze*'s deck were hauling the rope ladder back up. Rocek maintained his clutch on one of the rungs until his body and the ladder were pulled topside. He flipped onto the steel deck and rolled over facedown, panting heavily for several minutes. Covered in oil and wearing Japanese undress blues, he looked like any other pitiful survivor. But when one of the *Urakaze* sailors finally rolled him over to check on him, Rocek's luck took a turn for the worse.

"As soon as they recognized that I was not a Japanese, they began jabbering," he recalled. "Then I felt myself being picked up and carried to the fantail." It was a horrifying process that he had witnessed two weeks earlier when the destroyer *Yamagumo* had rescued *Sculpin*'s survivors. *They're going to throw me over the fantail!* he thought.

Japanese sailors hauled Rocek aft, but his streak of good luck prevailed once again. One of *Urakaze*'s senior officers apparently ordered them to retain the prisoner, and Rocek was carried back up to the amidships section, where he was thrown into a small laundry compartment. During his short time on deck and in being hauled to and from the fantail, he witnessed a heartbreaking sight. He saw Japanese sailors using long bamboo poles to poke at other survivors who were still trying to clamber onto the destroyer.

Ensign Smith and Maximo Barrera never made it on board. They and other Japanese survivors were jabbed with the poles as *Urakaze*'s deck hands hauled in the last of their lines. Moments later, Commander Yoshida's warship was underway, departing the scene of the sinking. His two-hundred-forty-man crew had hauled aboard 128 enlisted men, one *Chuyo* officer (Commander Eto), and one American prisoner of war. In the tossing seas, Yoshida's 2,500-ton destroyer was in danger of capsizing if he chose to overload it with more survivors.

Moon Rocek lay exhausted on the floor of the laundry compartment as *Urakaze* cleared the scene. In the confusion of the moment, his captors did not take the time to tie him up or even close the door to his little room. His heart went out to those in peril on the sea, but it was obvious this vessel was finished with her lifesaving efforts. He reasoned that in calm seas the Japanese would have attempted to bring more on board.

Rocek lay on the deck in his little compartment, wondering who else from *Sculpin* had been recovered.

★ ★ ★

Chuyo had been sunk with a heavy loss of life. *Urakaze* pulled only a hundred thirty men from the water before departing the scene, and only one of the survivors was an American POW. A short time later, the destroyer *Sazanami* passed through the flotsam and slowed long enough to scoop up only another thirty men, all Japanese. Some 1,250 men perished with *Chuyo*'s loss, including twenty of the *Sculpin* prisoners.[18]

One other officer, Lieutenant (jg) Azuchi, was fortunate enough to be pulled on board *Sazanami*. After hours of clinging to a makeshift raft, he was out of his senses. In a dreamy state, Azuchi suddenly found a line that had been thrown in front of him. He struggled to work his head and one arm through a loop at the end of the line, and he was only vaguely aware of the sensation of his body being pulled mightily through the waves by strong arms.[19]

Azuchi was hauled onto *Sazanami*'s deck, which pitched and rolled hard in the rough seas. Sailors carried his limp body down below and placed him in an enlisted man's bunk to recover. When Azuchi awoke, he was paid a sympathy visit by the destroyer's skipper, Lieutenant Commander Akiji Suga, and another officer. They told him that he had been hauled on board unconscious. Azuchi was soon able to swallow some thin gruel and recover enough strength to ask about his other comrades.

In due time, he would learn the gut-wrenching truth. He was one of only two officers rescued from *Chuyo*. Roughly ninety percent of the souls on board his former carrier had been lost in the sinking. "Life or death was determined only by a paper-thin difference," Azuchi recalled.

* * *

Motor machinist's mate George Rocek was the sole American survivor of the sinking, a dreadful fact that he would not come to realize for some time. He felt the rumbling of *Urakaze*'s engines as she picked up speed and cleared the scene of the carrier's demise.

As night came on, he became very cold as he lay in the laundry compartment. He noticed a metal tank filled with water and dipped his hand into it. It felt warm. "I climbed into the tub and sat down, with only my head above water," Rocek recalled. "I stayed there for the rest of the night."[20]

The next morning, December 5, he was visited by a young Japanese sailor who seemed genuinely interested in the American prisoner. Communicating largely through hand gestures, Rocek and the sailor learned that they both worked in the engine rooms of their respective ships. "He came back about fifteen minutes later and gave me a little hardtack cracker," said Rocek. The sailor made a shush sound with a finger to his mouth, his way of asking the prisoner to keep it their little secret. "I was elated," recalled Rocek. "If he was ever caught doing that for me, they'd have killed him."[21]

His only problem was in digesting the hard little cracker. Badly dehydrated, he could scarcely create enough saliva to swallow the dry snack. Rocek's next visitor was far less pleasant—a Japanese chief petty officer who acted and smelled like he had been partaking of plenty of sake. "He would come in there and yak, and then he'd slug the hell out of me," Rocek recalled. The chief departed, but returned about every hour to repeat the process of talking to and beating the American prisoner. "He also mentioned Tokyo, Doolittle, and gave me the cut-throat sign," Rocek remembered.[22]

During the morning hours, *Urakaze* arrived at the Kure Naval Arsenal, the second oldest dockyard in Japan. As the ship entered port, Rocek noted many damaged merchant vessels and warships. Shortly after the *Urakaze* docked, Rocek was visited by the abusive chief petty officer and three sailors carrying about fifty feet of heavy line. "They tied and blindfolded me so I couldn't even move," he related.

Hours later, a husky Japanese chief appeared. He untied Rocek and loosened his blindfold enough so that he could see down. "He then tied my wrists together and led me with the loose end to the gangway," said Rocek. There, he was given a pair of sandals, loaded into a small craft, and taken across the harbor. "I now began to realize I was the only *Sculpin* crewmember from the carrier to survive," he recalled.[23]

After reaching shore, he was led through part of the city. He could see shoes and the bottoms of women's kimonos. He felt awkward and embarrassed at first, as the seat of his pants had been ripped open while he slid along *Chuyo*'s deck. With his rear end exposed, his "Moon" nickname was back to haunt him once again. But that thought soon disappeared. *I don't give a damn! I've got more problems to worry about than my ass sticking out.*[24]

Upon arriving at a railroad station, the chief sat him down on a bench and began talking to a young woman. After a few moments, he removed Rocek's blindfold so she could see the captive was American. "She was a doll and dressed Stateside, with a short skirt and high-heel shoes," he remembered. A little while later, his blindfold was put back on and he was led onto a train.

An hour or two later, after standing the entire ride in the crowded car, Rocek was hustled off the train. The chief insisted that they run along a narrow, stony road. Rocek's sandals kept falling off, slowing their pace. Rocek pointed in protest at his sandals, at the stony ground, and at the proper shoes his captor was wearing. "He understood, but then motioned he wanted me to get there in time for eating, which we did," said Rocek.

Exhausted and feeling depressed over being the only *Sculpin* survivor, Moon Rocek was herded into a Japanese prisoner of war camp. His days at sea on Japanese warships were behind him, but a new and unknown fate as a special guest of the Japanese military was just beginning.

THIRTEEN

Sailfish on the Prowl

Bill Dillon was on radar duty three days after sinking the carrier. The date was December 7—two years to the day since the Japanese attack on Pearl Harbor—when *Sailfish* received her own surprise attack.

Although skipper Bob Ward would indicate in his patrol report that his boat was suddenly caught by surprise, duty radar operator Bill Dillon had a completely different take on the event that transpired.

"On our SD air-search radar set, we were reporting that there was an airplane out there," Dillon recalled. "We were down below in the conning tower, and we kept reporting that it was getting closer and closer. But I guess the lookouts topside didn't see anything, even though we're giving these reports. I was standing there wondering, *Why the hell don't they dive this damn boat?*"[1]

Finally, at 1440, one of the lookouts was startled to hear the chatter of machine guns and looked skyward to spot a Zeke fighter-bomber plunging through the cloud cover. "Plane!" he shouted.

Exec Bud Richardson happened to be topside at this time, getting an afternoon sun line using his sextant with assistant navigator Troy Ray. Nearby, Lt. (jg) Stan Cowin and his assistant, Ed Berghausen, had the deck watch. Richardson suddenly became aware of "a peculiar pipping sound off the starboard bow." He paid it little attention for about two seconds. Then, glancing to starboard, he saw "a very attractive little spray of bullets hitting the water, coming across our starboard bow."[2]

Richardson reached for the diving alarm but could not get to it. Cowin hit the alarm as Richardson shouted, "Dive! Dive!" A mad scramble of lookouts, three officers, and the duty quartermaster ensued as they piled upon one another in their haste to clear the bridge. One of the lookouts dropped from the shears and landed on Ray, knocking him to the floor. The last men down pulled the dazed quartermaster down with them.[3]

In the control room, the duty diving officer was shocked to hear Richardson shout, "For God's sake, take her down!"[4]

Somehow, in the midst of plunging down two sets of ladders from the bridge to the control room, Richardson still had his sextant in hand. He immediately took over the diving duties as the boat pointed downward.

Sailfish was still submerging as the first bomb exploded. No one was injured, but the Zeke banked around and released his second bomb. Lieutenant Commander Ward logged that it was "too damn close" for comfort. It exploded close aboard the starboard side abreast the after machinery space, lifting deck gratings and knocking a secured heater six feet in the air.[5]

In the conning tower, yeoman Bud Pike was on helm duty. "I was on the wheel and we had just started a zig when the bridge personnel came hollering and screaming through the hatch," he recalled. "I heard the loud explosion and saw blue flames shoot through the area."[6]

The two bombs could easily have been fatal hits for *Sailfish*. "We were lucky," Richardson recalled. "Maybe Providence was with us." But the resulting explosions still caused serious issues. All power to the engines was lost momentarily. Men were slammed against machinery, and Richardson had to work with manual power for a moment until order could be restored. In the forward engine room, John Good was tossed off his feet and knocked against a metal table covering the electric evaporators. As cork residue and paint peelings fluttered to the deck, Good instinctively shut down the engines, closed the outer exhaust valve, and closed the main induction valves as *Sailfish* headed for the depths. He was still securing his compartment for the dive when the second explosion sent him reeling across the port locker over the engine.[7]

Chief Electrician's Mate Les Bayles raced for the maneuvering cubicle in the after engine room. "The motors weren't running," he recalled. "The silence was eerie." A *Sailfish* plank owner with thorough knowledge of all electrical systems, Bayles swiftly traced the power problem to a faulty switch in the maneuvering space. He entered the electrical cage in the control cubicle, freed the burned contacts, reset them, and restored vital power to his submarine in less than one minute. But the bomb's blast created a different crisis nearby.[8]

"Water in the after engine room!" someone cried.

Damage control work began immediately. The severe concussion had snapped the studs of a saltwater line in the after engine room, and ocean water was pouring into the compartment. Engineers worked feverishly as water flooded the lower flats. They jacked the line against the flange and inserted new bolts. Chief Montie Walkup found a steady stream of water flowing into the ship at the hull flange from the main-motor-cooling-water overboard discharge, with salt water coming in over the starboard main motor casing.

One of the damage controlmen grabbed an offset box wrench and took position to tighten the nuts on the elongated studs that held the valve to the hull. But in his hurry, he dropped the wrench into the bilge. "I wasn't too sure that tightening the studs was a proper move," Walkup recalled. "If a stud snapped, we would be in a worse situation."[9]

Walkup found this was the perfect chance to employ the hydraulic jack he had brought on board at Pearl Harbor. In the after engine room, he worked to open the jack kit while Chief Bill Lyon—a husky, seasoned veteran of all previous *Sailfish* patrols—scurried to find two small boards. "He placed one board against the valve and the other board against an engine cylinder head exhaust," said Walkup. "As the jack was pressurized, the water slowed to a trickle and then stopped completely." The valve's gasket proved to be intact. Lyon and Walkup then tightened up the nuts on the valve's studs. Only much later would they learn that the force of the bomb's explosion had dished in *Sailfish*'s pressure hull. "I later looked on deck, and the wood planking was missing around a bent deck frame," Bill Bruckart remembered.[10]

For the remainder of the patrol, the engineers opted to leave the jack in place as a safety precaution. Bob Ward was proud of the swift work of his motormacs and electricians in saving the boat. In his patrol report, he praised Bayles for his "prompt and intelligent action" in preventing the boat from suffering a prolonged loss of power. He praised Lyon "for his cool and efficient action in gaining access to and stopping a hull flange leak" following the bombing.[11]

Ward maintained a northerly course submerged while his damage control parties shored up the leaks. Only after twilight did he return to the surface to clear the area. The only visible damage topside was a bullet hole in sheet metal near the doghouse entrance. *Sailfish* had been lucky.

★ ★ ★

Sailfish entered her patrol area south of the Japanese home islands on December 9 and patrolled submerged off the hundred-fathom curve on the navigation charts. During the next four days she was unable to close on any worthwhile targets. Her engineers worked to correct misaligned bow planes, noisy gears, and a damaged No. 2 periscope.

When Bob Ward found time to sleep, he remained prepared for action. Prior to the patrol, he had installed a large warning buzzer akin to a fire bell in his wardroom. Due to *Sailfish* having taken on one extra officer for this patrol, junior officer Bill Bruckart had ended up sharing Ward's cabin, sleeping on the upper bunk. When the captain-to-the-bridge bell rang during the late morning of December 13, Ward was gone in an instant. "I wakened only to see the skipper already heading through the watertight door to the control room," Bruckart recalled. "He was fast!"[12]

It was 1154. Lieutenant Pat Murphy's periscope watch had sighted light smoke on the horizon, about thirty thousand yards away and drawing south. Upon taking a sweep with the periscope, Ward ordered, "Station the tracking party."

Dutch Wetmore and Shorty Evans took their positions at the little plotting table in the control room as *Sailfish* began stalking this shipping contact. By 1408, with ten feet of periscope exposed, Ward could make out the tops of two sets of masts and an additional set of black smoke puffs. With three ships in the distance, he felt encouraged. But the presence of air cover and full daylight made it necessary for him to wait until sunset before bringing *Sailfish* to the surface for a 16-knot run to attain firing position.

Bill Dillon and Frank Dieterich monitored their radar sets as *Sailfish* raced toward an intercept. It was a bright moonlit night, with excellent visibility. From the bridge, Ward and his lookouts could plainly see their target ships and the escorting warships. By 2222, *Sailfish* was dead ahead of the convoy, and Ward soon submerged as two freighters, a small escort, and a large warship approached to within eight thousand yards.

At 2304, as his two primary merchantmen were about to overlap, Ward told talker Bud Pike to have the forward torpedo room open their tubes. Two minutes later, *Sailfish* shuddered four times as she cleared her forward nest. Ward then ordered helmsman Harry Tonden to swing her hard to starboard to bring the rear tubes to bear. Before his sub could complete the swing, the closest Japanese escort ship charged toward his periscope.

"Take her deep!" Ward snapped as he signaled for his periscope assistant, Troy Ray, to take the scope down.

Two minutes after firing, and as Ward's boat headed for the depths, he and his team heard two solid explosions from their torpedoes. The charging escort rocked *Sailfish* with two close depth charges but thereafter was heard to be making echo-ranging runs without further success in locating the American submarine. When *Sailfish* returned to the surface in the early hours of December 14, one of the Japanese merchant ships had clearly disappeared.

Ward eased in closer, but four Japanese escort vessels were stirred up, some sending blinker-light messages in the direction of the American submarine. With only one torpedo remaining forward and three functional tubes aft, Ward elected to forgo any further attacks on the remnants of this convoy.

Postwar analysis would later credit *Sailfish* with sinking the 3,194-ton troop transport *Totai Maru* south of Kyushu, Japan. The Japanese Army cargo ship had been steaming in convoy O-302 when she was torpedoed. She had departed Saeki on December 13 for Palau, in company with two other merchant ships and four escorts. *Totai Maru*'s cargo of incendiary bombs caught fire, which spread to a load of high-explosive bombs. The ensuing detonations finished off the ship, resulting in the loss of three passengers, twelve gunners, and twenty-two crewmen killed.[13]

With two successful shipping attacks under their belt, the newer hands on *Sailfish* had a sense of confidence. John Good overheard shipmates discussing their daring new skipper. "We all admired and respected him," Good recalled.[14]

★ ★ ★

The next sizable shipping target Bob Ward found a week later proved to be forbidden fruit. During the evening of December 20, *Sailfish*'s watch began an approach on a large ship with blinking lights.

Sailfish closed the contact until lookouts could clearly see a Japanese hospital ship. Illuminated red crosses were plainly visible. The large vessel was making 12 knots, burning normal running lights and deck contour lights. Ward could see a neon-light-type red cross on its stack and bridge structure, plus an illuminated red cross painted on its side amidships. Once he was convinced the hospital ship was not leading any other vessels, Ward secured his tracking party just before midnight. "We itched to send a torpedo into her bowels," recalled lookout Bud Pike. "We didn't, but it was a sight to behold."[15]

Ward decided to run up the reverse track of the hospital ship. Finding no other ships, he submerged at dawn on December 21 to patrol the Okino Shima–Shimanoura line. At 1020, the periscope watch sighted smoke on the horizon about ten miles away. Ward called the tracking party and commenced an approach. As the tops of four ships came into view, he logged: "This looks like a jackpot and we've only five torpedoes."[16]

By 1054, Ward had the complete picture. *Sailfish* had found a convoy of six heavily loaded freighters with three escort vessels. The most attractive target was the middle ship of the southern column of three cargo ships. Ward allowed the range to narrow and sidestepped a *Chidori*-class patrol boat before *Sailfish* began firing aft tubes 5, 6, and 7 at 1133. His torpedoes were set at eight feet, with a calculated run of 2,800 yards. As soon as the third Mark 14 was on its way, Ward called for hard port to swing his boat around to bring his last bow tube to bear.

The aft torpedo gang immediately set to work swinging their final replacement torpedo into Tube No. 7. Roughly two minutes after firing, the radio gang heard two distant explosions in the vicinity of the target. The characteristic breaking-up sounds could be heard as *Sailfish* completed her swing to set up for another shot. But at this inopportune moment, diving officer Stan Cowin lost depth control and *Sailfish*'s bow began to broach with a 5-degree up angle. He shouted for Chief Bayles to flood the negative tank to bring her nose down. All idle hands were ordered over the 1MC to run forward to help shift weight to bring the submarine down faster while the flood and vent valves on the variable tank manifold were opened.

Sailfish started down fast. "Caught ourselves at 52 feet, then started deep fast like a rock but regained control," Ward logged. He commenced evading the nearest *Chidori* patrol boat, whose screws radioman Bob Johnson could hear coming in fast. The first depth charge exploded at 1137, followed by a strangely light double explosion. A minute later, another close, heavy explosion rocked the boat. The next set of double explosions was equally perplexing. "A double affair which is not too heavy, with no warning crack," logged Ward. "Possibly two small charges dropped close together."[17]

Sailfish continued her downward plunge at a fast rate as the soundmen reported the screws of two destroyers and a patrol boat now stalking her. The sub's plunge was finally checked at 327 feet only by blowing an auxiliary ballast tank into the sea with compressed air. Ward eased *Sailfish* back up to two hundred feet under a negative break in a protective temperature gradient that would help mask her from echo ranging. During the next five minutes, his boat was rocked by another fifteen depth charges dropped in salvos of two and three. "All seem fairly close but not doing any visible damage," he noted.

In the after torpedo room, Bill Bruckart heard a disturbing thump above his head. "One of the depth charges must have dropped onto the deck, above my head, and bounced off without exploding," Bruckart recalled. "It was as loud a 'clank' as I've ever heard in an otherwise silent period during which no depth charges were exploding."[18]

By 1148, the sounds of his target ship breaking up were still evident on sonar. Ward regretted that this was his fifth torpedo attack in which he had still yet to see visual evidence of his war fish exploding in a target. The Japanese escorts continued pounding *Sailfish* for the next half hour, unloading another fourteen depth charges, some close enough to knock men from their feet. Another of the lighter, double-explosion-type charges felt very close. Had it been a full-sized depth charge, things could have been disastrous.

Due to her previous bomb damage and various mechanical challenges, *Sailfish* was producing far more noise than skipper Ward would have liked. "It was a laugh to think we could run silently," recalled Exec Bud Richardson.[19]

"The depth charging was well conducted and definitely of first team variety, with the Japs utilizing both their echo ranging and listening gear and attempting to work together," Ward recorded. "They had us boxed several times, with one fellow on one quarter and the other on the opposite bow, then vice versa." His quartermaster logged a total of thirty-one normal charges during the attack, plus many of the peculiar double light charges. In this counterattack, Ward felt that the Japanese "gave us a damn good working over—first-team stuff all afternoon."[20]

Once sound reported the enemy screws to have faded, Ward eased his boat back to periscope depth at 1310 to take a look. The Japanese apparently sighted him fifteen minutes later, as Johnson announced two sets of screws coming in fast. Ward headed back to two hundred feet and cleared the area submerged during the next two hours. His opponents were thoroughly whipped up, and this was no fight he wanted with only a single torpedo remaining in each of his torpedo rooms.

Postwar analysis would show that *Sailfish* had sunk her third ship of the patrol in the form of the 6,376-ton attack transport *Uyo Maru*. Originally completed as a cargo ship in the 1930s, the converted *Uyo Maru* was heavily laden this day with nine hundred fifty men of the 202nd Naval Construction Unit. She was steaming as part of convoy No. O-106, consisting of *Uyo Maru*, the light cruiser *Tama*, four other merchant ships, the patrol boat *PB-31*, and the auxiliary subchaser *Tama Maru No. 6*. The latter ship, ironically, had been attached to the convoy *Sailfish* had struck one week prior, and *Tama Maru* would make her second depth charge assault on the same submarine this day. *Uyo Maru* sank with a heavy loss of life, including 192 men from the construction battalion.[21]

Sailfish surfaced that evening and commenced searching along the convoy's presumed route while Ward sent out a contact report of his attack to ComSubPac at Pearl Harbor. Lookouts sighted another ship the following day, but it proved to be only a large white sampan with a radio antenna, clearly a radio picket vessel. *Sailfish* had to dodge these vessels to avoid being reported. While dodging another radio sampan on the morning of December 23, the boat was forced to make a hasty dive.

As *Sailfish* maneuvered ahead of the sampan, gunner's mates Frank Mullen and Lewis McCarty had come out on deck to check their main deck gun and to set spring tension on their bridge-mounted 20mm guns. But any hopes Ward might have entertained about a gun attack on this Japanese vessel were suddenly foiled when lookouts spotted a Pete-type float biplane about five miles distant, inbound.

"Clear the bridge!" OOD Pat Murphy shouted.

Ward, Murphy, and his lookouts began dropping down the conning tower hatch as the Japanese plane roared in. Gunner's mate Mullen had tense seconds as he found himself trapped. His lifeline had become tangled on the deck gun, making him the last man to finally reach the hatch. "He is now a Christian!" Ward wrote in his log as *Sailfish* headed for safer depths.[22]

* * *

With only two torpedoes remaining, Lieutenant Commander Ward set course for home that night. The crew celebrated both Christmas and New Year's Eve during the run back toward friendly waters. Ward paused his return trip only long enough on January 2 to offer his gun crews a little action against a floating cylindrical mine. Although several hits were obtained, it failed to explode.

As *Sailfish* resumed her run toward Hawaii, Chief Bayles and Freddie Wheeler decided it was finally time to test out the batch of homemade wine they had been fermenting in the engine room. John Good joined them, and the trio filled their cups from the tilted keg. "It was bitterly sour and did not even smell favorable," Good recalled. "We made sure it ended up over the side and into the ocean."[23]

On the evening of January 4, *Sailfish* was passed by a convoy of four destroyers and two American escort carriers. Troy Ray exchanged recognition signals with one of the destroyers, which was seen to alter course toward their submarine. Ward ran surfaced through the night and at 0630 on January 5, he rendezvoused with a patrol craft and proceeded to moor portside at Pier Sail-Four at the Pearl Harbor Sub Base. *Sailfish* had been at sea for forty-nine days, and had burned 87,590 gallons of fuel while steaming 9,521 miles.[24]

As *Sailfish* was secured to the dock, Admiral Chester Nimitz and Charlie Lockwood were on hand with their staff. They quickly strode across the gangway and greeted Lieutenant Commander Ward, who invited them down to his wardroom for coffee. Stewards R. D. Mosley and Morris Deas had only enough time to serve the group of officers before Ward opened up with an apology.[25]

"I failed to get that cruiser," he said. "I shouldn't have been so damn eager to get that carrier. But it happened."

Nimitz and Lockwood tried to reassure Ward. His boat had accomplished a supreme feat in sinking a Japanese aircraft carrier via radar in the midst of a typhoon. Ward explained that he should have known better. He had been personally critical in the past of the submarine *Nautilus* and her torpedo attack on the crippled Japanese carrier *Kaga* at Midway in 1942. He strongly believed that her skipper should have attacked a nearby Japanese cruiser first before firing on the derelict carrier. Now, when he had been presented with the very same opportunity, Ward had neglected to complete a full search that might have turned up the cruiser *Maya* as a primary target before he had finished off *Chuyo*.

Fortunately for Ward, if Pearl Harbor's intelligence analysts had any info that *Sculpin* survivors had been on board *Chuyo* when she was sunk, the admirals chose not to share that grim news with him.

Ward continued his discussion. He ran through the full events of the carrier attacks, of *Sailfish* being bombed on the surface, and of his subsequent successful convoy attacks. Once yeomen Bill Crytser and Bud Pike completed typing up the boat's tenth war patrol report, ComSubPac and his staff read it with great interest. Lockwood's staff credited the boat with three ship sinkings, totaling 35,729 tons, plus damage to another freighter of 7,098 tons. Postwar analysis was nearly the same: three ships sunk for 29,571 tons.

Captain Leon Blair, commanding Submarine Division 44, was pleased with Ward's "steady on" attack performance. "All attacks were persistent, vigorous, aggressive, and complete," he wrote. Swede Momsen, who had helped rescue the *Squalus* men in 1939, was now commander of Submarine Division 4. Momsen added his congratulations to the skipper, officers, and crewmen of *Sailfish* "on a vigorous and effective patrol." In his third endorsement to Ward's report, Admiral Lockwood heaped on additional praise. "This patrol can be considered one of the outstanding patrols of the war." Armed with classified intelligence, he added, "This is the first known unassisted sinking of an enemy carrier by a submarine of this force."[26]

For sinking three ships, including the first carrier by a U.S. submarine, Ward was awarded the Navy Cross. He in turn wrote up a number of his men for lesser awards. In due time, the Silver Star would be pinned on Lieutenant Bud Richardson for his work as assistant approach officer, on torpedo officer and TDC operator Pat Murphy, and on chief electrician Les Bayles. Ward also recommended the Bronze Star for diving officer Stan Cowin, senior radioman Bob Johnson, and chief of the boat Bill Blatti.

In his patrol report, he cited the "tireless efforts and exceptional skills" of his senior radar operator, Frank Dieterich, a man whom Ward recommended for promotion to warrant officer. Navy Letters of

Commendation were written up for other key members of his torpedo attack and plotting team, including fire controlman Jim Woody, senior signalman Troy Ray, assistant plotting officer Wayne Evans, and battle talker Bud Pike. For his "cool and efficient action" in helping to stop the hulk leaks after the bombing attack on *Sailfish*, CMoMM Bill Lyon would receive both a Letter of Commendation and the Navy and Marine Corps Medal for heroism.

Ward's lengthy report gave full details of all mechanical issues *Sailfish* had endured on the patrol, of the hot run that had disabled one of his after torpedo tubes, and of damage sustained by bombing and depth charge attacks. Lockwood's staff readily agreed that *Sailfish* was in need of a proper overhaul, one that would necessitate a return Stateside.

The crew's short stay in Pearl Harbor was jubilant. "We enjoyed our new status as conquerors of the sea and discussed proudly our achievements at sea with our old friends at the base," John Good recalled. The skipper soon passed the word that his boat was headed back Stateside for a lengthy overhaul.[27]

Ward's men had plenty of reason to celebrate. The boat's morale had been raised considerably in the wake of their recent successes. The foul mood that had hung over the crew during the tenure of its previous skipper was long gone. As SS-192 stood out to sea from Oahu on January 7, she was San Francisco bound. All hands eagerly anticipated the chance to see loved ones they had not seen in more than a year in many cases.

FOURTEEN

Prisoners of War

It was December 5, 1943, as George Rocek—having survived the sinkings of both his submarine, *Sculpin*, and the carrier *Chuyo*—arrived at a forbidding prisoner interrogation center called Ofuna.

A twenty-minute train ride from the Japanese naval port of Yokohama, Ofuna was a secret Japanese Navy confinement camp that had been opened on April 7, 1942, to temporarily house captured Allied prisoners. Unlike Imperial Japanese Army camps, the twenty-month-old Ofuna facility was designated for prisoners considered to be of high intelligence value, such as submariners and aviators. Those confined at this secret camp were not registered with the Red Cross as POWs. Ofuna consisted of three flimsy wooden barracks wings connected to a main building that housed latrines, the officers' headquarters, and a kitchen facility for feeding the prisoners. The three prisoner barracks were called by the Japanese numerals for one, two, and three—*Ikku*, *Nikku*, and *Sanku*.[1]

Although unknown to Rocek, another large group of *Sculpin* survivors had been herded into the Ofuna camp on the morning of December 5. The remaining warships of the Japanese task group, including the carriers *Unyo* and *Zuiho*, had continued on to Japan after *Chuyo*'s sinking. Upon entering Uraga Bay off Yokohama, the carriers anchored near the shore, and the American submariners were herded to the hangar deck. They were lined up in two columns, each man blindfolded but untied. "The Captain told us not to worry at all, to take good care of our health, and good luck to all of us," fireman Joe Baker recalled.[2]

It was one month since *Sculpin* had set sail from Pearl Harbor on her final war patrol. Now Baker and his comrades were loaded onto a motor launch, and then they headed for the shores of Yokohama, shivering from the cold air and salt spray. Each man was barefoot, with only Japanese Navy enlisted men's blues to cover their bodies. They were herded through the streets of the city and subjected to the abuse of citizens who threw sticks and other objects at them.

The twenty *Sculpin* survivors were moved onto an electric tram and taken southwest of Yokohama toward their new camp. They were marched the last five kilometers to Ofuna. Upon being received into camp, they were issued new clothing and placed in pairs into the *Sanku* barracks. *Sculpin*'s men would soon learn from other prisoners that Ofuna had been home in October 1943 to thirty-nine officers and men who had been captured from lost American submarines. This group included three officers and thirty men from *Grenadier*, which had been badly damaged and scuttled on April 22, 1943, in the Malacca Strait in the Indian Ocean. Her entire crew had been picked up by a Japanese merchant ship, taken to the port of Penang, and then moved to mainland Japan in the spring of 1943.[3]

The submariners housed at Ofuna heard rumors in late November that another large group of American prisoners was inbound to their camp. To prepare room for them, the Japanese had moved thirty prisoners to other camps on December 3, including thirteen *Grenadier* enlisted men and the skipper of the lost boat *Perch*, Lieutenant Commander Dave Hurt. Twenty *Grenadier* officers and men remained when the *Sculpin* crew arrived, plus five other U.S. submariners. Three of them were *Perch* radiomen, who were still undergoing severe interrogations about their electronics gear. *Perch* had been scuttled northwest of Surabaya, Java, on March 3, 1942, after the boat had been severely damaged by a depth charge attack and was unable to dive again. The other two American submariners at Ofuna were the only survivors picked up by the Japanese from *S-44*, Chief Torpedoman Tony Duva and Radioman 3c Bill Whitemore. Their *S-44* had been sunk on the evening of October 7, 1943, after a surface gun battle with the destroyer *Ishigaki*.[4]

Joe Baker soon learned of *S-44*, *Grenadier*, and *Perch* submariners being held in another of the Ofuna barracks. "Our first meal was a bowl of rice, two small baked fish heads—guts, bones, and all—and a couple of spoonfuls of soy sauce," Baker recalled. Ed Keller was scared after hearing an English-speaking Japanese guard announce to him, "You have survived the sinking of a submarine. No one survives the sinking of a submarine. No one knows you're alive." The guard explained that during interrogations, the *Sculpin* men would be shot if they refused to answer accurately, and the world would never know that they had even survived the loss of their submarine.[5]

Keller had been among the first to learn of other submariners when he entered camp. Suffering from a bad case of diarrhea, he had been unable to control his bodily functions during the long hike into Ofuna the first day. "When I arrived in camp, I was isolated," he recalled. Because of his stench, guards removed Keller and allowed him to use the bathhouse to clean himself. As he washed in a tub, another man entered the bathhouse to use the head. Through careful whispers, Keller learned that he was from the submarine *Grenadier* and that his entire crew had been captured.[6]

Quartermaster Bill Cooper collapsed into his cell, suffering from feet that were numb from the long hike to camp over frozen ground. As they regained feeling, Lieutenant George Brown helped Cooper with his agony by rubbing his feet to improve circulation. In small groups, the *Sculpin* survivors were escorted to the bathhouse to clean themselves and don their new clothing.[7]

Moon Rocek, still unaware of the other twenty *Sculpin* men who had arrived at Ofuna shortly before him, was initially questioned on how he had been captured. The leading interpreter was a well-dressed Japanese officer, Lieutenant Kunichi "James" Sasaki, who had spent time prewar in the United States and spoke excellent English. Known to wear fancy suits and oxford shoes, Sasaki had been nicknamed "Handsome Harry" by the American prisoners at Ofuna.[8]

Sasaki quizzed Rocek on the loss of his submarine. He passed the intelligence on to the Ofuna camp commander, who had been expecting forty-one total *Sculpin* prisoners to arrive from Truk. "The Jap commander of Ofuna could not speak English, and refused to believe a Jap carrier got sunk, but could never understand what happened to the other men," Rocek remembered.[9]

His first interrogation ended when Rocek told one of the guards that he was a survivor from the submarine *Sculpin*. "He apparently knew what had happened, because he didn't say anything more and led me into a bath," Rocek recalled. The warm water gave him great comfort for the shrapnel wounds in his legs. Even better, he found two other *Sculpin* crew members in the bath area, and learned that his shipmates transferred to Japan on *Unyo* had all survived. Once dressed in fresh clothes and deposited in the prisoner barracks, Rocek was slowly able to whisper details of *Chuyo*'s sinking to shipmates in neighboring cells.[10]

In the weeks that followed, the *Sculpin* survivors were interrogated frequently about their submarine and its bases. Lieutenant Brown fared the worst, fighting off various ailments while being offered frequent beatings and only reduced rations. Joe Baker was pleased when the prisoners were offered Red Cross packages as Christmas approached. He heated Australian bully beef from one of the containers and packed the warmed meat into the gunshot wounds in his left leg. "Doctors have since said that was the only thing that saved my leg, because the maggots got in there and they killed all the germs," Baker recalled.[11]

The deep wounds in Rocek's legs were becoming infected and beginning to turn gangrenous. Recalling advice from his father to urinate on an open wound if he was unable to obtain treatment, Moon called on Ed Ricketts—an avid outdoorsman who had heard of the same wound treatment—for help. Ed Keller later recalled that Rocek and Ricketts "cauterized themselves by urinating on each other's leg." After arriving at Ofuna, the fellow prisoners made the odd remedy a daily treatment. "Every one of the wounds healed up after that, except for one on my shinbone in my left leg," Rocek recalled.[12]

By January 6, 1944, the first snowfall of winter had coated the Ofuna prisoner compound with a white dusting. The drafty wooden barracks felt even more miserable when the Japanese elected to give the American prisoners close shaves and haircuts, leaving them shivering about the compound during their morning exercise periods. As Rocek sat on a bench, soaking up the warm morning sun, he was nudged by a shipmate as a Japanese guard approached with a sword, intent on preventing any man from resting. As the guard pushed his sword toward the eyes of any sleeping man, fellow prisoners would apply leg pressure to the man adjacent to them. "We had leg pressure warnings to let you be aware of the son-of-a-bitch," Rocek recalled, a gesture intended to warn the resting man not to move suddenly and risk eye injury. "The guard would finally move away. The guy next to you would cough, and you knew it was okay."[13]

By mid-January, after the arrival of additional captured airmen, eighty-two Allied prisoners were crowded into the Ofuna barracks. On January 24, the Ofuna camp commandant arranged for twenty-one Americans to be transferred to other Japanese camps to make room for incoming prisoners. Ed Keller was pleased to learn that such shuffling would include the men being officially registered as prisoners of war with the Red Cross. "That meant a lot to us," Keller recalled. "We knew everybody back home thought we were dead. They had been told we were presumed lost at sea."[14]

Joe Baker was deeply disappointed that he, George Brown, and seven other *Sculpin* survivors would remain at Ofuna. The transfer group included five sailors from *Grenadier* and a dozen from *Sculpin*, including Keller, Rocek, and Bill Cooper. The men were blindfolded and marched five kilometers back to the train station. Transported north to Tokyo, they were kept overnight at the Omori prisoner camp before being herded onto another steam train the following day. They were moved into the mountains northwest of Tokyo to Ashio, a mining village camp.[15]

Baker and his *Sculpin* comrades remaining at Ofuna endured rain, sleet, and snow during February and early March 1944. With his head shaved regularly and lacking proper winter gear, Baker looked forward to his twice-weekly baths in warm water. Among the captured aviators at Ofuna was a former famed Olympic runner, 1st Lieutenant Louis Zamperini, who had arrived in mid-September 1943 after surviving forty-seven days in a rubber raft after the crash of his B-24 bomber.

The next well-known American to be moved into Ofuna on March 7 was Major Gregory "Pappy" Boyington, the skipper of Marine VMF-214's "Black Sheep" fighter squadron.[16]

Boyington's Corsair had been shot down over Rabaul on January 3, shortly after he had achieved his twenty-sixth aerial kill. Thanks to American press releases about the fabled aviator and a Congressional push in America to decorate him with the Medal of Honor, the Japanese officials at Ofuna soon realized exactly who Boyington was. Nineteen-year-old Joe Baker found himself sharing a cell with the Marine ace. "He was a real tough guy," Baker recalled. "They made us all line up in the compound, and they beat the hell of out him."

Major Boyington was finally treated by the Ofuna medics for severe leg wounds he had received during the loss of his Corsair. Two fellow prisoners were ordered to hold down the Black Sheep skipper as the Japanese pharmacist crudely probed through one of his leg wounds to remove shrapnel. Boyington smoked a Japanese Cherry cigarette to keep his mind off the pain. *Grenadier* yeoman Bob Palmer, tasked with holding the major down, was appalled that the Ofuna pharmacist did not bother to stitch Boyington's leg up once his work was complete.[17]

His incision area simply wrapped with a dirty cloth, Boyington, per Palmer, "hobbled back to his cell on that homemade crutch he had, cussing all the way."

★ ★ ★

George Rocek could feel the difference in the thinner air as he was herded from the steam train on January 26, 1944. He and sixteen other U.S. submariners, including twelve *Sculpin* survivors, were marched into a new prisoner compound in the mountains northwest of Tokyo.

Officially, it was Ashio Camp 9-B, a mining camp for Allied POWs that would eventually see more than three dozen American submarine prisoners during 1944 and 1945. Located at the headwaters of the Watarase River in Ashio, the camp sat at an elevation of two thousand feet and was home to 252 Dutch prisoners, plus one other American and a British soldier when the submariners arrived. Ashio Camp 9-B was run by a forty-seven-year-old heavily built, bespectacled former school principal, Lieutenant Shigeru Numajiri.[18]

Rocek found that Ashio's prisoner compound consisted of two long barracks, with dirt floors and two tiers of bunks on each side. Lice-infested straw was used for bedding, with wood-pulp-filled Japanese blankets. At the rear of the barracks was the outdoors-type latrine facility. "During the winter months, the fresh water lines would freeze up; therefore, no baths for months," Rocek remembered.[19]

On January 27, the day after their arrival, Rocek and his comrades were put to work on mine duty—a grueling task that would be their way of life for more than a year. That morning, more than eighty of the most fit Allied prisoners were issued carbide head lanterns and led across a narrow river bridge through the streets of the Ashio mining community. They were halted at the rear of town before a square hole that was the mine entrance, which had railroad tracks leading into it. The POWs were ordered to bow before a Japanese shrine that stood before the mine entrance.

"You asked the shrine to protect you from disasters in the mine each day," recalled Ed Keller. Inside the dark mine, the prisoners would occasionally feel the terrifying tremors of minor earthquakes. As the months passed, Moon Rocek used the morning shrine-bowing ritual as a chance to say prayers for himself that he might survive each day.[20]

Inside the mine, in hot, air-starved confines, the prisoners were put to work mucking ore—breaking it up and shoveling it into small mine cars that were pulled to the surface. "Each man was required to muck eight tons of ore per day," recalled Bill Cooper. Suffering from a back injury sustained in *Sculpin*'s sinking, Cooper endured a great deal of pain hauling the heavy loads of rock.[21]

Japanese guards soon acquired names like "Four Eyes" for a former army lieutenant with thick glasses and "Slugger" for the guard who most frequently beat the prisoners who were caught stealing food. Rocek remained leery of the mine's overhead, which was prone to shed rocks that caused minor cave-ins. While on break one day with five men, Rocek felt sand drifting down from above. "We scattered quickly, but one man had his leg broken by a huge rock that fell from the overhead," he recalled.[22]

Men who were too ill or too injured to work were examined by a Japanese medic who determined whether they could work or not that day. He often used a primitive form of acupuncture for the wounded, rolling a quarter-inch ball of fuzz together to press onto the injured man's skin. The medic then lit the fuzz and let it burn into the man's skin. "Regardless of what you complained of, it seemed these punk balls were placed the farthest from your ailment," Rocek remembered. "For diarrhea, we were given charcoal to eat."[23]

Keller recalled that the burn treatment was usually given three times per day for three days. "The theory was that white corpuscles are germ fighters, and if they [the Japanese medics] burned you, the body manufactured more white corpuscles and sent them to that area to cure you," he stated. Keller noted that men who had undergone the medics' burn treatment had consistent scar areas, as opposed to the small cigarette-sized burn marks where guards snuffed out their smokes on Keller and other POWs.[24]

One of the few privileges Rocek enjoyed while working the Ashio mines was being allowed to mail a letter home to his family in early 1944. "Don't worry about me," he wrote his parents. "I am all right. Think and dream a lot of you and of times past and future." Rocek was later discouraged that this would prove to be the only parcel of mail he would be allowed to send to Cicero, Illinois.[25]

Among a fresh group of prisoners transferred from Ofuna to Ashio in March 1944 was a U.S. Army doctor captured at Bataan in 1942, 1st Lieutenant Basil Durbin. One of the POW miners he helped treat was *Sculpin*'s Ed Keller, who suffered a nasty fall down a thirty-foot muck pile while trying to blast apart a large boulder. Keller smashed a hand and lost some teeth in his fall. Durbin also helped treat the ugly wound still festering in Rocek's left shinbone, which was beginning to smell.[26]

Durbin had smuggled in a small quantity of sulfa tablets, which he used sparingly for such dire cases. "He ground one up and sprinkled it on my wound every day, and eventually it healed," Rocek remembered. "A year later, I had a small piece of metal work out of my left knee."[27]

The poor food, slavelike mining work, and frequent beatings began to take a mental toll on the *Sculpin* survivors by spring. Bill Cooper began scheming a plan to scale the camp fence, hike over the mountains, and escape to the coast with some of his shipmates. But Cooper was forced to abandon his dream when Japanese guards warned the inmates that if any one man escaped, all of his friends in his work group would be executed.[28]

After their first months of mucking ore in the Ashio mountains, few of the *Sculpin* survivors held much hope that they would ever enjoy freedom again.

FIFTEEN

Wolf Pack

It was a dream come true for Bob Ward. As a teenager, he had dreamed of commanding his own vessel as it steamed under the iconic Golden Gate Bridge. Now, on the morning of January 14, 1944, Lieutenant Commander Ward cupped his hands to light a cigarette. A brisk breeze greeted his face as he exhaled and noted officer of the deck Dutch Wetmore and a harbor pilot passing orders to the duty helmsman. The skipper relished the moment as *Sailfish* passed under the 4,200-foot-long burnt-red-hued bridge—its primer color officially called international orange—into San Francisco Bay.

Sailfish moored starboard side to the dock at the Bethlehem Steel Company Submarine Repair Basin at Hunters Point, where yard workmen would completely refit Ward's boat during the next five months and add various improvements, such as a powerful 4-inch, .50-caliber deck gun.

Radioman Bill Dillon managed to secure a spot on a military plane back to Pennsylvania when his time came for a thirty-day leave.

It had been more than a year since he had seen his family and his small hometown of Turtle Creek. He was most anxious to visit the young girl he had fallen in love with, a beautiful brunette named Janet Kugel he had first met in 1940.

Although she was just turning seventeen in March 1944, Janet had been corresponding with Bill since he shipped off to war. She had attended his football games in 1941, and her father had always enjoyed talking with Bill about the success of their undefeated team. Janet and Bill made the most of their days during his leave in Turtle Creek, eating pulled pork barbecue at the Lighthouse restaurant on William Penn Highway and walking four miles to the nearest movie theater to catch a show. They promised to write to each other often once his leave was complete.[1]

Before his son departed Turtle Creek, John Dillon pulled him aside and shared news about Bill's older brother. Bob Dillon, who had enlisted in the U.S. Army in April 1942, had just shipped out for Hawaii with the 77th Infantry Division, destined for deployment somewhere in the Pacific. "If you have a chance when you get back to Hawaii, see if you can find him," his father said. Bill promised to do so.[2]

During their leaves, some of Dillon's shipmates took the chance to get married. Among them was yeoman Bud Pike, who returned to Austin, Minnesota, in company with one of his best friends, electrician's mate Bob Kempf, who hailed from the nearby town of Red Wing. With their home state ties, the two had become close during *Sailfish*'s last patrol. Kempf, an accomplished cartoonist, also served as the pitcher for their ship's fast-pitch softball team with Pike. On January 30, Kempf took on the duty of best man as Pike married his hometown sweetheart, Evelyn Johnson, in Austin.

Chief Montie Walkup enjoyed a thirty-day leave home to visit his family. After his return to San Francisco, he set to work with his black gang on helping the yard workers tackle defects that had arisen during the prior patrol. He and Freddie Wheeler, the senior motor machinist in charge of the forward engine room, decided they should renew the crankshaft bearings on their No. 1 diesel engine. They obtained a set of new bearings, each prefinished by the manufacturer and ready for installation. After unwrapping them, Wheeler and Walkup decided to grab a cup of coffee before commencing the laborious project.[3]

When they returned, they found "a perfect stranger was scraping our new thrust bearing. We stopped him, but the thrust bearing was ruined." Walkup and Wheeler were furious, demanding to know who the hell he was and if he knew exactly what he had just done. To their surprise, the officer introduced himself as Lt. (jg) Joseph Sahaj, their new assistant engineering officer. "After we explained the situation, the new engineering officer apologized," Walkup recalled, but he was left with a less-than-glowing impression of his new officer.

Walkup would be further surprised by the mistake once he learned more about his new officer's experience in submarines. Sahaj, who hailed from Staten Island, New York, had been in the engineering gangs of older S-boats. After later service on destroyers, Sahaj had been appointed warrant machinist in June 1942 and returned to serve for a patrol on *S-40* before being assigned to *Sailfish*.

* * *

Early summer was approaching by the time most of the major work on *Sailfish*'s overhaul was accomplished. During those months, yeomen Bill Crytser and Bud Pike handled the usual shuffling of officers and men to new assignments. A full one-third of the crew would be replaced before the boat ventured into enemy waters again.

The only officer departing the *Sailfish* wardroom was Lieutenant (jg) Bill Bruckart, who had orders to report to *Pampanito* as her radar officer. In his place, *Sailfish* increased from eight to nine officers with the addition of Joe Sahaj and an unqualified new ensign, Craig Martell Hertsgaard. As the low-ranking officer, Hertsgaard became *Sailfish*'s newest "George," and as such assumed commissary duties from Ed Berghausen, who took over Bruckart's billet as radar officer. Heavyset and possessing an eager smile, Hertsgaard was a graduate of Concordia College in Moorhead, Minnesota, where he had met his future wife, Sylvia Gronseth. As the least experienced new officer, he would endure his fair share of tests from skipper Bob Ward prior to his first war patrol.

Among the numerous new faces among the enlisted personnel were two steward's mates. By the time the overhaul was nearing completion, the *Sailfish* wardroom was being served by Allen Batts and Killraine Newton Jr. Hailing from Petersburg, Virginia, Batts was new to submarines but he soon found close companionship with "Newt" Newton, who had also been raised in Virginia. Reared in a broken home, Newton had been drafted "kicking and screaming" in 1943, forced to leave his work as a supply clerk in the Yorktown Naval Mine Depot.[4]

A powerful man with a good education, Newton quickly became a favorite among his fellow sailors. "I was very strong, and people didn't mess with me," he remembered. "I qualified throughout the boat, just like everyone else." His father had long advised him that he would have to be twice as a good as any white man to succeed in America's military. On most naval vessels, Black men were still largely relegated to lesser roles, but Newton was pleased to find that Lieutenant Commander Ward was a very approachable officer who did not tolerate racism on his boat. Aside from his assigned duties as a steward, Newt soon earned himself a position as a machine gunner during surface actions, and he would man the phones in the forward torpedo room during battle stations. "After the torpedoes were fired, I counted off the seconds before they hit," Newt recalled.[5]

After a full six-month hiatus from the war zone, Bob Ward was itching to make his second command patrol. His boat's tenth war patrol had been one for the books. On June 1, newspapers began running a Navy Department press release that *Sailfish* was being awarded the Presidential Unit Citation for destroying "four important Japanese vessels."[6]

Sailfish departed the Hunters Point repair yard on Sunday, June 18, steaming back under the Golden Gate Bridge for Hawaii again. Soon after his boat was moored at Berth Sail-Six on June 26 at the Pearl Harbor Submarine Base, radioman Bill Dillon set out on a special quest.

Months before, he had promised his father that he would try to find his older brother, Bob, before his Army division shipped out. Bob Dillon's 77th Infantry Division had landed in Hawaii in late March 1944 and had since been camped on the west side of Oahu near Pali Pass, where Japanese aircraft had swept in by surprise on December 7, 1941. Bob's division had just completed its final training in amphibious and jungle warfare and was slated to ship out overseas on July 1 for the invasion of Guam.[7]

"Our radio gang was in charge of obtaining our own supplies from the base, so I went down to the motor pool and requisitioned a jeep for a couple of days' use," Dillon recalled. He spent the early afternoon inquiring around about the 77th Infantry, and found that they were camped at Pali Pass. But by the time he drove out to find his brother, the division had already broken camp and was boarding ships in Pearl Harbor. "Nobody could tell me exactly what the hell ship it was, so I drove my jeep back to Pearl, where I somehow finally managed to learn which ship he was on," Bill remembered.

Clad in his white cap and sailor's uniform, Dillon strolled up the gangway on the troop transport and inquired around with crewmen where Bob Dillon could be found. His brother soon appeared from belowdecks, and the two enjoyed a tremendous reunion. Bill invited him for a tour of the island on his jeep, with the two stopping to take souvenir photos along their journey.

As evening approached, Bill asked, "Hey, Bob, why don't you come over and stay on my boat for a while?"

"I'd love to," Bob replied.

Returning to *Sailfish*, the Dillon brothers strolled across the gangplank, saluted the crewman standing watch, and asked permission to come on board.

"You'd better get with the duty officer to make sure it's okay for him to be on board," the sailor advised.

Leaving his brother topside, Bill descended to the wardroom and approached the duty officer. He was shocked to find his request to have his brother aboard denied. "Hell, no, you can't do that," the OOD said. "We're in a war zone."

Dillon stomped topside and headed back across the gangplank. As he thought about it, he became even angrier. *Back in Mare Island, those damned officers brought their girlfriends, wives, kids, and anybody they wanted on board,* he thought. *We're in Hawaii, not a war zone. Why the hell can't I bring my brother on the* Sailfish*?*

"Hell's bells, you're coming aboard!" he snapped to Bob.

"I took him down the starboard side all the way to the back hatch, and we went down through the aft torpedo room hatch," Dillon recalled. "The crew knew what the hell was going on, and they treated Bob like a king." Cook Tom Sargent prepared whatever dish the infantryman desired, and Bob Dillon spent the evening sacked out in a bunk near his brother in *Sailfish*'s enlisted quarters. Other sailors helped keep tabs on officers so the two were not discovered.

The Dillons slipped off *Sailfish* very early the next morning and spent a second day motoring around Hawaii in their base jeep. As evening approached, Bob asked, "Hey, why don't you stay on my ship tonight?"

"Hell, I'd love to do that," Bill replied.

Getting the submariner onto the troop transport proved to be an easier task, but neither man relished the thought of sleeping belowdecks on a balmy vessel that lacked air-conditioning. They instead returned topside, talking into the evening hours before falling asleep on deck under a blanket beneath the stars. When Bill returned his jeep the next morning and boarded *Sailfish*, he was content. "Long after we sailed on our next patrol, my shipmates enjoyed comical discussions about the stunt we had pulled," Dillon recalled.

★ ★ ★

Skipper Bob Ward created his own form of entertainment breaking in his newest officers at Pearl Harbor. One of his challenges involved making odd requests to see how his young leaders would respond to challenges outside normal expectations.

Ensign Craig Hertsgaard, *Sailfish*'s new commissary officer, caught the brunt of this exercise. His to-do list included two special challenges: obtaining both an old-fashioned ice cream maker and a four-by-six rug for the captain's quarters. "It was too damn cold," Ward recalled. "I told him I wanted some fire-resistant rug in my cabin when I go to sea, something the Old Man could put his bare feet on."[8]

Ward instructed Hertsgaard to take his list and let him know if he had any trouble. The young ensign returned the next day to report that he had scrounged around the base but had no luck in obtaining the ice cream maker.

"It's a big island, and there's somebody here someplace that makes ice cream," Ward replied. "Find them! Get it! You don't just fool around here on the sub base and find it. It's a big island! Find it!"

Hertsgaard returned the next day all smiles, hauling on board a manual ice cream machine. He explained that he had visited the Montgomery Ward department store in Honolulu, where a clerk informed him of a woman who had purchased an ice cream machine two years earlier. Hertsgaard managed to strike a deal with her and returned to *Sailfish*, where his cooks rigged a motor to the machine to make it run automatically. "So, we could have ice cream now right in the middle of a depth charging, if we wanted to," Ward recalled.

Finding a rug for the skipper proved even more difficult. Hertsgaard finally returned one day with a big smile and announced, "I've found the rug." But he explained to his captain that it was the personal property of an admiral on the base's submarine tender who told the ensign that his skipper would have to come over and personally request some of the carpeting from him. Ward was amused that Hertsgaard had succeeded, so he paid the admiral a courtesy call to explain his challenging request. After the two had a good laugh over the whole episode, Ward returned with a piece of carpeting.

The whole ordeal was merely a gimmick, but it was one that Ward believed in. "We did all kind of screwball things, but it showed you the texture of the people you're leading," Ward recalled. He felt that his new commissary officer had shown great resourcefulness and would fit right in with the *Sailfish* wardroom.

* * *

Charlie Lockwood was eager to utilize his improved torpedoes in wolf pack strategy. The admiral's Submarine Force had adopted this method from German U-boat wolf packs in late 1943, the first pack having been commanded by his staff officer Swede Momsen, who had engineered the rescue of the *Squalus* survivors in 1943. Momsen's pack had turned in claims for five ships sunk and another eight damaged, enough to make sure the brass authorized further pack hunts.

The use of other packs in late 1943 had further honed tactics and at-sea communications, including the use of surface rendezvous between boats to exchange vital data during their patrols. In each use, the pack was led by a senior officer who rode one of the three boats as flagship commander, although the operation of each submarine remained in the hands of its skipper. The wolf pack being organized by Lockwood at the beginning of July 1944 would be the U.S. Navy's twelfth such outing.

Bob Ward's *Sailfish* would be heading for Empire waters in company with Lieutenant Commander Vernon Turner's *Billfish* and Lieutenant Commander Jack Gerwick's *Greenling*. The pack commander, Captain Stan Moseley, would ride aboard *Greenling* as his flagship, with the pack being known as "Moseley's Maulers." In preparation, the senior officers conducted meetings ashore at Pearl Harbor to work out tactics and communications techniques. The first week of July was then spent with the three boats participating in sound tests and special coordinated attack exercises to fine-tune their battle plans as a pack.

This training period was marred by a tragic loss reminiscent of the former *Squalus*. Lieutenant Commander Jack G. Campbell's *S-28*, an old boat now consigned to training duty after making seven war patrols, was participating in sound tests west of Oahu with the Coast Guard cutter *Reliance*. At 1730 on July 4, *S-28* dived to make an approach on *Reliance,* but the submarine and its crew of forty-nine simply disappeared without a distress signal in 1,400 fathoms of water.

Sailfish and other boats in the area were called upon to help scour the sea, but they found no trace of the missing submarine. Two days later, on July 6, an ominous oil slick was found on the surface near the last-known position of *S-28*. A court of inquiry later gave an opinion that the boat had lost depth control "from either a material casualty, or an operating error or personnel, or both." The officers and men of *S-28* were deemed to be competent, but something had gone terribly wrong.[9]

Upon returning to the sub base, Bob Ward—notified that he was soon being promoted to full Commander—passed the word that *Sailfish* had earned a special honor for her tenth war patrol. President Roosevelt went on national radio to hail the success of the former *Squalus*, authorizing a Presidential Unit Citation for *Sailfish* for sinking a Japanese aircraft carrier.

On Saturday, July 8, Admiral Chester Nimitz awarded the PUC to two boats in Pearl Harbor, *Bowfin* for her second war patrol and *Sailfish* for her tenth. Ward assembled his crew at 1130, with the main ceremony held topside on *Bowfin* as the Texas admiral congratulated both crews. "For obvious reasons of military security, the details of your operations cannot now be revealed, but the enemy knows their results to his sorrow," Nimitz said.[10]

Back on board *Sailfish*, base photographers snapped photos of officers and men holding the Presidential Unit Citation flag. Ward's seventy-two-man crew was dressed in their finest whites for the ceremony, and most were clean-shaven. Nimitz also presented skipper

Ward with the Navy Cross, while other officers and men were summoned forward to be pinned with the Silver Star and Bronze Star.

As *Sailfish* made ready to depart on her eleventh war patrol, Chief Electrician's Mate Les Bayles assumed the billet of leading enlisted man on board as chief of the boat. His predecessor, Bill Blatti, had received orders transferring him to another veteran boat, USS *Whale.* Bayles, freshly pinned with the Silver Star, had been with *Sailfish* since her commissioning, and was well respected by his shipmates. For the upcoming war patrol, his chief of the watch rotation would be filled by the other four CPOs on board: Bill Lyon, Montie Walkup, Bill Gray, and newly promoted Chief Radioman Bob Johnson.

Johnson's radio/radar gang included three new hands to help man the sonar, radio, and radar gear. RM2c Bill Dillon was Johnson's most seasoned veteran now, as radarman Frank Dieterich had been promoted from radio technician first class to warrant electrician on July 6. The *Sailfish* wardroom was now swollen to ten officers, forcing Dieterich to bunk in the CPO quarters. Ward named Stan Cowin as his new first lieutenant, moving Joe Sahaj up to engineering officer, with Shorty Evans as his assistant engineering officer. *Sailfish*'s newest officer was Lieutenant (jg) Tom "Snuffy" Smith from California, who joined as the boat's new radar and electronics officer and assistant first lieutenant.

Yeoman Bud Pike was now the boat's only yeoman, as his mentor, Chief Crytser, had received a transfer to Submarine Division 45 on July 8, following the awards ceremony with Admiral Nimitz. Pike sent the final typed-up sailing list over to the sub base command on the morning of July 9, as the ship's diesels were rumbling to life. Seven months after completing her prior patrol, *Sailfish* was finally heading out on her eleventh war patrol.

A bright sun warmed the skies as she stood out from the sub base with *Billfish*, *Greenling*, and their surface escort. Freshly painted in a gray war scheme, *Sailfish* eased through the harbor, continuing on past Pearl's entrance buoys and beyond Diamond Head. Near the huge cliffs, the Coast Guard cutter *Reliance* and other naval vessels continued to search over the area where the lost *S-28*'s oil slick had appeared. "We who were topside in reverence removed our white hats," recalled John Good.[11]

Shortly after passing over *S-28*'s watery grave, Ward gave the word for all hands to prepare for a standard trim dive as Hawaii faded from view. More than two dozen men were making their first war patrol, and serious business was at hand. For her eleventh patrol, *Sailfish* had a full load of two new types of torpedoes. In her after room, she carried the new, slower-speed electric Mark 18s, first introduced in the summer of 1943. In the forward room was another new weapon, Mark 23 torpedoes, a steam-propelled variety that had longer range than the earlier Mark 14s.

In the late afternoon, *Sailfish* would make her first trim dive of the patrol to determine the boat's balance from stem to stern. For the veteran sailors on board, it was a casual affair, one they had experienced hundreds of times. But working against the "norm" this day was the fact that the new diving officer, Lieutenant (jg) Joe Sahaj, was unaware that four torpedoes had been loaded into the forward room's tubes. The difference in forward ballast weight was roughly twelve thousand additional pounds, making the boat nose heavy. "[He] stated that no one had reported the weight change to him," Chief Montie Walkup recalled.[12]

The newest radar operator, James "Cal" Callanan, was celebrating his twenty-second birthday on July 9, and his first day ever at sea on a submarine. Because Callanan had no other duty assigned to him for the moment, Chief Johnson told him to take station near the dive gauge in the conning tower. "I was told to watch the depth gauge, and when we were ready to dive, when it passed sixty feet, to record the time," Callanan remembered.[13]

As the lookouts, quartermaster Harry Tonden, and the topside officers cleared the bridge, there was little reason for any concern. Belowdecks, Tom Sargent and his cooks were at work in the galley, and off-duty hands were sacked out in their bunks in the after battery. At the order to "Dive, dive," Chief Les Bayles at the manifold in the control room opened the vents for water to enter the tanks as ballast. Diving officer Sahaj passed orders to his planesmen to set their planes for a sharp dive, but he failed to adjust for the heavier-than-usual bow weight. Almost immediately, the boat took a very steep down angle.

"The men in their bunks grabbed for the side rails," motormac John Good recalled. An orange crate slid from one end of the compartment to the other, breaking open as it slammed into a sharp metal corner. "Sounds of falling and breaking dishes and the clatter of pots and pans came from the mess hall," Good remembered. "Some of the least suspecting sailors stumbled and fell over one another."[14]

Instead of monitoring the depth gauge as Johnson had requested, new hand Callanan found himself watching the bridge personnel spill down the ladder. Glancing back at the depth gauge, he was alarmed to see that it had already dropped past one hundred feet. "Seems I missed my assignment," Callanan recalled. "So, I looked at the timer that was there, and it was less than 30 seconds. We sure were moving fast! And down!" Within seconds, Callanan and others were pressed against the aft end of the conning tower's TDC panels, trying to retain their footing.[15]

In the control room, radioman Bill Dillon had just finished securing the radio antennas for diving. Standing outside the door to the radio shack, he grabbed for something to brace himself. "We were making more than a 20-degree plunge," he recalled. The nearby depth gauge showed two hundred feet, and seconds later was reading beyond two hundred fifty feet. For yeoman Bud Pike, it was "the scariest moment I had on the *Sailfish.* When we dove, the bow dropped so fast that we didn't know what was going on."[16]

Throughout the boat, many were immediately aware of their impending doom. "It was like falling in a dream," torpedoman Ray Bunt recalled. "That was the most helpless feeling a man could ever have." Fireman Larry Macek tried to cover himself as spare parts tumbled about his engine room. *Holy Christmas!* Macek thought. *I think we're heading for Davy Jones's locker!*[17]

Farther aft, Good heard cries of "Go aft! Go aft!" Men who had been asleep in their bunks seconds before were suddenly scrambling to all fours in a frenzy to shift human ballast aft. "Those that had reached the mess hall hatch formed a mass obstruction as they attempted to squeeze through the narrow opening at one time," Good remembered.[18]

"The only thing that saved us was the prompt blowing of the forward group of MBTs," Walkup remembered. Chief of the boat Les Bayles and an alert motormac had acted instinctively in blasting compressed air into the forward main ballast tanks. Skipper Bob Ward raced in from the wardroom and took over the situation. "All back emergency!" he shouted.[19]

Dillon joined other sailors who were grabbing at valves and helping to blow tanks to check the boat's plunge. "Nobody could stand up," he recalled. "As we tried to open valves, our feet were sliding out from under us on the deck. We simply couldn't get any leverage, and the boat was going down, down, down."

Before the alarming descent could be checked, *Sailfish* had plunged far below her test depth. The large depth gauge in the control room registered only four hundred feet, and that needle was pegged all the way to the right. Before the trim was finally corrected, Pike was alarmed to find that at one time "the screws were out of the water and backing emergency." The crew would never know exactly how far beyond test depth their old *Sargo*-class boat had gone.[20]

Like a wounded fish, the submarine finally blasted back to the surface so fast that Dillon felt the boat would break in half as it slammed back down. "That's how hard we came down," he recalled. Ward was thoroughly flustered with the mishap and gave Sahaj a stern chewing out on his failure to control the boat. Radarman Callanan was in the control room when he heard Ward announce to Sahaj, "I'd like to see you in the wardroom."[21]

Once order was restored, *Sailfish* proceeded on her course, but the nerves of the crew were badly rattled. "Prior to this day, everyone was in relax mode when we made a trim dive," Dillon recalled. "Off-duty guys who were playing cards in the mess hall, eating a meal, laying in their bunks, or shooting the breeze in a torpedo room had always continued doing what they were doing. From this day forward, we never relaxed again when they called, 'Dive! Dive!' Every man was out of his bunk and standing up, scared to death of a potential repeat of this near-fatal dive."[22]

The errant dive was not mentioned in the patrol report or daily deck log whatsoever. In light of the recent loss of *S-28*, this error on *Sailfish* would have had dire consequences in Ward's wardroom.

The crew set to work straightening up the mess created by the wild dive. During noon chow, a saltwater leak sprang in the forward engine room. Chief Montie Walkup led motormacs Freddie Wheeler and John Good in six hours of work belowdecks to sort through lines to find the leak. A hydrostatic pressure test ensured that all was in order, and it was dinnertime when the repairs were completed.[23]

As the crew's blood pressure subsided, other emotions swept over some of them. In the radio shack, Dillon was angry as he talked it over with Bob Johnson and his fellow radio operators on the performance of their new diving officer. "That is inexcusable!" Dillon snapped. "That guy should not be on this boat. The skipper ought to turn this boat around and put that son of a bitch on the shore!"

The first dive on *Sailfish*'s eleventh war patrol would never be forgotten. The crew had worked long and hard to remove any comments about their submarine being an "ill-fated" boat that had already once been sunk. One of the phrases now voiced by Dillon was felt by many:

"It was the *Squalus* all over again!"

* * *

During the four-day run toward Midway, Chief Johnson and Bill "Skip" Dillon began compiling news from home, particularly sports scores gleaned from nightly radio broadcasts, that was of interest to the crew. New radioman John "Saul" Miller helped Dillon type up the "Hot News," which was posted in the crew's mess for all hands to enjoy. Ship's cartoonist Bob Kempf contributed his share of humorous sketches, most depicting some misfortunate event that had occurred during the patrols.

School-of-the-boat sessions were aided by a new 16mm movie projector installed to show training films. Some were serious about their advancement. Fireman 1c Charles Pendleton, an eighteen-year-old who had made one patrol on *S-34*, set a boat record. Under the guidance of veteran electrician's mates Gail Lusk and Nick Charles Adinolfe, Pendleton was qualified within twenty-five days.[24]

Sailfish, *Billfish*, and *Greenling* arrived at Midway on July 13 and were underway again the following morning. The Moseley's Maulers wolf pack was on station by July 21, when *Billfish* made the first contact, which proved to be a worthless sampan.

On July 23, *Sailfish* received word to conduct a special search in the wake of American air strikes on the nearby Bonin Islands. "An American pilot was down in the sub's general area," Montie Walkup remembered. "The captain immediately ordered the lookouts doubled and the navigator to lay out a search pattern." The odds of finding a lone man in the ocean were not good from the low vantage point atop the periscope shears, but Ward was determined to do his best. Hours into the search, at 1540, one of Dutch Wetmore's lookouts spotted an object off the starboard bow.[25]

As *Sailfish* closed on the object, it was seen to be a lone man clinging to a spherical mooring buoy. The rescue party called topside included the boat's new pharmacist's mate, twenty-two-year-old John "Doc" Turver; expert swimmer Ray Bunt; and two gunner's mates with Thompson submachine guns. Ward carefully conned his boat toward the sailor. Bunt and another swimmer took a line and tied it around the man, who was found to be Japanese and appeared to be in his mid-thirties. "He was stocky, and one leg had a nasty cut running down the calf," Walkup recalled. "Some of his flesh had a grey discoloration from being in the water."[26]

Ward went down on deck to observe the prisoner, who attempted to bow, but he stumbled in the process because of his unsteady legs. After a short deliberation, the skipper announced, "Well, we can't throw him back in. Take him below and we'll patch him up."

The Japanese sailor was treated by Doc Turver, who had served on the *Henderson* before volunteering for submarine service. Turver had been a premed student at Cal Berkley when the attack on Pearl Harbor occurred. Turver's new patient, suffering from a moderate case of saltwater immersion, claimed to be a fisherman who had been in the water for four days after a submarine had sunk his sampan.

Bud Richardson ordered the prisoner to be taken to the forward torpedo room, where he could be guarded by the torpedoman on watch around the clock. Joe Mendel's gang put clean sheets on a lower bunk and offered the man a change of underclothing. After the Japanese sailor stretched out on the bunk, Turver began cleaning his leg wound and treating it with sulfa powder. The prisoner indicated he did not speak English but pointed to himself and announced, "Hinomoto." *Sailfish* sailors quickly shortened his name to "Moto."

Turver found the man to be worried about his fate. "His feet and legs were swollen twice their normal size and were covered with salt water ulcers," Turver recalled. "He made a chopping motion with his hand across his legs, asking by sign language if I was going to cut his legs off." Turver politely indicated to Moto that he had no such intention but that his patient would have to stay off his feet until the swelling in his legs subsided.[27]

The *Sailfish* crew found Moto to be respectful, but Turver heard that at least one of his shipmates would have preferred to throw the Japanese man back into the sea. Torpedoman Billie "Tex" Whitley, from Madisonville, Texas, was among the lookouts ordered to empty Moto's bedpan one night.

Whitley told his buddies he would have resigned if he hadn't been out on patrol. "I didn't join the Navy to carry a bedpan for no Jap!"[28]

Other crewmen soon took a liking to Hinomoto. Motormac John Good found him to be "highly humane and commendable." Other sailors offer him cigarettes and various gifts, treating him like "a newly found puppy." Turver found Moto eager to help polish brass in the forward torpedo room, so Richardson had him reassigned to the crew's mess. "The mess hall had never been cleaner," Walkup recalled.[29]

Doc Turver was alarmed to come off radar duty one night and find his prisoner alone in the galley, sharpening knives. But Moto quickly earned the trust of the *Sailfish* crew, the exception being Whitley. In the mess hall, he demanded extra service from Moto and prevented him from doing his cleaning duties in a timely fashion. Another crewman heard Moto muttering a phrase that was discovered to roughly translate to "pig" in English. Whitley's shipmates quickly began calling him by his new Japanese nickname, which only added to his distaste for the prisoner.[30]

Since *Sailfish* was already operating under a hot-bunking system, there was no spare bunk for Moto. When he was not working, he slept on one of the mess benches with a leg iron attached to one of his legs and to a bench support. Except for the baker, SC2c Austin Sundman, who worked through the night hours preparing fresh breads and pies, there was no other guard for Moto at certain hours. The only concern that some men had was that the ship's magazine was located directly below the mess hall.

One morning soon after Moto was brought on board, the duty chief prepared the boat for its morning dive. "Suddenly, a piercing cry which unmistakenly came from Hinomoto could be heard clearly in the control room," Walkup recalled. The auxiliary electrician on duty raced to the mess hall and found that Moto was seated on his bench, frantically pointing at his leg. Sometime during the night, Sundman had failed to properly secure the leg iron's latch, and it had come completely off while Moto slept. Sundman raced in and fastened the iron. After that, few on board had any worries that their prisoner intended any ill will toward them.[31]

* * *

Sailfish made passage through the Nansei Shoto island group on July 26, but found her patrol area void of targets. On August 7, Ward logged: "We have been one month out of Midway now and have had only one piddling sailboat contact prior to today. Now we have the quantity so far as quantity goes, but no quality. None of these spit kits could be remotely considered worthy of a torpedo, and battle surfacing is out because of our tactical situation."[32]

The situation changed by late afternoon, as *Sailfish* closed on distant puffs of black smoke from a small convoy. Ward approached and could soon make out masts and stacks of distant ships. He stationed his tracking party and continued to approach submerged during the next hour. Periodic shifts in the convoy's base course frustrated Ward, but by 1742 he was able to swing *Sailfish* hard right for a stern shot on a minesweeper.

With glassy sea conditions, Ward used his periscope sparingly for the setup. Dutch Wetmore and Shorty Evans worked out the plot, figuring the target's speed to be 9 knots. Bud Pike relayed orders for Chief Bill Gray and his after torpedo room gang to make ready three tubes. At this moment, the after gyro regulator went out of commission, forcing TDC operators Pat Murphy and Jim Woody to work with a manually set operation. At 1749, Ward ordered the firing of three aft tubes with their torpedoes set to run at only five-foot depth for a shallow-draft target.

Two minutes later, the skipper had the satisfaction of watching the third-fired torpedo impact his target ship. "This is the first time I've witnessed a hit through the scope, and the effect of a warhead on that Jap was amazing," Ward wrote. "He seemed to disintegrate. Everything went sky high. Within a fraction of a second, there was nothing there but smoke and debris in the air." Postwar analysis would show that *Sailfish* had sunk the 1,254-ton converted minelayer *Shinten Maru*. Submarine historian John Alden would also credit *Sailfish* with destroying the small Japanese coaster (coastal trading vessel) *Kinshu*

Maru in the Luzon Strait this night, although Ward turned in no claims for it.[33]

In the control room, new radar operator Cal Callanan was excited by the sounds of the explosions that could be heard. Turning to Chief Bayles, he asked, "Are those depth charges?"[34]

"No," replied Bayles. "It's just the ship breaking up."

Ward quickly invited his exec, Bud Richardson, and torpedo officer Pat Murphy to take looks through the scope to verify the demise of this target. As they did so, sound operator Bob Johnson suddenly announced at 1753 that his men heard high-speed screws on *Sailfish*'s port quarter and starboard beam.

"Take her down!" Ward called.

He lay in wait for eight minutes without hearing any further screw sounds before ordering Stan Cowin to bring her back up to periscope depth. There were no aircraft or anti-submarine vessels in sight, leaving Ward to assume that his soundmen had actually heard the torpedo screws of his other two fish in the distance. He could see a freighter from the convoy now running for the protection of islands to the north, so he commenced chasing him submerged, planning to overtake him upon surfacing that evening.

Ward tracked the ship by periscope until he surfaced at 2015 and commenced a high-speed surface chase. He had a dispatch sent to Commander Moseley to inform him of his pursuit, but his radar team was struggling to make contact. "SJ radar operating only intermittently," Ward logged at 2132. "Radar personnel placed knee deep in the conning tower, all working like mad on tubes, condensers, resistors."[35]

Bill Dillon, now the boat's senior radar operator, could not figure out what had gone wrong with the SJ gear. Chief Radioman Johnson and the others, including Cal Callanan, all pitched in. "I was fresh out of school, and we looked at this radar when we pulled it out of the case," Callanan recalled. "I was a smart-ass kid, because I sounded off, 'There's the problem right there: that resistor.'"[36]

The more seasoned Johnson instead continued to work with Dillon on other potential problem areas. But Callanan continued to point to one particular resistor, insisting that he knew the problem and had learned of it recently in school. Johnson and Dillon instead changed out the pulse transformer, and the choke for the radar's pulse. "Finally, we fired up the radar again, and it's still dead," Callanan recalled. Still determined that the resistor was fouled with carbon, he finally touched it.

With a flash and a zap, Callanan yelped as he was hit with a load of electricity from the resistor. "There, damn it! That proves it!" he snapped. "That's the bleed resistor for the pulse."[37]

Sailfish's radar set continued to frustrate the tracking party. Johnson and Dillon worked to install a new resistor in the SJ, but Ward was impatient. Deciding that his freighter had wisely chosen to anchor down in shallow water near a pair of islands, Ward reluctantly broke off the chase and followed Moseley's directions to proceed to the west.

* * *

Bud Pike had radar duty on the night of August 18, when *Sailfish* picked up another worthwhile shipping contact. The PPI screen showed the distance to be 22,650 yards, and Pike was commended for his alert reporting of the long-range pip.[38]

In the crew's mess hall, engineman John Good was playing cards after finishing his watch duty. As the Bells of St. Mary's gonged for battle stations torpedo, he stood to head for his engine room and glanced at the Japanese prisoner. "I motioned to Moto and said, 'boom-boom.' He just grinned," Good recalled.[39]

Ward called his tracking party and flashed an alert to his pack mates. With *Sailfish* on a parallel course with the radar contact, the range closed rapidly during the next twenty minutes. By 0127, the range had narrowed to 6,900 yards, and Ward found that he had a large ship with one escort ahead of it and another trailing on each quarter. *Sailfish* had stumbled onto a prime target, the thirty-six-thousand-ton Japanese battleship *Haruna*, which was on a southwest course from Sasebo, Japan, to Singapore with three destroyers: *Michishio*, *Yamagumo*, and *Nowaki*. *Sailfish* encountered this important warship group southwest of the Formosa Strait, near the latitude of Laoag City on northern Luzon to the east.[40]

Five minutes later, Ward ordered, "Open the forward tube doors."

The battleship *Haruna* was still too hazy to identify, but it had a large superstructure forward and appeared to be twice as large as its escorting destroyers. "Believe he is battleship or heavy cruiser," Ward noted. As the range to target suddenly began increasing, he gave the orders to fire all four bow tubes at a distance of 3,600 yards.[41]

Ward remained on the bridge with his lookouts, watching the phosphorescent wakes of all four torpedoes heading out hot, straight, and normal. Two minutes after firing, he heard, felt, and saw the flash of a torpedo hit, followed twenty seconds later by another hit. Ward was in the process of moving to the after torpedo bearing transmitter and could not see the exact location of the explosions on his target. "Both hits were solid," he wrote. "All bridge personnel saw the flash and heard and felt the hits but also lost sight of the targets in our turn."

The sharp turn into the swollen seas threw a heavy spray over the bridge that foiled the view of those topside, but radar operator Bill Dillon reported that the escort ship on the main target's port quarter had disappeared from his SJ radar screen in the conning tower. Dillon further reported no change in position of the main target or the two remaining escorts. "Would like to think we had two hits in target with good possibility of slowing him down but apparently the destroyer took them," Ward wrote.[42]

The other two torpedoes were assumed to have missed astern. Ward called for full-right rudder in order to trail on the main target's course. In spite of losing one of its escorts, *Haruna* and her two remaining destroyers did nothing but continue straight on course. By 0145, the three ships had increased speed to 20 knots, and Dillon reported that the third destroyer was definitely now missing from his radar screen.

Sailfish was unable to gain position on the fleeing Japanese ships. Almost immediately after the sub increased speed to chase the warships, two of *Sailfish*'s engines overheated and shut down. *Haruna* and her remaining escorts pulled away, and a prime opportunity was lost.

Sailfish was later credited with sinking a 1,500-ton destroyer. But postwar analysis of Japanese records would fail to show any Japanese warship lost on this date. *Haruna* and her three destroyers arrived in Singapore without damage. In hindsight, one of two scenarios occurred: Two of *Sailfish*'s torpedoes had exploded prematurely, or *Sailfish* had hit an escort ship that Japanese records failed to later document. When this came to light years later, it was highly frustrating to her crew. The men topside had seen, heard, and felt two torpedoes explode.

Bill Dillon would forever believe what he had heard and seen, and then had not seen, on his radar scope. Like many other U.S. submariners whose important sinkings were robbed in postwar "official" paperwork analysis, Dillon remained bitter. "We knew then and later what we sank," he recalled.

★ ★ ★

Dillon's radar team was frustrated with a different sort of SJ issue two days later. Glassy sea conditions, combined with strong riptides, created on the radar screen ghostly phantom "pixies" that looked at times like either distant ships or fast-approaching torpedo boats. During the early-morning hours of August 20, Commander Ward called his boat to battle stations to track numerous contacts that alternately appeared and disappeared from the radar screen. "One of them came in from 1400 yards to 0 yards at high speed and we still couldn't see him," Ward logged.[43]

The following days of patrol produced more radar pixies, numerous aircraft contacts, and small Japanese vessels unworthy of a torpedo attack. After more than a month at sea, the crew had taken on a motley appearance in its confined, mostly lightless world. "Beards have grown to various lengths and the owner's sense of a trimmed beard has surpassed the wildest conceptions of a writer's imagination," Good wrote in his journal. "From a Van Dyke to a full bush." Most men wore only shorts, with few still wearing trousers and shirts. "Those whose duties are confined to within the boat wear only shorts and the exhibition of fat bellies, skinny frames, and hairy bellies is as humorous as the attendance of a sideshow for the first time," Good added.[44]

A number of crewmen took on the Vandyke look, a style with both a mustache and a goatee with all the hair on the cheeks shaved. Among the engineers, Good, Bob Bradley, and engineering officer Joe Sahaj sported another look—thick, bushy beards sans mustaches. Two other officers, Shorty Evans and Pat Murphy, kept their beards trimmed but grew out thick mustaches.

Sailfish's days of frustration finally paid off on August 24, as an SJ radar contact at 0220 soon materialized into three good-sized merchant ships, a smaller cargo vessel, and two escort ships. Ward started in at high speed on the surface, sent out contact reports to his pack mates, and, after an hour of pursuit, fired all four bow tubes from a range of 3,020 yards.

Two minutes after firing, Ward witnessed a beautiful explosion on his target freighter between her midsection and stern. Ten seconds later, a second torpedo exploded just forward of the vessel's midsection. "Target immediately lost in cloud of smoke," Ward wrote. One minute later, at 0336, he added, "Can see target's stern with a 60-degree down-angle, just to right of the smoke. Radar reports he had broken in two."[45]

Three minutes later, Bob Johnson on sound reported two end-of-run explosions, believed to be the third and fourth war fish having missed astern of the target. *Sailfish* remained on the surface as Joe Mendel's forward gang raced to reload their tubes. Three random depth charges were heard to explode in the distance. For *Sailfish*'s blooded veterans, they seemed miles away. Fireman James Roberson, a young Texas throttleman on duty in the engine room, calmly remarked to another motormac, "Boy, you guys have been talking about how bad these things are. That wasn't bad at all."[46]

One of his grizzled fellow engineers simply replied, "Just wait."

Roberson's introduction to severe depth charging would come in time. Following this attack, radarman Dillon reported at 0345 that both ends of the stricken vessel had disappeared from his scope. *Sailfish* would receive wartime credit for sinking a four-thousand-ton freighter on August 24, but postwar analysis would again strip Ward of this credit. Japanese records failed to show any ship lost in this area during this time—something that *Sailfish* sailors could simply not fathom.

Sailfish commenced a high-speed end around to obtain a good firing position on the remaining merchant ships. Not wishing to foil his night vision by using his bridge target bearing transmitters (TBTs), Ward continued to rely solely on radar ranges and periscope bearings that were fed to him. At 0446, he fired all four forward tubes again. To his shock, the orange glow of explosions erupted on a different ship in the column than the one he had been concentrating on. Taking quick radar bearings on another freighter astern of his boat, Ward then fired all four stern tubes.

Another explosion was heard and felt by those topside, but nothing was seen. Radarman Dillon reported one stern tube target had disappeared from radar, but Ward was perplexed as his boat cleared the scene at high speed. Having fired a dozen torpedoes in less than ninety minutes, *Sailfish* radioed to *Greenling* and *Billfish* that she had only one torpedo remaining and was retiring from the scene.

While submerged that day, he and the plotting team ran through the scenarios to figure out what had gone wrong. They discovered that in the twisting, confused surface attack, *Sailfish* had fired on the same freighter twice.

"It was a stupid error and an expensive lesson," logged Ward.[47]

Assistant approach officer Bud Richardson acknowledged a "foul up of the control party down below, which was largely me." Several months after this attack, Richardson stated, "In the process of swinging to shift targets, the resulting confusion down below ended up that we shifted off the target, back again, fired the stern tubes at the same target at which we fired the bow tubes."[48]

Ward would work with his plotting team, conning tower crew, and bridge personnel to better coordinate any future attacks when multiple targets were presented. Upon surfacing that evening, Ward headed back toward the scene of his early-morning attacks. He had his radio gang update Moseley that the remnants of the convoy were out of range now, and offered its last-known position course and speed. *Greenling* radioed back two minutes later with word from Moseley that Ward should return to base.

Sailfish set course to the southeast. In spite of the mistakes made in tracking numerous ships, Bob Ward was pleased with this crew in their relentless series of attacks. Over the 1MC, he announced that his men would have steak and brandy for dinner that night, along with strawberry shortcake, followed by ham and eggs for breakfast the next day. Better yet, as John Good logged, "field day was to be postponed for another day."[49]

★ ★ ★

During the return run toward Midway, *Sailfish* dodged airplane contacts and skirted a typhoon. By midday on September 3, the winds had reached 40 knots, and the seas were so rough that Ward refused to put lookouts on the periscope shears while surfaced. For the next forty-eight hours, the boat could manage no better speed than 10 knots at any time.

The storm and the lack of provisions were wearing the crew thin. Fireman James Roberson had grown accustomed to helping himself to sandwiches, leftover roast, or slabs of Austin Sundman's pineapple upside-down cake early in the patrol.

"We ran out of everything," Roberson recalled. "I remember eating nothing but spaghetti without any sauce on that last leg. That gets pretty old."[50]

At 1215 on September 6, *Sailfish* moored near the tender *Proteus* at Midway as the tender's band triumphantly blared "America the Beautiful" to welcome *Sailfish* after two months at sea. Commander Ward greeted the welcoming party of Midway officers after a gangplank was extended from the pier. Base sailors hauled over crates of fresh fruit and milk as the *Proteus* band continued to blast out music for sailors who began devouring fresh oranges. Likely the most eager to see *Sailfish* arrive was Lieutenant (jg) Ed Berghausen, who happily reported back on board after having been detached at Pearl Harbor two months prior.

John Turver watched as two Marine guards from Midway came on board to haul his healed prisoner, Moto, to the brig. “He was strictly GI, with clean dungarees, white hat, and his ditty bag full of cigarettes, all gifts of the crew,” said Turver. “When he left, he had more cigarettes than I had!”[51]

SIXTEEN

The Mines of Ashio

After more than six months at Ofuna, *Sculpin* survivor Joe Baker was excited to be moving. On July 15, 1944, he and the final seven enlisted men from his submarine were blindfolded and marched the five kilometers from camp to the local train station. Although they were being moved into the mountains to join their other shipmates at the Ashio Camp 9-B facility, Baker knew that he would now at least be properly registered as a prisoner of war.

With their arrival, the Ashio mining camp now included thirty-four captured American submariners: three officers and eleven enlisted men from *Grenadier*, and all twenty *Sculpin* enlisted men. The camp compound held about two hundred eighty prisoners, the largest contingent being Dutchmen, although they were joined in mid-August by a hundred fifty American soldiers who had survived the Bataan Death March.[1]

The final *Sculpin* survivor, Lieutenant George Brown, remained at Ofuna until mid-January 1945. His treatment as an officer continued to be severe. The camp commandant made it clear to Brown where he stood. "We were lower than the lowest Japanese seaman, no matter what our rank had been in our own country, and that we would be treated as such," Brown recalled. In early September, he had been roused from sleep in his cell and was publicly beaten for the entertainment of civilian guests of the compound. During the months that Brown remained the sole *Sculpin* man kept at Ofuna, he witnessed terrible abuse handed out to other submariners and aviators.[2]

Around the first of November 1944, Brown noted the arrival of nine new prisoners of war, the only survivors from the submarine *Tang*. They included the skipper, Commander Dick O'Kane; two junior officers; and six enlisted men. During her five war patrols, *Tang* had sunk at least two dozen Japanese ships, but the sub was lost during the early hours of October 25, when she was struck by her own final torpedo, which was seen to broach and curve left in a circular run. O'Kane and two other men were able to swim through the night after their submarine sank. One officer escaped from the flooding conning tower to be rescued with them. *Tang* settled to the bottom at a hundred eighty feet, where about thirty survivors attempted to swim up from the forward torpedo room hatch in small groups.

It was the only known attempt to do so using Momsen lungs, an emergency breathing device designed by Swede Momsen. Of thirteen men who attempted the escape from *Tang*, five were rescued later that morning by a Japanese frigate. On November 6, just days after arriving at Ofuna, the nine *Tang* survivors were lined up in the compound to witness how prisoners would be punished for various offenses. Eight veteran prisoners, including *Sculpin*'s George Brown and *Grenadier* skipper John Fitzgerald, were subjected to brutal beatings.

O'Kane felt that Fitzgerald and two of the prisoners looked like "walking skeletons." They were beaten with clubs until they could no longer stand, at which point other guards lifted them up so the beatings could continue. *Tang* radioman Floyd Caverly, a tough former boxer, was so sickened by the sight that he vomited. When the *Tang* prisoners were led away, Japanese guards were still kicking the limp bodies of Fitzgerald and others. O'Kane later stated, "We believed them dead."[3]

When Lieutenant Brown was finally moved to Omori, he remained an unofficial prisoner. "I was never registered officially or unofficially as a prisoner of war, nor was my family ever notified," he recalled. Brown was put to work in a leather factory, sewing canteen covers for the Japanese military. Months later, he would be shipped to yet another Japanese POW camp, but he remained separated from his twenty fellow *Sculpin* men.[4]

* * *

John Rourke and some of the newly arrived prisoners at the Ashio camp were sent to work in the mine. Joe Baker and six others were put to work in the town's copper smelter, where they labored in an environment full of damaging gas and sulfur fumes. Two of his comrades, Ed Ricketts and Julius Peterson, had been beaten for refusing to work in the mine. Laboring over the sulfur vats, they became tired of the fumes, which were so strong that some of the Korean laborers, who worked alongside the American POWs, passed out.

"We crapped out between the boilers," Ricketts recalled. Guards found them, beat them severely, and cut their rations as punishment. "They never really could understand us," he added. Finally tired of beating Ricketts for his arrogance, the Japanese assigned him to work in camp commandant Numajiri's personal garden. There, Ricketts pocketed vegetables and broke into storehouses when the Japanese took cover during air raids. "I was stealing them blind," he admitted.[5]

By early fall of 1944, several more American submariners had joined the work details at Ofuna, among them *S-44*'s only two survivors, Tony Duva and Bill Whitemore, and the sole survivor of the submarine *Tullibee*, Gunner's Mate 2c Cliff Kuykendall from Texas. Making her fourth patrol off the Japanese naval base at Palau, *Tullibee* had made a surface attack on the night of March 27 against a Japanese convoy but had the misfortune of being sunk by one of her own torpedoes, in a rare circular run of boomerang fashion. Kuykendall, standing watch as a lookout, was blown into the ocean by the force of the explosion. After an hour of treading water, he was the only American survivor picked up by a Japanese destroyer.[6]

Deposited at Palau, Kuykendall had the further misfortune of riding out two days of intensive American carrier air strikes against the Japanese facilities. Moved to mainland Japan in April, Kuykendall had spent five months at Ofuna prior to his arrival at Ashio. There, he worked alongside other submariners from *Sculpin*, *S-44*, and *Grenadier* and slept in an unheated barracks cell full of lice, fleas, and rats. "Prisoners working in the mine were beaten by the Jap work foremen if they didn't like the way the prisoners were working," Kuykendall recalled.

Winter weather crept into the Ashio mountains, leaving the American prisoners shivering at night from the bitter cold. Japanese guards routinely inspected the barracks, forcing many prisoners to kneel on their pallets throughout the process. One man was smashed with a rifle butt because his fingers were touching a bunk railing. Enraged, *Sculpin* gunner's mate Bob Wyatt jumped from his second-tier bunk onto the guards. Such an assault would normally end in a beating that could have proven fatal, but Ed Keller was pleased that his shipmate behaved so irrationally that he convinced the Japanese guards he was simply crazy. "From then on, they went down the barracks on the opposite side from Wyatt," Keller recalled.[7]

The dry rice-and-barley mix fed to the Ashio inmates, along with some watery soup, was barely enough to sustain life. "We were weighed about every month, and I seemed to lose about six pounds per month," recalled *Sculpin*'s chief, Bill Haverland. "Now and then, you'd get a little piece of fish. Sometimes, you'd get a small piece of horse meat, about a half an inch square."[8]

By early 1945, many of the *Sculpin* men were suffering from dysentery, diarrhea, and beriberi, the last ailment causing severe swelling of the legs and persistent joint pain. Food rations were inadequate for the men to ever fully recuperate, and Japanese guards pilfered the Red Cross packages that were delivered during the Christmas season. Tony Duva and others who helped serve as camp cooks did what they could with their limited food offerings. George Rocek considered it a treat to occasionally receive ground-up horse bones. "These were boiled for a week to make them soft, and then rationed out to the men," he recalled.[9]

During early 1945, seaman Ed Keller developed a serious case of pneumonia, which removed him from mining work for some time. As he was carried from his cell to the camp infirmary, Keller weakly said to other prisoners, "I'll be back."[10]

"Yeah, that's what they all say," one of them replied. Fortunately for Keller, his body proved strong enough to eventually fight off the infection, and he was then returned to the Ashio mines.

Rocek found that some of the Korean mine laborers treated the Americans well, occasionally even offering him small portions of their own food. News from the outside world was difficult to obtain. "Occasionally, a newspaper would be stolen by the prisoners working the night shift," Rocek recalled. The paper was then delivered to an Australian POW in camp who could read and speak Japanese. "He would write down the condensed war information, which was then passed throughout the camp," said Rocek.

The abuse, the cold weather, the hard labor, and the frequent beatings eventually began to claim lives. Some simply lost the will to survive. Keller found one older prisoner to be like a zombie who simply sat on his pallet at all hours of the night just staring at others. "His eyes reminded you of the devil," Keller recalled. "They had a weird glow to them, even though he was very sick." Finally, the ailing inmate lay down in his bunk one day and never rose again. Although others would perish at Ashio, this POW stood out to Keller more than any others.[11]

"I swear he willed himself to die."

SEVENTEEN

Lifeguard League

At Midway's rest camp, torpedoman Ray Bunt set to work on a special project. From his seabag, he produced a brass gallon container with little pipe openings at its top. In short order, various rubber hoses were attached and the brass container was resting on a burning electric hot plate liberated from *Sailfish*'s officer pantry. Utilizing a freshwater sink, Bunt's still operation began.

"Another copper tube projecting from its extreme face end dripped a pure white liquid into a half-full water glass set below it," John Good wrote. "The alcoholic still was their dream, and to watch it work on its first operation filled the minds of youth with acute satisfaction."[1]

During the wee hours of the morning, Bunt's team ran the still in the washroom of their enlisted shack. They used the pink-tinted torpedo alcohol as their brewing base. All went well until around 0300, when a watch guard sailor rushed in to announce that the shore patrol was on its way. Men rushed to stash the boiling still; then they raced out a back door. The following day, there was great discussion about the near discovery of the still and one poor sailor who was found passed out after consuming a healthy quantity of the new concoction.

Aside from operating their bootleg still, the *Sailfish* sailors amused themselves with laughing at the clumsy gooney birds, playing softball, drinking beer, and writing letters. One afternoon, a fishing charter was set up on a twenty-foot launch, complete with beer, sodas, and sandwiches. Dragging trawl lines, crewmen caught enough bonito to hold a fish fry. By the time the two weeks' rest at Midway was complete, some were almost eager to help with the final refit of their boat.[2]

Bob Ward would be making his third command patrol with two new faces in the wardroom. Dutch Wetmore, Frank Dieterich, and Bud Richardson had new orders, with Richardson serving briefly as operations officer of Submarine Squadron 4 before taking command of the submarine *Tarpon*. He departed with the satisfaction of knowing that *Sailfish* under Ward was a transformed boat. "The success of that ship was due largely to the effect of the commanding officer's own personality transmitted back through those people," Richardson remembered.[3]

Richardson's place as XO was ably filled by former third officer Pat Murphy, whose role as torpedo officer was assumed by a newcomer. Lieutenant Dave Gaston was a seasoned submariner who would also assume commissary duties from Hertsgaard, who in turn took on the role of communications officer. Gaston had started the war as commissary officer and assistant first lieutenant on *Trout* before making the first patrol on the new boat *Pipefish* as torpedo officer through July 1944.

Also leaving the boat for new duties were chief petty officers Bill Lyon and Les Bayles, the latter heading Stateside to new construction. "When Bayles left the boat, the crew was really upset," recalled Bill Dillon. "He had tremendous experience, and we really liked that guy. When Bayles spoke, we followed him like sheep." To fill his shoes as chief of the boat, Ward selected Chief Montie Walkup, the most seasoned CPO still on the boat. Only two men remained on board who had made all eleven prior war patrols: Chief Radioman Johnson and electrician's mate Harry Blundell.[4]

Loaded with a dozen Mark 14-3A and eight Mark 18-1 torpedoes, *Sailfish* departed Midway on September 26, 1944, bound for her twelfth war patrol between Formosa and Luzon. Outbound to his patrol area, Ward worked out his gun crews with mock firings. The men passed their time gossiping, reading books, and listening to radio reports. Motormac John Good was pleased with the newer hands now manning the galley. "The chow situation is under control, to the pleasure of the crew," he wrote in his journal. "Joe Adams, SC1c, is the best cook we've ever had and it's a pleasure to sit down to his meals."[5]

The *Sailfish* crew had their first enemy plane contact on October 8. Two days later, Ward attempted to attack a Japanese transport ship near Batan Island, but could not attain firing distance. That night, he sent a contact report and gave up the chase. His boat had an important mission: lifeguard duty off the southwestern tip of Formosa.

★ ★ ★

Bill Dillon was on the radio at 0552 on October 12, exchanging calls with planes on his VHF radio, as *Sailfish* headed for a reference point to await the day's air strikes. At daybreak, Admiral William "Bull" Halsey's Third Fleet, consisting of four carrier groups, began sending waves of strike planes against Formosa, where they would encounter stiff resistance in the form of more than two hundred thirty Japanese aircraft. The first wave of American attackers downed nearly a third of their aerial opponents, but U.S. plane losses were inevitable.

En route to her lifeguard station, *Sailfish* encountered a small fishing sampan sitting right in her path. Ward decided a battle surface was in order for his 20mm gunners and the 4-inch deck gun. Gunner's mates Frank Mullen, Ben Davis, and Maurice Barnes and their teams raced through the conning tower hatch and manned their weapons. Radioman Dillon joined the enlisted men who hurried out on deck to begin hoisting ammunition for the gun loaders. "The shells were heavy and difficult to handle under sea conditions, and it was in close quarters with no real space to move around," he recalled. Glancing back at the 20mm machine gun, he noted one of his buddies, steward Killraine Newton, swinging his weapon toward the Japanese vessel. For the *Sailfish* crew, this surface duel would mark the first time Commander Ward had called them into action against an enemy ship.[6]

At 0735, the 20mm gunners opened up on the little sampan, which was manned by three fishermen. "20mm shells streaked at the sampan, with tracers blazing the air," recalled motormac John Good, who served as the deck gun's sight setter. Once the range was established, multiple hits soon shredded the little wooden vessel into pieces on the surface.[7]

Dillon and Bob Johnson reported at 0846 that the overhead aviators from Task Force 38 carriers had placed a call for *Sailfish*'s services. Columns of billowing smoke reached skyward from Formosa, and thunderous explosions reverberated across the water. The downed-pilot location was sixty miles to the southeast. Ward headed that way, hoping the given position was an error. He was rightfully nervous to keep *Sailfish* on the surface. By 0925, more than a hundred carrier planes were overhead. In the radio shack, Dillon used his VHF to establish friendly contact with the pilots, and he kept up running chatter with them until the promised air escort planes finally appeared a while later.

At 1007, *Sailfish* received two additional calls for help for downed aircraft, both close to her early-morning lifeguard station position. Ward decided to abandon his sixty-mile rescue and return to a point where he could be more effective. He would have good reasons to support this decision, including later intelligence that showed the first downed plane report to have been made in error.

By 1130, the results of the air strikes on Formosa were visible to the men manning *Sailfish*'s bridge and periscope shears platforms. Forty minutes later, lookouts saw a U.S. plane trailing smoke that finally crashed well to the north. Four Hellcats appeared overhead to provide cover as *Sailfish* headed for the downed pilot. Lt. (jg) Stan Cowin supervised a deck rescue crew that consisted of line handlers, expert swimmer Ray Bunt, pharmacist's mate Doc Turver, and junior officers Joe Sahaj and Shorty Evans. At 1235, *Sailfish* approached a bobbing yellow rubber boat. It contained Lieutenant Samuel M. Tharp and Aviation Radioman Second Class (ARM2c) Richard Sullivan Hodel from VB-20 off *Enterprise*.

Ward conned his boat in fast until close aboard. Cowin's team then tossed a life ring to the aviators. The deck crew swiftly pulled the raft alongside as a Jacob's ladder was dropped down the hull. Bunt dived in to help the airmen and used his knife to puncture the raft so it would sink. The ladder was quickly hauled on board and all men were hustled down the forward hatch as *Sailfish* built up speed again to clear the scene.

The day's work as a rescue boat was just beginning. With numerous fighter pilots engaged in aerial dogfights and others calling out the locations of downed comrades, communication soon became chaotic. "Everyone on the circuit was talking at the same time," Dillon recalled. "It was difficult to know who was in trouble and who was not. The one in trouble had to shout louder than the rest."

Twenty minutes after scooping up the Helldiver crew, the *Sailfish* rescue party pulled aboard a fighter pilot from the carrier *Wasp*, Ensign Arlington Reid Arnold from VF-14. Another VF-14 pilot then reported a damaged Helldiver making a water landing. Before Commander Ward could turn to help these men, the air cover team reported yet another downed plane even closer to the lifeguard sub.

This one proved to be a Grumman TBM Avenger torpedo bomber crew from the carrier *Essex*. Ensign Houston Ray Copeland of VT-15 made a controlled water landing after his engine was hit. As he and his two crewmen, ARM2c Russell J. Bradley and Aviation Machinist's Mate Second Class (AMM2c) William C. Poppel, scrambled into their yellow life raft, they were suddenly approached by a small Japanese lugger that had changed course in hopes of capturing the Americans.[8]

An *Essex* Hellcat pilot made repeated strafing runs on the small enemy vessel to drive it away as *Sailfish* raced in. By 1314, the TBM crew was safely on board and in the hands of Doc Turver. With six rescued aviators on board his boat, Ward now raced toward the position where the Helldiver crew was reported to have gone into the drink. At 1353, he nudged his boat up to the rubber raft of the two downed SB2C aviators. They were from VB-20 off *Enterprise*: Ensign George Muinch Jr. and his rear-seat gunner, ARM2c Charles Weldon Anderson Jr. When they came on board, they found that Lieutenant Tharp and gunner Hodel from their VB-20 squadron were also on *Sailfish*.

The rescue of Muinch's crew came with high drama. A small Japanese ship, appearing to be a patrol boat or a tug, tried to race from shore to beat *Sailfish* to the recovery. Ward called for gunner Frank Mullen to have his guns take over. As Mullen's team manned the 4-inch, .50-caliber main gun, the overhead American pilots began bombing and strafing the enemy ship. Irritated, Ward grabbed the transmitter from Dillon and shouted, "Leave him alone! He's mine!"[9]

Mullen's crew fired three rounds of shells. The second was a solid hit and explosion that appeared to cripple the Japanese ship. Ward then called for a cease-fire, as eager U.S. warplanes were diving one after the other on the hapless vessel. He cleared the range to allow his topside crew to enjoy the show as the planes strafed and bombed the little ship into a blazing, sinking wreck.

In the course of this rescue and others that *Sailfish* made, Commander Ward entered into forbidden areas where he was under direction not to attempt a rescue. "One was within 30,000 yards of Apo Hill at Takao," Ward logged. To recover Muinch's crew, he took his boat into a large cove with shallow water. "A large cliff bordered the cove and on top of the cliff was a gun emplacement," Chief Walkup recalled. "It was calculated that if we went in far enough, the gun could not depress enough to fire on us."[10]

In order to edge into the shallow cove, Ward had ordered the ship to flood down to present a low profile. One of the pilots placed a call to *Sailfish*—whose handle this day was "Girl Chaser"—to inquire whether they should take out the gun emplacement. "The Captain reasoned that we should leave them alone," recalled Walkup.

Just as this action was winding down at 1430, one of the Hellcat pilots overhead announced that he was out of gas and making an emergency landing close aboard *Sailfish*'s bow. The pilot, Ensign Dale W. Fisher from VF-14 on *Wasp*, was landing parallel to the submarine when he suddenly turned and crash-landed directly ahead of *Sailfish*. "Had to back emergency to avoid ramming," Ward wrote in his log. As the Hellcat slammed into the water, Ray Bunt dived overboard and swam to assist. The latch to Fisher's canopy had jammed shut, and Bunt saw the pilot struggling to get free as his F6F bubbled under.[11]

"Although Bunt went deep, he successfully brought the pilot up," Walkup remembered. "The pilot was choking and he had some bruises and minor cuts, but in short order, he was put into a bunk in the CPO quarters where he fell asleep." Fisher was the second pilot fished from the water who had flown off *Wasp* earlier that day.[12]

In the midst of the sub's crew rescuing Fisher, another dive-bomber made a perfect water landing just off *Sailfish*'s port bow after suffering flak damage. At 1435, Lieutenant Cowin's deck rescue team pulled from the rubber boat two more SB2C men from *Wasp*'s VB-14: Lieutenant (jg) Dominic Nicholas Scatuorchio and ARM2c J. C. Seeley. In his log, Ward triumphantly recorded: "We now have six officers and five crewmen on board—a score of one plane crew every twenty minutes, or one person every eleven minutes since 1235."[13]

By 1440, a check of the radio traffic revealed that all rescue calls had been taken care of except one: an *Essex* fighter pilot who had been downed twenty miles away from *Sailfish*'s early-morning position. Ward proceeded to this point, remaining on the surface during the morning of October 13 as further strikes against the Japanese were made by Task Force 38. Around 0930, a fighter escort pilot reported that he had discovered a rubber boat to the north.

During lifeguard duty, two radio watch standers were kept in the radio room at all times. Chief Johnson and his radio gang—Dillon, Leon Labrecque, Joe Lang, John "Saul" Miller, and Richard Owen—had worked tirelessly the previous day, manning both the radar and VHF communication gear. They had been able to talk with friendly planes to a distance of thirty miles, but the constant chatter on the airwaves made it tough to effectively communicate. Throughout the second morning of lifeguard duty, Johnson's radio gang used their four newly recovered rear-seat radiomen to assist on VHF duty. "It apparently takes an aviator to really understand the language and procedure of an aviator," Ward logged.[14]

Sailfish soon had a yellow life raft in sight, and the rescue party moved out on deck to prepare. As they tossed their life ring to the lone pilot, Ward was amused to see the pilot casually smoking a pipe. Swimmer Ray Bunt, who went over the side for the seventh time in two days, would later be written up for a Navy Letter of Commendation by his skipper.

Once the man was hustled below, the *Sailfish* men learned that he was Lieutenant (jg) John Paul Van Altena from VF-15 off *Essex*. During the early-morning strikes the previous day, Van Altena had shot down an Imperial Army Ki-44 "Tojo," but the Japanese fighter's wingman had hit Van Altena's F6F in the engine. Forced to ditch, the Hellcat pilot had spent the night sailing toward China. He reported to Ward that he was the pilot whom the submarine had been searching for during the past twenty-four hours.[15]

Ward remained surfaced throughout the day's air strike actions. His radio gang sent a message to an airplane overhead, giving names and initials of all twelve aviators rescued to date. By midafternoon, the only new reports of downed aviators were of planes that were forty-four and eighty miles northwest of *Sailfish*. Due to the distance and the fact that the airmen were in shallow water off the coast of a small island, Ward sent word that a seaplane rescue would be required.

By 1630, all air escorts over *Sailfish* had departed following TF 38's third and final air strikes. *Sailfish* commenced retiring to the southwest as her lookouts spotted two Japanese Betty bombers returning toward their coastline. Five minutes later, the topside watch was surprised by a Japanese Tojo fighter that came diving out of the clouds without warning. Ward cleared the deck as the fighter passed close aboard to port—so close that the men topside could see the red meatball insignia on his fuselage.

As *Sailfish* made a crash dive, the pilot began strafing. Bullets were heard to hit the boat as she reached thirty feet. "He didn't have any bombs left, but he hit us with a strafing run," Bud Pike recalled. "I was in the front end of the forward torpedo room and I could hear his bullets beat a tattoo on our deck. He shot up our radio antenna."[16]

When *Sailfish* resurfaced at 1844, a topside inspection was conducted. One slug was found in the wood decking of the after 20mm platform, and one of the aerial radio antennas had been shot away.

Dillon, Johnson, and their team spent the night hours removing the broken portside aerial antenna and replacing it with a spare. During removal of the severed antenna, the gasket-securing nut on the lead-in to the standoff insulator was inadvertently loosened, allowing water to enter the trunk during the morning dive on October 14. The drain became fouled with loose cork insulation, and upon the sub's surfacing after the morning dive, the trunk was found to be flooded with salt water, which had passed completely through the TBL-3 transmitter. When the transmitter was powered on, it simply flashed as it shorted out.[17]

Dillon and his comrades had a complete mess on their hands. *Sailfish* was now operating blind, unable to transmit any reports. *Sailfish* exchanged voice calls with the submarine *Sawfish* on October 14, giving data on downed aviators Ward had been unable to rescue. He had no further calls for lifeguard services this day, so he proceeded with his war patrol.

The radiomen worked around the clock during the next two days trying to sort out the mess. When *Sailfish* was surfaced at night, they cleaned out all the salt water from the antenna trunk, and then rebuilt the unit with dummy transistors. "Bob Johnson and I attempted to clean every place that water might have penetrated our connections," Dillon recalled. "We took out just about everything possible, cleaned as best we could, reinstalled all that was removed, air-dried with a blower, and then tried to test the transmitter."[18]

As soon as they turned on the power, there was a sharp flash as the transmitter shorted out. Nothing worked, leaving *Sailfish* powerless once again to send any messages to Pearl Harbor or to other submarines. In their cramped radio room, Dillon and Johnson started all over again, trying to clean and rebuild their burned-out transmitter. In the midst of their labor, communications officer Craig Hertsgaard still had to decode messages in the cramped space on the ECM as other radiomen stood their normal watches.

In his patrol report, Ward wrote of the radio-gear fiasco, "In view of the existing tactical situation, this casualty was a most serious one." It soon became evident that *Sailfish* might have to cut her patrol short.

* * *

Effectively silenced, *Sailfish* lurked about Formosa the next two days, able to hear only transmissions from other boats. Admiral Charlie Lockwood, apprised of the fact that *Sailfish* was having radio problems, sent another boat that was patrolling near Luzon, Commander Lawson "Red" Ramage's *Parche*, to rendezvous with Bob Ward.

During the evening of October 18, Ward was directed to proceed with *Parche* into Saipan to unload her dozen rescued aviators and repair her radio transmitter. After transiting the Balingtang Channel, *Sailfish* and *Parche* remained in close contact through the remainder of their run into Saipan. By this time, the twelve rescued aviators were in good spirits. The crew was more than happy to trade with them for items they carried on board from their rescue kits, such as medical supplies, tourniquets, and souvenirs. Engineman Freddie Wheeler even managed to secure a .38-caliber pistol from one of the thankful pilots, while another sailor traded for a lightweight summer flight suit.[19]

Out of boredom, the aviators often gathered in the control room to observe the operations of their rescue submarine, although Commander Ward had requested they try to remain in the wardroom or in the after battery mess hall. "The Captain decided that he would shake them up by simulating a flooding casualty," Chief Montie Walkup recalled. "He instructed the quartermaster to take a five-gallon bucket of water up to the conning tower and then instructed the OOD to simulate a Jap plane attack. He then ordered the OOD to dive and that the quartermaster report that the bridge hatch was jammed open, and then throw the water down into the control room."[20]

The OOD dived the boat as instructed, but the quartermaster failed to toss the water on cue. Ward then approached the ladder to the conning tower to find out what had gone wrong. As he did, Troy Ray finally tossed the bucket of water down the hatch toward the control room, drenching his skipper. "The fliers commenced to laugh as the Captain chewed out the quartermaster," wrote Walkup. *Sailfish* cartoonist Bob Kempf soon produced a sketch of the mishap that graced the next issue of the radio gang's newspaper.

On the morning of October 24, *Parche* and *Sailfish* reached Saipan and moored alongside the tender *Fulton* in Tanapag Harbor. The rescued aviators were sent ashore while engineers set to work on repairing their patrol damage. Work was completed on the TBL radio transmitter and the No. 2 periscope, in addition to overhaul and refitting work tackled by the engineers on the sub's engines and shafts. Chief electrician Ralph Kitterman and two of his senior petty officers, Harry Blundell and Al Kasuga, worked closely with the *Fulton* repairmen during this work. The work was marred by one serious mishap, when a young *Fulton* electrician, Fireman First Class Willard T. Jeffress, was electrocuted on October 24 while calibrating motors on the main control cubicle.

During the repair work, Bill Dillon and many of his fellow crewmen took the chance to go ashore for liberty in watch sections.

The smell of dead bodies from the recent fighting still permeated the air. Around the island, there was ample evidence of the massive ship bombardments and aerial bombings that had leveled many of the structures. "The only thing left standing was a tall smokestack," Walkup recalled. "Stricken landing craft were scattered all over a lagoon, which had been used as a landing area."[21]

Ashore, the crew found that most of the island's native people had been relocated to the top of a small mountain. Most of the dead had been buried, but the bodies of slain Japanese in destroyed bunkers were a grim reminder of the realities of war. The men found the island swarming with flies, but were happy to also find that Saipan's vast frog population was doing its best to eradicate many of the pesky things. Young and foolish, Bill Dillon and several of his buddies strapped on their Colt .45s and decided to go hiking up into the hills in search of any remaining Japanese soldiers. Although they encountered their share of bodies, Dillon was later relieved that "we didn't see any Japs. I don't know what we would have done if we saw any."

On October 28, *Sailfish* departed Saipan with *Parche* and *Pomfret* for a coordinated wolf pack patrol. The new pack would be under direction of Commander Red Ramage on *Parche* and was dubbed "Red's Rowdies." But only one hour out from port, *Sailfish*'s port bearing shaft failed. Ward returned to Tanapag Harbor to allow the *Fulton* crew to get both shafts operating again. *Sailfish* was underway again on October 29, releasing her escort *PGM-9* in late afternoon.

Ward made good speed to catch up with his Red's Rowdies pack mates, and he was in his assigned patrol area by November 2. At 2110, his radio gang received a coded message that *Pomfret* was in contact with a seven-ship convoy seven miles northwest of Sabtang Island. By the early minutes of November 3, *Parche* reported that she was in contact with the convoy. At 0304, *Sailfish* picked up the enemy ships at fifteen thousand yards, and Ward sent notice to his wolf pack commander that he was closing to attack.

In the control room, Joe Sahaj, the diving officer, was standing near plotting officers Craig Hertsgaard and Shorty Evans at the small desk. Pat Murphy was now Ward's assistant approach officer, with Dave Gaston running the TDC with assistant Jim Woody. The battle stations officer of the deck was Stan Cowin, while Murphy helped manage the conning tower and control room crews.

The wildly swerving convoy presented its challenges to Ward, and at 0350, Bill Dillon reported that his SJ radar had gone out of commission. Operating at radar depth, Ward waited as the convoy escorts approached. By 0401, two of the destroyers swung toward the position of his periscope, leaving him to assume he had been detected. Ward had already ordered the forward torpedo room doors opened, so he commenced firing all four tubes a minute later from 2,700 yards. *Sailfish* went deep to evade, and four minutes later, the first of seven explosions was heard.

Ward deemed them depth charges by the nature of their sound and the fact that two were close enough to part the causing cables on his No. 2 periscope and flood the rudder angle indicator on the bridge. It had been a long shot to even fire on these vessels. "The decision to fire using the meager data available was based on the 'bird in hand' theory, and a fervent hope that four fish with small gyros and a small target angle would overcome the deficiency in data," he admitted.[22]

Sailfish patrolled south of Sabtang Island the following day. Ward radioed Commander Ramage that he believed Japanese freighters had anchored there for the night. On the morning of November 4, his hunch proved correct. His periscope watch found two small *Chidori*-class patrol boats, two *Wakatake*-class destroyers, and three other patrol boats, all on various courses and all employing echo ranging at slow speed. Ward presumed this to be a hunter-killer group that was sweeping the area for submarines before the anchored freighters got underway.[23]

By early afternoon, Ward sighted the smoke of the freighters as they lay anchored. As he continued to wait them out, a pair of destroyers was spotted, and the *Sailfish* crew was called to battle stations. Throughout the boat, there was a rush of adrenaline stronger than that experienced in most prior attacks. The Old Man was lining up to punch at a killer pack, and repercussions would be expected if he drew blood. In each compartment, the sailor on the headphones whispered the orders being relayed by talker Bud Pike to his eager listeners.

At 1600, *Sailfish* fired all four forward tubes at the easternmost destroyer, from a range of 1,600 yards. Using a slight spread with three-foot depth settings, Ward motioned to Troy Ray to lower the scope as he ordered Dave Gaston and Jim Woody on the TDC to shift to Mark 18 torpedoes in preparation for firing at the western destroyer.

Ward returned to the scope at 1601 in time to see his first torpedo hit the destroyer "and blow everything aft of his number two stack sky high." He immediately swung his periscope onto the second destroyer and put the setup into the TDC. The destroyer was swinging hard, rapidly decreasing the angle on the bow toward zero, so Ward held check. During these seconds, his crew heard a second explosion as another of their torpedoes was believed to slam into the first destroyer.

Analysis by historian Anthony Tully shows *Sailfish*'s November 4 victim to have been the Japanese destroyer *Harukaze*. A torpedo struck her port side aft around frame 155, shattering her fantail. Her shafts were left dangling downward and *Harukaze* went dead in the water, shipping water through her shaft alley.[24]

The second destroyer steadied on a course that presented a 10-degree angle on the bow, which headed him toward his stricken cohort, *Harukaze*. After checking the bearings several times with his TDC operators, Ward ordered the firing of three aft Mark 18 torpedoes from a range of 2,700 yards. During the final setup and launching of these war fish, *Sailfish* had been bracketed by somewhere between six and ten bombs close aboard from Japanese aircraft that had apparently spotted the American submarine's periscope.

"Take her deep!" Ward called. "Rig for silent running."

As *Sailfish* started down, additional aircraft bombs or depth charges began exploding. Men were thrown from their feet and loose equipment slammed into bulkheads and bodies. Then Bud Pike relayed an urgent call from Chief Bill Gray's after torpedo room: "Fire in the after torpedo room!"

One of the aircraft bombs had forced open the inboard poppet vent valve on Tube No. 7 in the after room about fifteen seconds after that tube had been fired. "The water streamed through the six-inch pipe in rushing volumes," recalled motormac John Good. The vent could not be closed, but the master inboard vent and the outer door were immediately shut when water was seen entering the torpedo room. At the time of the initial flooding, *Sailfish* was in a 5-degree dive, which had forced all the water past the after bilges, flooding the forward end of the room to a depth of six inches above the deck.[25]

The water quickly rose above the electric torpedo charging panel, located about four inches off the deck on the forward bulkhead, and short-circuited the panel. "A bright flash blazed out and rubber-burning stench filled the compartment with huge billows of black smoke," Good remembered. The fire was quickly stopped by men who rushed in with fire extinguishers and by an electrician's swift pulling of the supply circuit in the maneuvering room.

At 1605, Ward's sound operators heard a torpedo explosion in the second destroyer that perfectly matched with the estimated time of run. In a matter of minutes, the fire was put out and *Sailfish* was no longer taking in water, but considerable ocean water had flooded in aft, dragging the boat downward and causing a large up angle. *Sailfish*'s nose was heading for the surface.

Over the 1MC, Ward ordered all spare men to race forward to help bring the bow down, and shouted for full reverse speed on the screws. A mad stampede ensued as watertight doors were opened and some three dozen officers and men sprinted through the hatches for the forward torpedo room. In the after battery compartment, talker Allen Batts dashed out of his pantry still wearing his headset and was jerked to the deck by its extension cord. With nearly five thousand pounds of human ballast jamming into the forward torpedo room, the bodies pressed forward of the torpedo racks in a mass of humanity, *Sailfish*'s severe rise was quickly checked. "Caught her with 25 degrees up angle at 170 feet," Ward logged. "Knew we had a fire and were flooding aft, but everybody took it in stride as though it were an everyday occurrence."[26]

At 1610, Johnson reported another heavy explosion on the bearing of the second Japanese destroyer, while diving officer Joe Sahaj battled to get the boat back under control. At silent running and in near darkness, the sailors on the bow and stern planes sweated profusely as they guided the large steel wheels that controlled the diving planes. Sound operators continued to report on the presence of screws above from the remaining hunter-killer warships.

With the fire and the near broaching of the boat under control, Ward called for all spare men to help correct the ballast. "All buckets were taken to the after torpedo room and a human chain formed, reaching to the forward torpedo room," Good recalled. "Filled buckets of water passed hands the length of the submarine." The excess water was dumped into the forward washroom, where it drained into the No. 1 sanitary tank, and into the forward torpedo room bilges. The net effect gradually brought the boat to a more level trim. Ward's engineers also pumped from the after trim tanks to the negative tanks and blew enough from negative to compensate for the added weight.[27]

During this forty-five-minute period, the sound operators reported five different sets of light screws from Japanese patrol boats pinging for their boat. At times when the pinging was weaker, Ward allowed both torpedo rooms to begin quietly reloading their tubes. Men dripped with sweat and trousers clung to wet skin from sloshed buckets of water. The acrid stench of burned-rubber smoke hung in the air as the heat continued to rise through the boat, whose air-conditioning had been shut down during silent running. "Condensation dripped from the overhead lines or rolled down the glistening bulkheads," Good remembered. "Breathing became heavy and difficult." As the excitement died down, unnecessary men were allowed to crawl into their bunks to conserve oxygen.[28]

By 1900, Joe Mendel's room reported all four forward tubes reloaded. Aft, Bill Gray and his gang could load only one Mark 18 torpedo due to the boat's trim and the noise that would have been required to shift the excess water that had collected. Johnson and Dillon's sonar team reported that five ships were still pinging, one apparently stopped and four others moving about in the distance. "Moonrise is at 2054 and the battery is close to flat, so we have to get up soon," Ward logged.[29]

Sailfish eased up to radar depth at 1911. Dillon found the nearest patrol boat to be at 6,500 yards, so Ward changed course to put it astern and brought his boat to the surface two minutes later. "The sudden onrush of fresh air into the boat miraculously revived the physically and mentally distraught men," Good recalled. Although the fresh air brought new energy, the crew was far from out of the woods. The PPI scope in the conning tower showed five different Japanese warships, with ranges from 6,900 yards to 13,400 yards. The electricians began jamming a charge into *Sailfish*'s depleted batteries while their skipper aimed for the largest gap in enemy targets on the PPI screen.[30]

The circle began tightening at 1930, so Ward ordered flank speed on all four engines to race out of harm's way. His crew had thoroughly stirred up a hornet's nest, and he simply did not have the battery power for another long, submerged assault on this killer group for the time being. During the next half hour, the dimly visible silhouettes of the last three Japanese vessels slowly disappeared from view topside. By 2015, radar contact had faded out.

According to historian Anthony Tully, *Harukaze* had been crippled by *Sailfish*'s strike. After its attack on the American submarine, *Patrol Boat No. 38* took *Harukaze* in tow to Takao, arriving at noon the next day, November 5. *Harukaze* had suffered sixty-seven sailors killed or missing and another eighteen severely wounded. The destroyer was later towed to Mako, and repairs would continue slowly. It was not until March 1945 that *Harukaze* was able to steam under her own power back to Sasebo, Japan. *Sailfish*'s strike had essentially ensured that she never served in an essential offensive role again during the war.[31]

In celebration of sinking one destroyer and crippling another, Ward approved pharmacist's mate Doc Turver to make the rounds through the boat, passing out shots of medicinal brandy to all willing participants.

Sailfish crew members continued charging her batteries, effecting repairs, and pumping out bilges from the earlier flooding mishap.

Shortly before midnight, Ward had his diving officer complete a quick trim dive to ensure that all was in order. The after torpedo room reported their situation back to normal, and all four tubes had been reloaded. The most interesting sidebar to the attack on the hunter-killer group occurred as the topside watch made a sweep of *Sailfish*'s upper works to inspect the damage from the Japanese aerial bombs and depth charges.

They found attached to the forecastle a Japanese G-string and, on the forward 20mm gun, a pair of Japanese pants. "We hereby claim to be the first submarine to not only catch a Jap with his pants down but also to actually take them off," Ward wrote. One sailor proposed to Ward that their boat should return to port with the Japanese trousers flying as a pennant.[32]

* * *

When *Sailfish* surfaced on the evening of November 9, the seas had grown heavy, and the sub began riding out a moderate typhoon. *Sailfish* pitched and rolled to the point that standing watch topside was hazardous. During the worst of the storm, Commander Ward lashed himself to the bridge. Before going topside, he ordered chief of the watch Montie Walkup in the control room to dive the boat if, in his judgment, the ship was going to turn over. *A brave and dedicated man,* thought Walkup.[33]

At one point, a giant wave passed over *Sailfish*. With the main induction shut and only a small auxiliary motor running, the only air came through the conning tower hatch. Considerable water poured through the open hatch, but the engineers below were able to maintain depth control by running their drain pump continuously. Ward was eventually forced to take his boat to a hundred fifty feet to ride out the storm the next day, as the eye of the typhoon barreled over them during the morning hours.

By that evening, the worst of the storm had passed and the boat returned to the surface. For the first time in many hours, the crew was able to relax long enough to enjoy a meal. Just before dawn on November 11, navigator Pat Murphy and Troy Ray were able to take their first navigational fix in forty-six hours.

Hours later, at 1035, Joe Mendel's forward gang was performing routine maintenance on their torpedoes. During this process, the starting lever on one torpedo was tripped, causing it to begin running in its tube. Mendel immediately seated the starting piston, but before he shut it down, a considerable amount of smoke was carried into the boat. Officer of the deck Dave Gaston was forced to surface the boat for an hour to draw out the choking smoke, which had permeated into all compartments.[34]

Red's Rowdies rendezvoused during the early-morning hours of November 12 to exchange orders from the pack commander. The following evening, the three submarines received a contact from *Gunnel* that enemy warships were headed north into their area. *Parche*, *Pomfret*, and *Sailfish* searched diligently but were unable to obtain attack positions. Commander Ward found only small patrol boats on November 14, and made an attempt to close SJ radar targets during the early-morning hours of November 15. But his tracking team was unable to obtain visuals on these small ships, which appeared to be employing radar jamming. "They may be Jap submarines," Ward surmised.[35]

During the week that followed, *Sailfish* evaded various aircraft contacts and fought heavy seas while searching for targets worthy of her remaining torpedoes. On November 22, the boat was still struggling to reach her new patrol area, due to heavy seas and consequent slow speed. The following day, ComSubPac sent word to Ward authorizing him to extend his patrol with *Pomfret*, with *Parche* having been ordered back to Midway for a refit.

Sailfish celebrated Thanksgiving Day on November 23 at sea on patrol. "We had no chicken today, as word has been given the commissary to ease up on chow," John Good wrote in his journal. "We are slowly running out of certain commodities; butter today. Our meals show signs of this condition." By the following day, the cooks had run out of salt. The sodium chloride tablets used by Doc Turver for perspiring individuals were ground up in the galley's meat grinder for use in the saltshakers. In return for commissary officer Dave Gaston having his cooks ration the food supplies, Commander Ward spread the word that *Sailfish* would be back in Oahu by Christmas Day, and that all hands would enjoy a hearty dinner together.[36]

Pomfret and *Sailfish* made contact with a convoy during the early evening of November 24 and made their approaches, exchanging frequent update reports. With a three-quarter moon, visibility was excellent, and Ward soon found that he had four freighters, plus escorts, making about 7 knots' speed. With *Pomfret* visible on radar at 7,750 yards, Ward informed his fellow submarine crew of his position, and the two skippers decided *Sailfish* would attack first.[37]

As Ward set up to fire, one of the convoy's escorts changed direction and headed toward *Sailfish*'s periscope. Ward fired three torpedoes down the throat of the incoming ship. Minutes later, the first torpedo hit and exploded with a bright yellow flash. Eight seconds after that, another torpedo was heard to hit. Radar operator Bill Dillon announced that the target warship had disappeared from his screen, as the approach party verified the timing of the hits to coincide with the length of the torpedo runs. On the bridge, Ward could see no visible damage to the Japanese destroyer charging toward his submarine.[38]

Gun blasts fountained the water near *Sailfish*. Ward made a crash dive to escape the charging destroyer. Two patterns of three depth charges each erupted close above *Sailfish*, forcing her down faster but causing no serious damage. Joe Sahaj's diving team managed to check the boat's rapid plunge at 345 feet and thereafter leveled her off at three hundred feet. Ward rigged for silent running and passed the word for only eighty turns on both shafts to slowly clear the scene. During the next twenty minutes, three different sets of screws were audible as the Japanese scoured the ocean with pinging in an effort to locate *Sailfish*.

Each time *Sailfish* eased up for a periscope observation during the next two hours, one of the Japanese warships raced in to attack her. The worst of the enemy's depth charges came at 2221, when a well-executed pattern of fifteen ash cans exploded directly above and uncomfortably close. "These charges jarred the boat considerably, opening valves, knocking the hands off four gauges, breaking a few light bulbs, and chipping cork and paint," Ward wrote.[39]

For motormac John Good, these were "the loudest and worst charges any of us have ever heard or felt. They came fast and furious upon us." The force of the blasts shoved *Sailfish* downward, so the diving team leveled her off at three hundred twenty feet, making efforts to put the attacker astern once and for all. At 2249, another series of tooth shakers commenced erupting in groups of three. Four such volleys, seemingly closer than the previous drops, slammed the boat sideways and sent men tumbling as light bulbs shattered.[40]

Motormacs and firemen worked as quietly as possible to stop the fresh leaks that sprang out. As the minutes ticked by, the air in the boat grew hot and stuffy. Damp with perspiration, those who needed to move across the slick decks did so in drenched undershorts. Only emergency lights burned as Doc Turver moved through the boat to distribute CO_2 absorbent in each watertight compartment to help alleviate headaches.

The severe depth charge attack took its toll on some, but skipper Bob Ward made the rounds through the boat to reassure his crew. Throttleman James Roberson, on duty in the engine room, felt Ward pat him on the shoulder and ask, "How are you son? Are you alright?"[41]

"Yeah, I'm doing fine, Captain," he said.

"Well, it's all right to be scared," Ward said. "I'm scared, too."

Such little events went a long way to humanize the skipper to his men. "He was a great guy," Roberson recalled. "He was hard! But he knew what he was doing. I'd follow him anywhere."[42]

By 2330, the Japanese warship was hanging on with impressive ability. "This fellow has apparently been to sound school," wrote Ward. "Am not sure we haven't an oil slick or something helping this fellow stay on us."[43]

Torpedoman Ray Bunt was sweating out the attack in the forward torpedo room. "You could hear the screws through the ship getting louder, louder, and finally right over our head," he recalled. "Our hearts were all doing double-time, but we were helpless." At one point, Bunt thought, *How much longer can this go on? If he is going to get us, do it now, and get it over with. Don't make it so drawn out.* He felt that he and his fellow crewmen "were living in hell down there."[44]

Confounding Ward's efforts to shake the attacker, his boat was experiencing its fair share of problems. The starboard sound head training gears had gone out of commission from the explosions, and the port sound head could be trained only by hand. *Sailfish*'s rudder jams were very noisy, the port shaft had a pronounced chirp above 80 rpm, and the No. 4 motor was producing a slight click. Ward was forced to use his rudder sparingly while heading submerged northeast, running on only sixty turns with the port screw and seventy turns on the starboard screw.

Finally, at 0135—after six hours of tense counterattacks—Johnson's sonar gang reported no more pinging from above. Both periscope motor hoists were out of commission, but Ward decided at 0157 that he would have to take his chances. "We surfaced, depending on our sound equipment and praying," recalled John Good. "We put the radar up and the skipper whispered, 'All clear,' and we slowly and quietly broke surface to make our way the hell out of there."[45]

* * *

Upon surfacing, Ward found that his diving alarm, the rudder angle indicator, and other equipment had been knocked out of commission during the violent attacks. He quickly headed on all four main engines toward the east. The *Sailfish* crew had been at battle stations since 1830 the previous evening, and all hands had missed evening chow. The cooks set to work cranking out food while emergency repairs were made.

After completing further inspections, Ward became convinced that it was time to call a halt to his patrol. "Do not believe our mediocre condition warrants completing the remaining three days of the patrol extension granted to us," he wrote. At 2230, he had Craig Hertsgaard's radio gang send a message to Admiral Lockwood and to *Pomfret* alerting both that *Sailfish* was returning to base.[46]

Sailfish experienced heavy aerial traffic during the next week en route back to Midway. Ward conducted training dives, field day cleanings, and drills, while new hands worked on their qualification notebooks. On Sunday, December 3, Ward finally allowed his cooks to serve a proper, although belated, Thanksgiving dinner of turkey, dressing, nuts, and a shot of brandy.[47]

Upon crossing the 180th meridian on December 7, *Sailfish* repeated the date to return to the proper time zone and arrived in Midway on the second December 7 at 0813—three years to the day since the Japanese surprise attack. The boat moored at Midway's Berth Sail-Three, wrapping up her twelfth war patrol. After taking on fuel and provisions, *Sailfish* was underway again for Pearl Harbor, in company with pack mate *Pomfret*.

Bill Dillon wondered if the damage incurred by *Sailfish* on this patrol would be enough to send her back Stateside for a proper overhaul. Two years had passed since he had entered sub school at New London in late 1942. Dillon was now the boat's most experienced radar operator. He had high hopes of seeing his family again, and his girlfriend, Janet. After five runs in the war zone, he was beginning to feel like he was living on borrowed time.

EIGHTEEN

The Last Nine Months

Pale-skinned motormacs, standing topside for the first time in weeks, strained to see in the blinding sunlight. It was December 11 as *Sailfish* steamed into Pearl Harbor under clear skies, seventy-five days since her departure from Midway at the beginning of her twelfth patrol. She had covered 14,269 nautical miles in that time and had burned 185,434 gallons of fuel. Dozens of bags of mail awaited the crew, who were soon sprawled out on deck reading letters and opening early Christmas packages. While the boat took on provisions and was refueled, the men were taken ashore for routine physicals, and then they returned to the boat for crew photos.

The following morning, the men were hustled off to the Royal Hawaiian, where they expected the usual two weeks of rest before preparing for another patrol. "We had no idea we were heading back Stateside," recalled Bill Dillon. "We thought we were going back on war patrol, so we really lived it up and trashed the Royal Hawaiian Hotel."

Sailfish's departure from Pearl Harbor came with sweeping personnel changes, particularly in the wardroom. Admiral Charlie Lockwood awarded the Submarine Combat Patrol Insignia on December 20 for the boat's "outstanding" twelfth run, in light of sinking one destroyer, damaging another, conducting two gun attacks, and rescuing a dozen naval aviators. Due to the availability of so many newer-class boats, most sporting more powerful deck guns and more torpedo tubes, ComSubPac made a difficult choice. Once *Sailfish*'s battle damage was repaired, he decreed that *Sailfish* would proceed to the Atlantic to serve as a training boat. "Her illustrious combat record will long be remembered," Lockwood wrote on December 21.[1]

Leaving the boat for new assignments from Pearl Harbor were skipper Bob Ward, Shorty Evans, Tom Smith, Ed Berghausen, and Dave Gaston. To fill Ward's shoes, Lockwood selected Lieutenant Commander Lincoln Marcy, a 1939 Academy graduate from Massachusetts who had made ten war patrols on *Searaven* and *Ronquil.* Marcy reported on board on December 16, allowing several days for him to learn the boat with his predecessor. The crew was lined up on deck at 1000 on December 20 to receive their latest Submarine Combat Patrol Insignia pins and to witness the official passing of command of the vessel from Ward to Marcy.

Radarman Dillon, for one, was pleased to learn that his skipper had orders to take command of a newer submarine. "While we were glad for Captain Ward to get a new boat, we were also sorely disappointed," Dillon recalled. "He was always a strict disciplinarian, but did it ever pay off for us." When he heard that a thirteenth war patrol was not in the cards for *Sailfish*, Dillon was equally grateful and saddened. He relished the chance for liberty back in the States, but felt equal dismay that his boat's time of fighting was complete. Dillon had no bonds with new skipper Marcy. "He had one hell of a job trying to fill Ward's shoes."[2]

On December 26, the sub base band cranked out popular tunes such as "Auld Lang Syne" as *Sailfish* backed away from Pier Sail-Three at Pearl Harbor. Motormac John Good watched his former skipper Ward tearfully observing his boat's exodus. "Several of us who were on deck saluted our skipper in farewell, and he returned our salute," said Good.[3]

Sailfish proceeded through the Panama Canal en route to the Atlantic, stopping for a day and night in Panama City to allow the crew to drink in the local bars. Good, who had received word of his promotion to motor machinist's mate first class on January 12, was tossed into the canal by his shipmates, in spite of his pleas of "I can't swim!" Only when Good failed to resurface did shipmates Al Kasuga, Ray Bunt, and Bill Schilling dive in to save him amid much laughter.[4]

Dillon and his forward torpedo room companions enjoyed being able to "let it all out" during their time in Panama. "Many of us went to the highest point of the *Sailfish* and dove into the canal," he recalled. *Sailfish* continued her journey through Panama's locks the following morning. When their boat reached New London, Connecticut, on January 26, the balmy temperatures in the seventies they had enjoyed at Hawaii had been replaced by brisk, subfreezing air. For the next four and a half months, *Sailfish* would operate as a training submarine for the school at New London, where the majority of her men had once learned the ropes. They had now come full circle, being seasoned hands helping to break in classes of fresh greenhorns.

During this time, former skipper Bob Ward was at work helping to bring a new boat, *Sea Leopard*, into commission at the nearby Portsmouth navy yard. His *Tench*-class fleet boat was launched on March 2, 1945. As final construction continued through late March and early April, Ward poached liberally from the crew of his former command and received on board eleven of his former *Sailfish* men.

Those eager to leave their training boat in favor of more war in the Pacific included electrician Al Kasuga, steward Killraine Newton, baker Austin Sundman, Doc Turver, gunner Frank Mullen, and torpedoman Ray Bunt. In addition, Ward brought on board chief electrician Gerry McLees, one of the *Squalus* survivors who had served on *Sailfish* earlier in the war. *Sea Leopard* was placed into commission at 1130 on Monday, June 11, 1945, at the U.S. Navy Yard in Portsmouth.

By that date, Lieutenant Commander Marcy's *Sailfish* had received a special new training assignment and put to sea from New London on June 4. Seasoned officers Pat Murphy and Joe Sahaj, each having served stints as exec, had been rotated to other boats. *Sailfish*'s new duty was to serve in Guantánamo Bay, Cuba, as a training vessel for Italian sailors who were learning about diesel engines and a new snorkel device for extended periods of submergence.

Bill Dillon returned to the boat narrowly in time for its departure for Cuba. He had departed New London early on Friday, June 1, hoping to make it back to Turtle Creek, Pennsylvania, in time for his girlfriend's graduation ceremonies from high school that afternoon. After hitchhiking nearly five hundred miles, Dillon arrived late, borrowed his future father-in-law's vehicle, and raced to the school, only to find that the ceremonies had ended. He found Janet Kugel that evening and relished his time with her during the next forty-eight hours. He returned to *Sailfish* late Sunday evening, far past the limits of his leave. Lieutenant Commander Marcy confined Dillon to the boat after a captain's mast, but with the voyage to Cuba only hours away, the seasoned radar operator took his "punishment" in stride.

During the first week of August 1945, events were shaping up that would soon negate the need for *Sailfish* as a Cuban training boat. On August 6, a U.S. Army B-29 bomber named *Enola Gay* dropped an atomic bomb on the Japanese city of Hiroshima that killed or wounded two-thirds of the immediate population and destroyed nearly seventy percent of Hiroshima's buildings. President Harry Truman warned Japan to accept surrender terms or "expect a rain of ruin from the air, the like of which has never been seen on this earth."[5]

By August 9, *Sailfish* was underway from Cuba back for the East Coast, due to the events that were unfolding. "We received word about an atomic bomb being dropped on Japan," recalled yeoman Bud Pike. "None of us had any idea what it was all about." That same day, another atomic bomb, nicknamed "Fat Man," was dropped on Nagasaki, resulting in tens of thousands of additional deaths. By the following day, Emperor Hirohito made the decision that Japan must accept terms of surrender. One of the few blessings made possible by the unprecedented atomic bombing of Japan was that survival was afforded to thousands of long-suffering Allied prisoners of war—who had been warned of their own execution should America ever begin an invasion of the Japanese mainland.[6]

★ ★ ★

For George Rocek, January 26, 1945, marked his one-year anniversary of mining labor at Ashio prisoner of war camp 9-B. Eleven of his *Sculpin* shipmates had endured the same twelve months of hell at Ashio, where they had been joined in mid-July 1944 by another eight former *Sculpin* enlisted men.

They were all in pitiful condition. By early February, two Ashio prisoners had died. The camp commandant, Lieutenant Numajiri—called "the Goat" by his inmates—showed little concern. He called them out one morning into the snow-covered compound yard for inspection, to see who was still physically able to return to the mine. "We were naked and told to do six knee bends," Rocek recalled. "From this, he designated about thirty men that were to work."[7]

One of the inmates who perished at Ashio collapsed beside Ed Keller. "I carried him on my shoulders coming out of the mine," recalled Keller, who chastised the dying man for continually trading his food rations for cigarettes. "I had the compassion to carry him, but I was very angry that he was dying." As the men were paraded for work the following day, Keller felt guilty for scolding the man, whose body lay on a rickshaw for transport to the local crematorium.[8]

Gunner John Rourke continued to work even after a battle with dysentery left him with crippled feet. He tried complaining to one of the "honchos"—the Japanese civilian mine bosses—that he was too weak to push mine cars onto the elevator. "The Jap civilian replied that I was not weak, and then beat me with his fists about the face and body, knocking me to the ground," Rourke recalled.[9]

Those not assigned to the mine continued working at the local copper smelter or on camp duties. Men who were injured were treated by Dr. Katoku at the Ashio hospital. *Sculpin* electrician Eldon Wright, who had suffered a hernia while mucking ore, was given burn treatments with a material resembling spun glass by Katoku. "This substance would be lighted and it would burn slowly," recalled Wright. Over a period of twenty days, the burn treatment resulted in festering sores, "each approximately the size of a twenty-five-cent piece," on Wright's upper back.[10]

Moon Rocek had burn scars on his legs from the odd treatment from the doctor for the shrapnel wounds he suffered during the loss of his submarine. He returned to the mine, where he had worked his way into a driller's position after a year of mucking ore. Determined to sabotage the Japanese mining efforts, he and his fellow miners poured carbide powder into the air drills when their guards were not paying attention to them. "The drill would work for a short time, and then was put out of commission," Rocek recalled. "We screwed them as best we could."[11]

During the spring of 1945, the Japanese allowed distribution of some Red Cross items to the prisoners, although the guards often pilfered many of the items first for their own consumption. The occasional soybeans, fish heads, and shark entrails added to the daily rice allotment left many of the POWs longing for food they had once known. Keller resorted to compiling little booklets of his favorite dishes, including full recipes for maple peanut ice cream, fruit salad Alaska, and main courses.[12]

Rocek and another inmate had the satisfaction of stealing a Red Cross food package from camp commandant Numajiri's room. They hid the package under a floorboard in the outhouse stall, ate from it each night, and later watched the Japanese ransack their whole camp days later, looking for the items. Beatings continued for the smallest of incidents. *Sculpin* ship's cook Andy Anderson was beaten in the head with a stick of firewood for preparing special food in the kitchen for inmates who could not consume the regular diet.[13]

By July 1945, the Ashio prisoners were wasting away at an alarming rate. Torpedoman Herb Thomas, normally weighing a hundred fifty pounds, had dropped forty pounds. Shipmate Paul Murphy had withered from a hefty hundred eighty pounds down to a mere hundred ten pounds. Teenage sailor Mike Gorman, 156 pounds in 1943, was a mere ninety-four pounds by the end of summer.

Fortunately for them, the Allied effort to end the war took a drastic turn with the atomic bombs dropped on Hiroshima and Nagasaki. Ed Keller was stunned to hear from a Japanese civilian guard that one bomb had destroyed a whole city. Bill Cooper and Keller narrowly escaped their own deaths in the mine the day before Japan surrendered when a large rock came loose and tons of rocks crashed down, cutting in two the hose that led to their drill. Cooper remembered another drill on the other side of the mine and they went to get it. While they were in the process of locating the second drill, the rest of their work area caved in, buried their drill gun, and effectively ended their labor. "I guess my mother's prayers brought me through the whole thing," Cooper recalled.[14]

The following day, August 15, the prisoners in the mine were ordered to quit working at noon and board a truck back to camp. Slowly, the *Sculpin* men learned that the war had ended and that the Allies were landing in Japan to liberate the prisoner camps. Commandant Numajiri began distributing long-withheld Red Cross packages, and his guards ordered the POWs to paint twenty-foot-tall "PW" letters on the roof of their barracks. "The old guards quickly disappeared from camp, and they were replaced by new ones, who were just as nice as they could be," Cooper recalled.[15]

On August 25, American fighter pilots swooped in over the Ashio camp, having spotted the large "PW" painted on the roof. The Hellcat pilots roared over the compound, dumping candy, cigarettes, provisions, and even a note that liberators were on their way and would arrive soon. During the next several days, B-29s and carrier planes dropped crates of provisions for the Ashio prisoners.

Cliff Kuykendall, the lone survivor from the submarine *Tullibee*, was greatly relieved, as he had been told that all prisoners would be executed if America ever invaded Japan. "The atomic bombs saved my life and everyone else's," he reflected. In a letter he was allowed to write to his family back in Texas on August 31, Kuykendall noted the frequent food drops, adding, "We are certainly a happy bunch of fellows."[16]

On September 5, more than two hundred fifty American, Dutch, and British survivors of the Ashio mining camp were loaded into train cars and moved south toward the port of Yokohama. Moon Rocek, down from half his former weight to about ninety-five pounds, was happy to see two beautiful U.S. Army nurses standing at the terminal, handing out cigarettes and candy bars. The former prisoners were moved by bus to Yokohama's main wharf area, where they were fed as much as they could stomach, treated, and sorted for eventual transportation back home. At the naval base, the twenty *Sculpin* men were reunited with Lieutenant George Brown, newly arrived from another prison camp where he had been held for months.[17]

Some were fortunate enough to secure flights out. Among them were Brown, Cooper, and *S-44*'s Tony Duva. While waiting for his flight, Cooper sifted through a Japanese hangar and collected a Japanese rifle and bayonet as souvenirs. When he reached Pearl Harbor, he was treated to a steak dinner in officers' country and was given the Purple Heart and five hundred dollars in back pay for his homeward journey. Vice Admiral Lockwood cornered Cooper and asked him about the seven *Sculpin* survivors.[18]

"No, there's twenty-one of us," Cooper corrected the admiral. "I've got a list of everybody and their addresses."

Many of Cooper's shipmates—including Keller, Rocek, Joe Baker, and Mike Gorman—boarded the hospital ship *Ozark* (LSV-2) on September 8 for passage from Yokohama. On September 12, *Ozark* reached Guam, where intelligence officers took their first statements from the submarine survivors whose boats had once been declared "overdue and presumed lost." From Guam, the freed men traveled to Pearl Harbor for a brief layover. When their ship finally reached San Francisco on October 2, the submariners were the first to leave the ship. The Submarine Force had individual cars, with an officer assigned to each returning submariner. They were carried to a hotel for a large welcome dinner. "We were all impressed and proud to be submariners, and knew that we were not forgotten," Rocek recalled.[19]

Seven U.S. submarines of the fifty-two boats lost in World War II had survivors picked up by the Japanese. Of 196 men captured, 158 American submariners would survive their internment in Japan. None of the men captured from *Robalo* survived, but officers and men from six other U.S. boats ultimately returned to their homes in 1945. This total included two enlisted men from *S-44*, one from *Tullibee*, nine officers and men from *Tang*, the majority of the *Grenadier* and *Perch* crews, and twenty-one from *Sculpin*.[20]

Rocek was treated at the Oak Knoll Hospital and then released to take a train cross-country to his home in Chicago. He was met by his sister in a heart-wrenching reunion complete with many tears of joy. He soon took an elevated train from Chicago to Cicero and walked into his father's tailor shop. His mother greeted him in tears as James gazed at his son's rail-thin body, but for Moon Rocek, his journey through hell had ended.[21]

During the latter weeks of October 1945, many other *Sculpin* survivors returned to their homes to greet families who were equally overjoyed and in some cases shocked. From San Francisco, fireman Joe Baker called back home to Boston to talk with his parents, only to find that they had never even been informed that he was a POW. Upon taking his phone call, his mother fainted when she heard his voice. His younger sister angrily snatched up the phone and was equally dumbfounded to learn that her brother was indeed alive. "My name had already been put on the town memorial as lost in war," Baker recalled. "It was quite a shock for her."[22]

During the same weeks that newly returned *Sculpin* survivors made their way home, the final days of her sister submarine, *Sailfish*, were coming to a close.

* * *

Sailfish had departed from Cuba on August 9, 1945, the day the second atomic bomb was dropped on Japan. Her return to the East Coast was slowed by severe weather. "We got caught off Cape Hatteras in a storm that was so rough it almost tipped the boat over," Bud Pike recalled. "We had to go down 100 feet to get away from the seas."[23]

The weathered submarine sailed into the Philadelphia Navy Yard on August 14, the date declared by the U.S. as V-J Day, or "Victory over Japan Day." Harbor sirens, church bells in town, and whistles from nearby factories pierced the air as *Sailfish* docked on the afternoon that the war ended in the Pacific Theater. The crew was soon dismissed for leave ashore, where they proceeded to get drunk and revel with civilians and servicemen in the streets of downtown Philadelphia. "Everyone was given liberty, and I spent that night on the streets of Philadelphia getting hugged and kissed," Pike remembered.

Six weeks later, *Sailfish* departed Philadelphia on October 1 for her final voyage up the Atlantic Coast. She was destined for Portsmouth, New Hampshire, where the *Squalus* story had begun six years earlier with great tragedy. Dubbed "ghost ship" by some and "ill-fated" by others, *Sailfish* had covered more than 192,000 miles at sea and a dozen war patrols. Raised from the depths, she had survived aerial attacks and depth charges, and she had been the first U.S. submarine to sink a Japanese aircraft carrier. She had earned the Presidential Unit Citation and carved a name in the annals of submerged warfare in World War II.[24]

But the history of *Squalus* and *Sailfish* was coming to a close, as the crew readied their beloved vessel for decommissioning ceremonies. By this date, there remained only sixteen crewmen who had been on board *Sailfish* for her attack on *Chuyo* nearly two years prior: Donald Bowers, Elmer Charlton, Bill Dillon, John Good, Edwin James, Bob Kempf, Marion Lohmeier, Larry Macek, Philip Makley, Lewis McCarty, Bud Pike, Henry Robertson, Robert Smail, Harry Tonden, Lester Warburton, and Bernard Williams. Of them, only McCarty had been with the boat since the start of the war and made eleven of her twelve patrols.

Sailfish spent two days traveling past New London and the New England coast to reach Portsmouth. She sailed past the Isles of Shoals, where *Squalus* had gone down in 1939, and toward the mouth of the Piscataqua River; she was soon docking in the Portsmouth Navy Yard to the cheers of yard workers who welcomed her back to her birthplace. The crew spent the next three weeks preparing the boat for decommissioning, set to take place on Navy Day, October 27, 1945. Tens of thousands of people packed into Portsmouth for the event.

At 1100, her final skipper, Lieutenant Commander Berkley Irving Freeman, conducted one final dive of the boat in the river as the crowd watched. *Sailfish* resurfaced and returned to the dock; then Chief Bill Gray assembled the entire crew on deck for the ceremony. Freeman addressed the crowd, stating that the submarine was "an eternal symbol of what courage, fine workmanship and faith in God and one another can accomplish."[25]

As the boat's commissioning pennant was lowered to end her service, Bill Dillon struggled to fight back his tears. He reflected on the thirty-one months of his life spent on board *Sailfish*. His countless hours of tracking enemy pips on his PPI radar screen, the bone-jarring eruptions of depth charges, and the distant explosions of torpedoes in Japanese shipping seemed a distant memory. Before departing *Sailfish*,

Dillon took the liberty of removing some of his tools from the radio shack, and the ship's clock, which he gave to his son Joe years later.

Dillon's buddy Bud Pike later reflected, "Never did I dream that I would be the last one off that boat." As the crew soon scattered to their next assignments, Yeoman First Class Pike elected to use the service points he had accumulated to be discharged at the Fargo Building in Boston. He had spent three years in the Navy, all but his training periods being in submarines. "I wouldn't trade the opportunity to serve my country for anything in the world," Pike recalled in 2009. "God Bless America, and all those who sailed the seven seas in submarines."[26]

Epilogue

July 2022

Seventy-seven years after the decommissioning, only one *Sailfish* veteran remains who was present at both that 1945 ceremony and on the boat's final five war patrols: Bill "Skip" Dillon. Nearing his ninety-eighth birthday, Dillon still sports a hearty smile on a tanned face that looks decades younger than his true age. He is still full of energy, eager to recount his service accomplishments and how a Great Depression–era high school dropout went on to achieve so much. He is a shining example of the men author Tom Brokaw rightfully dubbed the "Greatest Generation."

In Bill's words, "The Depression instilled almost a fantastic willingness in me to deprive myself of anything wasteful. It provided me with a great personal drive to excel in anything I undertook." He applied that logic throughout his electronics training during World War II. His submarine service taught him his life's trade and provided him with the vision that continuing his education was crucial. But first

Dillon signed on for another two years in the Navy after the war ended. During leave, he married his hometown sweetheart, Janet, on January 5, 1946, in a Catholic church in Swissvale, Pennsylvania, ironically by a Father Dillon. Following his thirty-day leave, Bill reported on board the submarine *Odax* for duty.

He served six months on *Odax* during 1946 before being transferred on September 1 to serve under Commander Bob Ward again on *Sea Leopard*. Dillon remained for a year before electing to retire from naval service to earn his high school GED. He immediately signed up for college and earned an electrical engineering degree in 1951 from the University of Florida. He proceeded to earn his master's degree in systems management while he and Janet were raising their family of seven kids.

After graduation, Dillon spent five years with Western Electric, assigned to work on electronics and guidance systems on U.S. Navy warships in Guantánamo Bay, Cuba, and in the Philadelphia, New London, and Portsmouth Naval Shipyards. On September 8, 1955, Dillon and Janet attended the launching of the second submarine *Sailfish* (SSR-572) in Portsmouth, the same shipyard where his original *Squalus*/*Sailfish* had been built.

Bill then worked in Cape Canaveral, Florida, for the next fourteen years. His initial job was with Pan America/RCA, where he became director of program management; his role was to support the development of launch vehicles and missile tracking systems. Working alongside German aerospace engineer Dr. Wernher von Braun, Dillon was the Eastern Test Range planning director for thirteen downrange tracking stations. He directly supported the Army/Jet Propulsion Laboratory (JPL) launch team under General John Medaris that launched the first U.S. satellite, Explorer 1, into space on January 31, 1958. He was in the blockhouse with the launch team monitoring range support for the tracking system on each of the stations. Dillon was given a cherished replica of the Explorer 1 by JPL for his support of the launch. After the first successful satellite launch, he chalked out hopscotch squares on the floor of the hotel in Melbourne, Florida. "Dr. von Braun and I hopscotched in celebration," Dillon recalled.

He also supported all of the Army Redstone and Jupiter launches, all accomplished under the first U.S. projects to develop space launch systems. Dillon's staff at that time included a large group of knowledgeable engineers and four PhDs.

When Bill left RCA/Pan American after almost seven years, he went to work for the Aerospace Corporation at the same Eastern Test Range. Instead of supporting the Army/JPL organization, he worked directly supporting the U.S. Air Force in developing Air Force launch vehicles. He supported the Titan 2 and the first seventeen launches of Titan 3. Bill's work at the Eastern Test Range included the development of the first electronic checkout on launch vehicles.

All initial tests were evaluated manually, which took up to three days to complete. While with Aerospace, Bill worked with IBM for almost two years developing and installing electronic checkout systems. He convinced IBM to loan the Air Force, at no cost, all of the systems needed to accomplish electronic checkout. This system was called Onboard Computer and Launch Assistance (OCALA). Upon completion of this effort, all equipment was returned to IBM. All launch system checkouts eventually were accomplished electronically, with the results known immediately instead of waiting three or more days![1]

Dillon also became the solid rocket booster manager for the Air Force Titan 3 program at the Eastern Test Range, and he traveled extensively to Huntsville, Alabama, to review and report on the seals involved with stacking its solid rocket boosters. He found that in many cases one of the two seals between the booster stacking had burned through, leaving only one seal to contain the rocket thrust. (It was just such seal issues that later caused the shuttle *Challenger* disaster.)

Bill was then transferred by Aerospace to the Los Angeles Air Force Station located in El Segundo, California, to head a team of twenty-one engineers in the initial development of Near Term (first five years) and Far Term (next five years), which had been requested by Deputy Defense Secretary David Packard in 1970. It was from this request that the initial development of the Global Positioning System (GPS) occurred.

"We worked ninety hours per week, seven days per week, with no overtime pay, on that project," Dillon recalled. "We did it just for the country, and at great sacrifice to our families." The study resulted in five classified documents, one of which Dillon authored himself. "While the GPS idea has been claimed by others, the work we did in developing how it could be accomplished was done by our group," Bill added. "We calculated all of the trajectories in each constellation, how many satellites would be in each constellation, and defined the trajectories and the areas to be covered."

Although busy building his postwar career, Dillon still found time to renew bonds with his former World War II shipmates. During the first five days of August 1979, the first reunion of the *Squalus*/*Sailfish*/*Sculpin* Association was held in Mobile, Alabama; it was organized by two former *Sailfish* yeomen, Bud Pike and Aaron Reese. The veterans were pleased to welcome Rear Admiral Bob Ward, who attended while still recovering from open-heart surgery. When Ward encountered Moon Rocek, the sole American survivor from the carrier *Chuyo*, which his boat had sunk, he embraced Rocek warmly. "There was not a dry eye in the room," recalled *Sailfish* veteran Larry Macek. Nine months later, Ward suffered a fatal heart attack and was buried in the Arlington National Cemetery with full military honors.[2]

Veterans from the three boats would continue annual reunions for more than two decades. On May 23, 1989, a special ceremony was held for these men before the bridge of the *Sailfish* at the Portsmouth Naval Shipyard. Jutting from the earth near them was the conning tower, with the large numerals 192 painted on its side. A crowd numbering more than three hundred was on hand when the boat's eighty-five-year-old former skipper, Rear Admiral Oliver Naquin, spoke at 1000, exactly fifty years to the hour from that day in 1939 when *Squalus* had sunk to the ocean floor. Among those present with Naquin were eight other survivors, including Jud Bland, Lenny de Medeiros, Gene Cravens, and Gerry McLees. Naquin, who would pass away six months after the ceremony, shared how he and the other survivors had lain huddled under blankets, shivering as they tried to keep warm until rescuers brought them to the surface in Swede Momsen's diving bell. "We owe our lives to them," said Naquin. "We were lucky."[3]

During the various reunions of the boats, Skip Dillon had the chance to become close with a number of the *Sculpin* survivors who attended, including Rocek, Bill Cooper, and Ed Keller. After liberation, Keller opted to return to naval service and would spend his next twenty years in submarines before returning to his home state of New Jersey.

Dillon learned that Cooper had to spend weeks in the Oak Knoll Hospital in San Francisco in 1945 before he could be flown back to the naval air station at Millington, Tennessee, close to his home. "All of us had shrunk down to less than 100 pounds by the time the war was over," recalled Cooper. "I don't believe I would have lasted another year because I was coughing up blood from working in that mine."[4]

Cooper's most prized possession upon returning to the States was a cross engraved in Dutch from a fellow Ashio prisoner, who added both Cooper's name in Dutch and the U.S. submarine emblem to the back of the cross. "Underneath in Dutch, he put 'Christ has risen.'" After another five months of rehabilitation, he left military service and spent his next four decades in the insurance industry. Cooper retired to Florida, where he passed away in 2008.

Dillon spent time with Moon Rocek at these reunions, where in 1989 the two reminisced in detail about their submarine service. Bill explained his duties on radar during the repeated attacks on *Chuyo* and professed to Moon that the crew of *Sailfish* had had no idea that *Sculpin* POWs were on board the carrier until long after the war. Dillon was surprised to learn that Rocek had also served postwar on *Sea Leopard*, joining the boat in January 1948, a short time after both Dillon and skipper Ward had been transferred to new assignments.

A survivor of the Japanese prisoner of war camps, Rocek felt that experience, combined with being a youth during the Great Depression, taught him to forever appreciate "the most minute things" that he later witnessed younger generations simply take for granted. Rocek spent twenty-two years in the Navy before retiring to civilian life, where he worked at various Illinois factories, including seventeen years as a mechanic for International Harvester.

Although he blended back into civilian life with success, the memories of his torture in the POW camps would haunt Rocek forever. He often flailed and fought in his sleep as nightmares took over. His wife learned to keep picture frames and other breakables away from her husband's side of the bed. "But all my wife had to do was holler out my name, and then I'd snap out of it," Rocek recalled. He retired to Jacksonville, Florida, where he passed away in 2007 at the age of eighty-six.[5]

The final reunion of *Squalus* and *Sailfish* veterans took place at the Portsmouth memorial in September 2002. Dillon led his shipmates in the Pledge of Allegiance to open the ceremonies before one of his former officers, Pat Murphy, addressed the crowd to relate some of the history of their twice-christened boat. Among those present were *Squalus* survivors Carl Bryson, Gerry McLees, and Nate Pierce, and numerous *Sailfish* veterans, including Dillon, Bud Pike, Craig Hertsgaard, Bill Bruckart, Cal Callanan, Royal Harrison, and Ray Bunt. Twenty years later, only Harrison and Dillon remain from these veterans. Bryson, the last of the *Squalus* survivors, passed away in December 2008, and Joe Baker was the last of the *Sculpin* POWs when he died in September 2012.

The young men who fought the war on *Sculpin* and *Sailfish* were resilient by nature. In their youth, they had already struggled through America's Great Depression, a trying time that taught them to make the most of their opportunities. As teenagers enlisting in the service to help protect their country, most thought little about what they would do when, or if, they survived World War II.

In the case of Bill Dillon, he will tell you today that the Second World War was but a tiny sliver of his life's journey. But it was an important part. "Joining the Submarine Service was one of the best decisions of my life. The Navy found what my best interests were, based upon my talents in radio and electronics gear," he reflected. "As a high school dropout at the time, I had no idea of what a good electrical engineer I would become, or that I would actually go on to earn my GED, my bachelor's degree, and my master's degree. I guess the Navy's decision on my career path worked out perfectly!"[6]

Although Bill recalls his submarine service fondly, he is most proud of the citation he received from the Air Force upon his retirement from his work as systems director. Signed by Lieutenant General Edward Barry and three other senior officers, the citation reads in part: "Your selfless devotion, perseverance, and expertise transformed a desolate prairie into the most advanced satellite control facility in the world."

Now, in the final years of his life, Skip Dillon is often requested to speak at military assemblies and museums, and he has been a featured guest of the United States Submarine Veterans Inc. He was honored at a Los Angeles Rams football game in 2021, the season that ended with their Super Bowl victory. Months later, he was the veteran hero of the game for the Los Angeles Kings hockey team on March 15, 2022, and tossed out the first pitch for the Los Angeles Dodgers on Memorial Day 2022.

Thoughts of his submarine service still bring a smile to his face. More often than not, those memories have little do with the success of *Sailfish*. Many are minor blips on the radar screen of his Silent Service days. Dillon laughs as he recalls standing a four-hour shift on the bridge of SS-192, with his binoculars sweeping the horizon in search of enemy planes or the distant smoke from a Japanese convoy. On one occasion, he began daydreaming of his girlfriend, Janet, and unwittingly broke into one of his favorite songs.

> *You are my sunshine, my only sunshine.*
> *You make me happy when skies are gray.*
> *You'll never know, dear . . .*

Before he could finish belting out his tune, the annoyed officer of the deck hollered, "Dillon, knock it off!"

In the end, he went through hell in World War II, but achieved his number one goal: coming back home in one piece. To *Sculpin* survivor George Rocek, to *Sailfish* veteran Skip Dillon, and to other World War II submariners who have chosen to share their many stories of life in the Silent Service, this book is dedicated.

Acknowledgments

First and foremost, I wish to thank the veterans who directly contributed to this project: Bill Dillon and Royal Harrison from *Sailfish*; and Joe Baker, Bill Cooper, George Rocek, and Herb Thomas from *Sculpin*.

The idea for this book began with my chance meeting of Skip Dillon on a flight from Dallas to London in September 2021. He was wearing his Sub Vets cap and a blue *Sailfish* jacket, evidence enough for me to provoke a conversation with this World War II veteran. He was at first astonished that I knew anything about his boat, its accomplishments, and its strange ties to *Sculpin* and the sole American survivor of the *Chuyo* sinking, Moon Rocek. In the months that followed, Dillon and I had frequent exchanges about his service days in person, on the phone, and via texts and emails. I came to know a man who was rightfully proud of his service to America in the Second World War, but who was tenfold more proud of the things he accomplished in the decades after 1945.

Two of Bill's daughters, Linda Musler and Tania Kaiser, were very generous in their support of this work, coordinating my meetings with their father and helping to copy ample sets of materials for my research. The children of other *Sailfish* veterans were equally helpful in fleshing out keepsakes. Among those deserving special praise are: Louise Walkup for sharing her father Montie's memoirs and photos; Hank and Mark Bayles for supplying information on their father, Lester; Dwayne Newton for details on his father, Killraine; David Pike for sharing photos, stories, and articles on his father, Bud Pike; Ray Bunt Jr. for providing copies of his father's papers and photos; Lorraine Naquin Tyler for sending various papers regarding the service of her father, Rear Admiral Oliver Naquin; and Traci Griffin for the photos and materials from the collection of her grandfather, Rear Admiral Bob Ward.

Many other researchers and authors kindly assisted me in gathering other documents needed to flesh out the *Squalus/Sailfish/Sculpin* story. Rory Grennan, manuscripts archivist with Florida State University Libraries, provided a copy of Bill Cooper's oral history transcript. Joseph Mathis, maintenance supervisor for the Arkansas Inland Maritime Museum and archivist for the U.S. Submarine Veterans association, went above and beyond in spending countless hours searching through back issues of USSVI magazines for articles of interest. Charles Hinman from the Pacific Fleet Submarine Museum once again granted me permission to use images for this book.

Carl LaVO, author of *Back from the Deep*, assisted me years ago with materials for my book on American World War II submarine POWs. For this project, Carl generously supplied reunion videotapes of the *Sailfish* and *Sculpin* crews, in addition to fielding a number of questions regarding details about the men he had previously interviewed. Carl also allowed me to review original audiotapes of his interview sessions with Edwin Keller, provided courtesy of Ed's son, John Keller.

Professional researchers Susan Strange and Karen Needles are appreciated for their work in the National Archives and Records Administration for securing various documents. Archivists Laura Waayers and Shana Rittierdot pulled personnel records from the Naval History and Heritage Command. Wendy Gulley of the Submarine Force Museum in Groton reviewed files on *Sculpin* and *Sailfish* and provided requested materials for me. For assisting with *Sailfish* photos, I must thank Rebecca Chasse from the Special Collections and Archives of Dimond Library, University of New Hampshire.

As always, I am indebted to my agent, Jim Donovan, and Caliber/Penguin Random House editor Brent Howard for their input, edits, and combined efforts in bringing this story to light. Brent's crack editorial team has gone to great lengths to fact-check the book. Any mistakes that slip through are mine, and they are regretted. Bill Dillon spent plenty of his own time trying to keep me on path through his readings of the rough drafts. I know he wants this to stand as a worthy tribute to his Silent Service comrades—for those fortunate enough to return from the war zone of the Pacific with him, and for those who did not.

Appendix A

Roster of USS *Sculpin* (SS-191) for Ninth War Patrol
Sunk November 19, 1943

Personnel Killed in Action or Lost on Board *Sculpin*

NAME	RANK/RATING
Allen, Nelson John	Lt.
Apostol, Eugenio (n)	CK1c
Arnath, Eugene (n)	S2c
Beidleman, Edgar Melrose Jr.	RT2c
Bentsen, Fred George	S2c
Blum, Arthur George	EM3c
Clements, Kenneth Burl	MoMM2c
Coleman, Charles Steele	MoMM1c
Connaway, Fred (n)	Cdr.
Cromwell, John Philip	Capt.
Daylong, James Edwin	MoMM2c
Defrees, Joseph Rollie Jr.	Lt.
Diederich, Donald Lawrence	EM3c

Embury, George Roderic	Lt. (jg)
Fiedler, Wendell Max	Ens.
Gabrunas, Philip Joseph	CMoMM
Goorabian, George (n)	S1c
Guillot, Alexander Benjamin	F1c
Harper, James Quinton	TM3c
Hemphill, Richard Earl	CMM
Holland, Erwin Raymond	MoMM1c
Johnson, Gordon Everett	MoMM2c
Kanocz, Steve (n)	EM3c
Lawton, Clifford Joseph	F1c
Maguire, Stanley Wayne	EM2c
Marcus, Grover Wade	RM3c
Martin, Merlin Guy	FC3c
McTavish, John Francis	S1c
Miller, Charles Edward	TM3c
Moreton, Arnold Frank	EM1c
Murray, Elmon Truett	SM3c
Partin, William Henry	S1c
Salava, Frank (n)	FC3c
Schnell, Elmer Virgil	TM3c
Schroeder, Delbert Eugene	Y2c
Shirley, Dowdy Buel	SM3c
Smith, Laroy Harold	EM2c
Suel, James Thomas	S1c
Swift, John Barlow	EM1c
Taylor, Russel Hershel	S1c
Warren, Ellis Edward	EM2c
Weade, Claiborne Hoyt	CTM

Appendix A

Sculpin Personnel Recovered by Japanese Destroyer *Yamagumo*

NAME	RANK/RATE	NOTES
Anderson, Edward Niles	SC2c	Recovered from POW camps
Baglien, Jerome Warren	RM3c	Died in *Chuyo* sinking
Baker, Cecil Eugene	F1c	Recovered from POW camps
Baker, Joseph Nicolas Jr.	F1c	Recovered from POW camps
Barrera, Maximo (n)	CK1c	Died in *Chuyo* sinking
Berry, Warren Rawling	TM1c	Died in *Chuyo* sinking
Brannum, Bill Clifton	F1c	Died in *Chuyo* sinking
Brown, George Estabrook Jr.	Lt.	Recovered from POW camps
Brown, Thomas Vincent	S2c	Died in *Chuyo* sinking
Carter, Robert William	S2c	Died in *Chuyo* sinking
Cooper, Billie Minor	QM2c	Recovered from POW camps
DeLisle, Maurice Simon	F1c	Died in *Chuyo* sinking
Elliott, Henry Leonidas	F1c	Died in *Chuyo* sinking
Eskildsen, Leo Aage	F1c	Recovered from POW camps
Gamel, John Worth	Ens.	Died in *Chuyo* sinking
Gorman, Michael Thomas	S2c	Recovered from POW camps
Haverland, William Herbert	CMoMM	Recovered from POW camps
Keller, Edwin Karl Frederick	S2c	Recovered from POW camps
Kennon, John Bowers Jr.	SC3c	Died in *Chuyo* sinking
Laman, Harold Dewitt	MoMM2c	Died in *Chuyo* sinking
McCartney, James William	EM3c	Died in *Chuyo* sinking
Milbourn, Harry Smith Jr.	MM3c	Recovered from POW camps
Moore, Weldon Edward	CSM	Died in *Chuyo* sinking
Morrilly, Robert Michael	EM3c	Died in *Chuyo* sinking
Murphy, Paul Louis	F1c	Recovered from POW camps
Murray, Leo Joseph	MoMM1c	Recovered from POW camps

Parr, John (n)	RM3c	Died in *Chuyo* sinking
Peterson, Julius Grant	RM2c	Recovered from POW camps
Pitser, Charles Earl	TM2c	Died in *Chuyo* sinking
Ricketts, Edward Forest	MoMM2c	Recovered from POW camps
Rocek, George (n)	MoMM1c	Survived *Chuyo* sinking; recovered from POW camps
Rourke, John Paul	GM2c	Recovered from POW camps
Smith, Charles Gold Jr.	Ens.	Died in *Chuyo* sinking
Taylor, Clifford Gene	RM3c	Died in *Chuyo* sinking
Thomas, Herbert Joseph	TM1c	Recovered from POW camps
Todd, Paul Allen	PhM1c	Recovered from POW camps
Toney, Harry Ford	TM3c	Recovered from POW camps
Van Beest, Henry (n)	S1c	Died in *Chuyo* sinking
Welsh, William Henry	S1c	Wounded; thrown overboard
White, Duane Joseph	MoMM2c	Died in *Chuyo* sinking
Wright, Eldon (n)	EM3c	Recovered from POW camps
Wyatt, Robert Orlin	GM2c	Recovered from POW camps

Appendix B

Muster Roll of USS *Sailfish* (SS-192) for Patrols 10 to 12
November 17, 1943–December 11, 1944

Note: This roster does not include personnel who served briefly during refit periods and did not make a war patrol. Advancements in rank/rating are noted during this period.

NAME	RANK/RATING	PATROLS
Adams, Joseph Lee Jr.	SC1c	11, 12
Adinolfe, Nunzio "Nick" Charles	EM3c	11, 12
Allen, Clarence Edward Jr.	F2c	10
Atkins, Eldred Russell	EM1c	10
Bandy, Vernon William	F1c/SC3c	10, 11, 12
Barnes, Cyrus Lee Jr.	TM3c	11, 12
Barnes, Maurice Drummond	GM3c	10, 11, 12
Barnett, Harris (n)	RM2c	11
Batts, Allen (n)	StM2c	11, 12
Bayles, Lester Wallace	CEM	10, 11
Berghausen, Edward Justus II	Ens./Lt. (jg)	10, 12
Blatti, Willard Wayne	CTM	10
Blundell, Harry Lester	EM1c	10, 11, 12

Bowers, Donald Elliot	MoMM2c	10, 11, 12
Bowman, George Luther Jr.	S2c	10
Bradley, Robert (n)	MoMM1c	10, 11, 12
Breit, Gene Franklin	F1c/MoMM2c	10, 11, 12
Brown, Richard Andrew	F1c	11, 12
Bruckart, William Lee	Lt. (jg)	10
Bunt, Raymond Charles	TM3c	10, 11, 12
Burrows, Hudson Harold	S1c	12*
Callanan, James Bartholomew	RT2c	11
Charlton, Elmer Allen	TM3c	10, 11, 12
Chivers, Homer Lawrence	S1c	11, 12
Clark, Norman Eugene	TM1c	11
Clay, Robert Lewis	TM3c	11, 12
Cowin, Stanley Joseph Jr.	Lt. (jg)/ Lt.	10, 11, 12
Crytser, William Baker	CY	10
Darragh, James Joseph	S1c	10
Davis, Benjamin (n)	GM3c	11, 12
Davis, Harold Amos	MoMM2c	10
Deas, Morris (n)	StM1c	10
Dieterich, Francis Lewis	RT1c/WE	10, 11
Dillon, William Joseph	RM2c	10, 11, 12
Earl, Kenneth (n)	S1c	12*
Evans, Wayne Anthony	WE/Lt. (jg)	10, 11, 12
Falcon, Doward (n)	S1c	11
Gaston, David William	Lt.	12
Gleeson, Cyril James	SC2c	10
Good, John Michael	MoMM2c	10, 11, 12
Gouker, Zelbert (n)	SM3c	10, 11
Gray, William Howard	CTM	11, 12
Hannum, Harry Lincoln	TM2c	11, 12

Henry, Lawrence Seymour	TM2c	10, 11, 12
Hertsgaard, Craig Martell	Ens.	11, 12
Itzen, Eugene (n)	TM3c	11, 12
James, Edwin Lafayette	F1c/MoMM3c	10, 11, 12
Johnson, Albert Joseph	SC3c	10, 11
Johnson, Robert William	RM1c/CRM	10, 11, 12
Kahler, Wellington Berrymore	MoMM1c/CMoMM	10, 11, 12
Kasuga, Albert Alexander	EM2c/1c	10, 11, 12
Kelly, Paul Joseph	RM3c	10
Kempf, Robert Charles	EM3c/2c	10, 11, 12
Kitterman, Ralph Randolph Jr.	CEM	11, 12
Kreitzmann, Earl William	F1c	11, 12
Labrecque, Leon Eugene	RM2c	11, 12
Landon, Max Oliver	MoMM2c	10, 11
Lang, Joseph Henry	RdM2c	11, 12
LaRose, Leo Roger	S1c	12*
Lloyd, Herbert "I"	F1c	10
Lohmeier, Marion Howard	EM3c/2c	10, 11, 12
Lucas, Emmett (n)	TM2c	10
Lusk, Gail Cooke	EM3c/2c	10, 11, 12
Lyon, William Homer	CMoMM	10, 11
Macek, Matthew Larry	F1c/MoMM2c	10, 11, 12
Makley, Philip Charles	S1c/FCS3c	10, 11, 12
Masterson, John Leo	SM3c	10, 11, 12
McCarty, Lewis Frederick	GM2c/TM2c	10, 11
McClellan, Frederic Chester	MoMM2c	10
McGrath, James Robert	CMoMM	10
McGuire, Warren Ellsworth	EM2c	10
McMurtrey, Emerial Afton	CPhM	10
Melstrand, Howard Walfred	TM3c	10, 11

Mendel, Joe Francis	TM1c	10, 11, 12
Miller, John Joseph	RM3c	11, 12
Mosley, Robert David	StM1c	10
Mullen, Frank Warren	GM1c	10, 11, 12
Murphy, Walter Patrick Jr.	Lt.	10, 11, 12
Newkirk, Clemon Eugene	MoMM2c	11, 12
Newton, Killraine Jr. (n)	St3c	11, 12
Niccolai, Albert Louis Jr.	EM3c	10, 11
Owen, Richard Salladay	RT2c	11, 12
Pendleton, Charles Frank	F1c	11
Perez, William (n)	F1c	11, 12
Peters, James Bostick	F1c	11, 12
Peterson, Arnold Andrew	MoMM3c	11, 12
Pierce, Edwin Everett Jr.	EM3c	11
Pike, Luverne Carl	Y3c/2c	10, 11, 12
Plummer, James Calvin	TM3c	10, 11
Poole, Andrew Driscoll	MoMM1c	11, 12
Ray, James Troy	SM1c	10, 11, 12
Reynolds, Jack Lamar	S2c	11, 12
Richardson, George Floyd	Lt./Lt. Cdr.	10, 11
Ring, Joseph John	MoMM2c	10, 11
Roberson, James Earl	F1c	11, 12
Robertson, Henry Keith	MoMM2c	10, 11, 12
Rogers, Frank Everett	S1c	11, 12
Sahaj, Joseph (n)	Lt. (jg)/Lt.	11, 12
Sandvik, John Mathew	TM3c	10
Sargent, Thomas Andrew	SC2c	10, 11
Sayles, Paul Hermann	EM3c	11, 12
Schilling, William Howard	S1c	12*
Scholander, Harry Thomas	S1c	11, 12

Sebree, Thomas Woodrow	F2c	11, 12
Simpson, Paul Shelton	S2c	11, 12
Skinner, Clifford Ray	TM3c	11, 12
Smail, Robert William	F1c/MoMM3c	10, 11, 12
Smith, Thomas "S"	Lt. (jg)	11, 12
Stevens, Glen Allen	GM3c	10
Sundman, Austin Theodore	SC2c	11, 12
Swaim, Charles Leslie	TM2c/1c	10, 11, 12
Thomas, Glenn Clifton	EM3c	11, 12
Thomas, Louis Edward	EM3c	10, 11
Tonden, Harry Arthur	QM2c/1c	10, 11, 12
Traxler, Paul Gilbert	MoMM1c	10
Turver, John Turton	PhM1c	11, 12
Tweedell, Robert Asbury	S1c	11, 12
Uhlman, Thomas Luellan	MoMM1c	10, 11, 12
Van Dusen, William Roger	TM2c	10
Walker, Freeman Dewberry	TM2c	10, 11, 12
Walkup, Montie DeWitt	CMoMM	10, 11, 12
Warburton, Lester (n)	F2c/MoMM3c	10, 11, 12
Ward, Robert Elwin McCraner	Lt. Cdr./Cdr.	10, 11, 12
Waterhouse, John Wellington	SC2c	11
West, Benjamin Freeman	RT2c	10
Wetmore, Irving Earl	Lt. (jg)/ Lt.	10, 11
Wheeler, Fred Elwood	MoMM1c	10, 11, 12
Whitley, Billie (n)	S1c/TME3c	10, 11, 12
Williams, Bernard Joseph	MoMM2c	10, 11, 12
Woody, James Herrold	FC3c/FCS2c	10, 11, 12

* Indicates a sailor received on board at Saipan midway through the twelfth patrol.

Notes

PROLOGUE

1. Maas, *The Terrible Hours*, 24–28.
2. LaVO, *Back from the Deep,* 40.
3. Calogero, "Sub *Squalus* Sank 25 Years Ago," 2.
4. Ibid.
5. LaVO, *Back from the Deep,* 41.
6. Ibid., 44.
7. Maas, *The Terrible Hours*, 97.
8. "U.S.S. *Squalus* (SS192) Report of Rescue Operations."
9. "Survivor of Ill-Fated '*Squalus*' Describes Its Sinking and Rescue," 1.
10. Bland, speech.
11. "Routine Test Dive Turned into Tragedy," 1.
12. LaVO, *Back from the Deep*, 57–59.
13. Ibid., 74.

ONE ★ *SCULPIN* ON THE WARPATH

1. Anthony Tully, in a November 29, 2021, email to the author, confirmed the time of Admiral Lockwood's Ultra to *Sculpin*, ComSubPac 060347.

2. Other accounts of *Sculpin*'s attack this night list that she might have attacked the carrier *Hiyo*, but Japanese warship researcher Anthony Tully confirmed with the author in a November 29, 2021, email that the carriers in question this night were indeed *Chuyo* and *Unyo*. During the morning of June 9, *Hiyo* was anchored in port at Kisarazu in Tokyo Bay. See also "IJN *Chuyo*: Tabular Record of Movement" on Tully's site, www.combinedfleet.com/chuyo.htm.

3. Galatin, *Take Her Deep!*, 39.

4. USS *Sculpin*, "Report of Seventh War Patrol," 4.

5. Parshall and Tully, *Shattered Sword*, 302–3.

6. Mendenhall, *Submarine Diary*, 142.

7. Ibid.

8. Ibid., 145.

9. USS *Sculpin*, "Report of Seventh War Patrol," 10.

10. Ibid., 11.

11. Blair, *Silent Victory*, 410–11.

12. USS *Sculpin*, "Report of Eighth War Patrol," 2–3.

13. Cooper, telephone interview with author.

14. Ibid; Cooper, interview with Jason Jewell, 1–2.

15. McCullough, *A Tale of Two Subs*, 176.

16. USS *Sculpin*, "Report of Eighth War Patrol," 8.

17. McCullough, *A Tale of Two Subs*, 212.

18. USS *Sculpin*, "Report of Eighth War Patrol," 21.

19. Ibid., 30.

TWO ★ RUNNING FROM TARGETS

1. Dillon, personal interview with author, September 30, 2021; Dienesch, "Radar and the American Submarine War," 31–32.

2. Dienesch, “Radar and the American Submarine War,” 32.

3. Blair, *Silent Victory*, 435.

4. USS *Sailfish*, Lefavour, “Report of Ninth War Patrol,” 2.

5. Naquin Tyler, telephone interview with author.

6. Blair, *Silent Victory*, 120.

7. Ibid., 273, 434.

8. LaVO, *Back from the Deep*, 115.

9. Dillon, “Biography of William J. Dillon,” 1–5.

10. Ibid., 5.

11. Dillon, personal interview with author, October 31, 2021.

12. Accessed ussseaowl.com/Text/Spritz_Navy.html on April 4, 2023.

13. Edwin Keller, audiotaped interviews with LaVO; LaVO, *Back from the Deep*, 122; John Keller, email, August 15, 2022.

14. Dillon, telephone interview with author, December 4, 2021.

15. Edwin Keller, audiotaped interviews with LaVO.

16. Dillon, email to author, November 28, 2021.

17. Dillon, telephone interview with author, December 4, 2021.

18. Walkup, “Memories of WW II,” 1–31.

19. Ibid., 63.

20. Ibid., 65.

21. LaVO, *Back from the Deep*, 119.

22. USS *Sailfish*, Moore, “Report of Eighth War Patrol,” 7.

23. Ibid., 11.

24. Blair, *Silent Victory*, 435.

25. LaVO, *Back from the Deep*, 119.

26. USS *Sailfish*, Lefavour, "Report of Ninth War Patrol," 6.
27. Ibid., 11; Dillon, personal interview with author, October 31, 2021.
28. USS *Sailfish*, Lefavour, "Report of Ninth War Patrol," 12.
29. Ibid., 13–14.
30. Blair, *Silent Victory*, 435–36.

THREE ★ "A CLEAN SLATE"

1. Bruckart, "Personal Experiences," 1.
2. Ibid.
3. Harrison, telephone interview with author.
4. Langenfeld, "He Served Under the Sea," 18.
5. Ward, interview at Pearl Harbor, 1.
6. Ibid., 18.
7. Ward, interview with Blair; Ward, interview at Pearl Harbor, 2.
8. Ibid.
9. Blair, *Silent Victory*, 414.
10. Ward, interview with Blair.
11. Richardson, officer biography sheet.
12. Richardson, interview, 2.
13. Ward, interview with Blair.
14. Walter P. Murphy, "*Sailfish* vs. *Chuyo*," 1.
15. Walter P. Murphy, "Wedding," 1–2.
16. Walter P. Murphy, "*Sailfish* vs. *Chuyo*," 1–2.
17. USS *Sailfish*, Ward, "Report of Tenth War Patrol," 50.

18. Dillon, personal and telephone interviews with author, September 24 and 30, 2021.
19. Bruckart, "Personal Experiences," 2.
20. Ward, interview with Blair.
21. USS *Sailfish*, Ward, "Report of Tenth War Patrol," 56.
22. Good, *The Submarine* Sailfish, 36–42.
23. Walkup, "Memories of WW II," 68.
24. Ibid., 69.
25. Ibid., 70–71.
26. Pike, "L. C. (Bud) Pike."
27. Ward, interview with Blair.
28. Bruckart, "Personal Experiences," 2.
29. LaVO, *Back from the Deep*, 172.
30. Bruckart, "Personal Experiences," 2.
31. Raymond C. Bunt Jr., interview with author.
32. Raymond C. Bunt, letter, March 2, 1944, 3.
33. Richardson, interview, 2.

FOUR ★ "THEY HAVE US"

1. John Pope, "Commander Fred Connaway."
2. LaVO, *Back from the Deep*, 122–23.
3. Edwin Keller, audiotaped interviews with LaVO.
4. Ibid; LaVO, *Back from the Deep*, 123.
5. Blair, *Silent Victory*, 495.
6. LaVO, *Back from the Deep*, 124.

7. Ibid.
8. Accessed combinedfleet.com/Chogei_t.htm on February 3, 2022.
9. Brown, "The Last Engagement," 1.
10. Cooper, telephone interview with author.
11. LaVO, *Back from the Deep*, 126.
12. Accessed combinedfleet.com/yamagu_t.htm on February 3, 2022.
13. Edwin Keller, audiotaped interviews with LaVO.
14. Ibid; LaVO, *Back from the Deep*, 126.
15. Brown, "The Last Engagement," 1.
16. Rocek, videotaped oral history with Robert Wright.
17. Ibid.
18. Ibid.
19. LaVO, *Back from the Deep*, 114.
20. Accessed combinedfleet.com/kashima_t.htm on February 3, 2022.
21. LaVO, *Back from the Deep*, 126.
22. Brown, "The Last Engagement," 1.
23. LaVO, *Back from the Deep*, 127.
24. Brown, "The Last Engagement," 2.
25. Ibid.
26. Rocek, videotaped oral history with Robert Wright.
27. LaVO, *Back from the Deep*, 128.
28. Accessed combinedfleet.com/kashima_t.htm on February 3, 2022.
29. Brown, "The Last Engagement," 2.
30. Accessed combinedfleet.com/kashima_t.htm on February 3, 2022.

31. Joseph Baker, telephone interview with author.
32. Accessed combinedfleet.com/kashima_t.htm on February 3, 2022.
33. Brown, "The Last Engagement," 2–3.
34. J. N. Baker, "The Last Days."

FIVE ★ BATTLE SURFACE!

1. Cooper, telephone interview with author.
2. Todd, statement.
3. Cooper, telephone interview with author.
4. Brown, "The Last Engagement," 2–3.
5. Accessed combinedfleet.com/kashima_t.htm on February 3, 2022.
6. Brown, "The Last Engagement," 2–3.
7. Joseph Baker, interview with author; J. N. Baker, "The Last Days," 2.
8. Rourke, statement; Brown, "The Last Engagement," 5.
9. J. N. Baker, "The Last Days," 2.
10. Cooper, telephone interview with author.
11. Accessed combinedfleet.com/kashima_t.htm on February 3, 2022.
12. Cooper, telephone interview with author.
13. Baker, "The Last Days," 1; Ricketts, statement.
14. Ricketts, statement.
15. LaVO, *Back from the Deep*, 132.
16. Brown, "The Last Engagement," 2–3.
17. LaVO, *Back from the Deep*, 132.
18. Ibid., 133.

19. Ibid.; Edwin Keller, audiotaped interviews with LaVO.

20. Edwin Keller, audiotaped interviews with LaVO.

21. Rocek, videotaped oral history with Robert Wright.

22. Brown, "The Last Engagement," 2–3.

23. Ibid.

24. Toney, statement; Wright, statement.

25. Joseph Baker, interview with author; Thomas, telephone interview with author; J. N. Baker, "The Last Days," 2.

26. Ricketts, statement; Toney, statement.

27. LaVO, *Back from the Deep*, 134.

28. Rocek, videotaped oral history with Robert Wright.

29. Edwin Keller, audiotaped interviews with LaVO.

30. LaVO, *Back from the Deep*, 134.

31. Brown, "The Last Engagement," 2–3.

32. Accessed combinedfleet.com/kashima_t.htm on February 3, 2022.

33. Cooper, telephone interview with author.

34. Rourke, statement; Rourke, war crimes testimony, 99.

35. Thomas, interview with author.

36. Joseph Baker, interview with author.

37. LaVO, "Footprints in the Sand," 85–87; Link, *US Submarine Veterans of World War II*, vol. 1, 244.

SIX ★ "A LIVING HELL"

1. Edwin Keller, audiotaped interviews with LaVO.

2. LaVO, *Back from the Deep*, 135.

3. Joseph Baker, interview with author.

4. Wright, war crimes testimony, 1; Thomas, interview with author.

5. Cooper, telephone interview with author.

6. Rourke, war crimes testimony, 99.

7. George Estabrook Brown Jr., affidavit, 2.

8. LaVO, *Back from the Deep*, 135.

9. Brown, affidavit, 2.

10. J. N. Baker, "The Last Days," 2.

11. Rocek, videotaped oral history with Robert Wright.

12. Michno, *Death on the Hellships*, 143.

13. J. N. Baker, "The Last Days," 2.

14. Brown, affidavit, 3.

15. Edwin Keller, affidavit.

16. Cecil Baker, war crimes testimony, August 10, 1948, 111.

17. LaVO, *Back from the Deep*, 138.

18. Cecil Baker, war crimes testimony, August 10, 1948, 111.

19. "Saga of a *Sculpin* Survivor," 18; Rourke, war crimes testimony, 100.

20. Cooper, telephone interview with author.

21. Brown, affidavit, 3.

22. Ibid.

23. Rourke, war crimes testimony, 99.

24. Eskildsen, statement.

25. Peterson, affidavit; Thomas, statement; Ricketts, statement.

26. Rocek, videotaped oral history with Robert Wright.

27. Edwin Keller, affidavit, 2.

28. Joseph Baker, affidavit, 2.

29. LaVO, *Back from the Deep*, 138.

30. Rourke, war crimes testimony, 103, 106.

31. Joseph Baker, affidavit, 2.

32. Paul Louis Murphy, war crimes testimony, 1; Cecil Baker, war crimes testimony, August 10, 1948, 113.

33. Cecil Baker, war crimes testimony, August 10, 1948, 114.

34. Rourke, war crimes testimony, 109; Rourke, affidavit, 3; Cecil Baker, war crimes testimony, August 10, 1948, 114.

35. Edwin Keller, affidavit, 2.

36. Joseph Baker, affidavit, 2.

37. Rourke, war crimes testimony, 102; Edwin Keller, affidavit, 2–3.

38. Thomas, interview with author.

39. LaVO, *Back from the Deep*, 139.

40. Joseph Baker, affidavit, 3.

41. Rourke, war crimes testimony, 101.

42. Rocek, statement; Rourke, war crimes testimony, 101, 108.

43. Edwin Keller, affidavit, 3; Edwin Keller, audiotaped interviews with LaVO.

44. Ricketts, statement; Rocek, videotaped oral history with Robert Wright.

45. Cecil Baker, war crimes testimony, August 10, 1948, 119.

46. Rourke, war crimes testimony, 101.

47. J. N. Baker, “The Last Days,” 3.

SEVEN ★ "CHANCE OF A LIFETIME"

1. Raymond C. Bunt, letter, March 2, 1944, 4.
2. Good, *The Submarine* Sailfish, 44.
3. Blair, *Silent Victory*, 411.
4. Good, *The Submarine* Sailfish, 59.
5. Dillon, personal interview with author, September 30, 2021.
6. USS *Sailfish*, Ward, "Report of Tenth War Patrol," 1.
7. Good, *The Submarine* Sailfish, 58.
8. Sasgen, *Red Scorpion*, 74; Michno, *USS* Pampanito, 144.
9. Michno, *USS* Pampanito, 144.
10. Bruckart, "Personal Experiences," 2.
11. Good, *The Submarine* Sailfish, 45–50.
12. Ibid., 52–53.
13. Jourdan, *Operation Rising Sun*, 171.
14. Winton, *Ultra in the Pacific*, 144.
15. Walter P. Murphy, "*Sailfish* vs. *Chuyo*," 3.
16. Bruckart, "Personal Experiences," 3.
17. Ibid., 5–6.
18. Ward, interview with Blair.
19. USS *Sailfish*, Ward, "Report of Tenth War Patrol," 40–41.
20. Ibid., 41; Bruckart, "Personal Experiences," 4.
21. Bruckart, "Personal Experiences," 3.
22. USS *Sailfish*, Ward, "Report of Tenth War Patrol," 41.
23. Good, *The Submarine* Sailfish, 63.

24. Pike, "L. C. (Bud) Pike," 2.

25. Richardson, interview, 5.

26. Good, "The *Ryuho*'s Last Stand," 18; Good, *The Submarine* Sailfish, 63.

27. Walter P. Murphy, "*Sailfish* vs. *Chuyo*," 3.

EIGHT ★ CARRIER PASSAGE TO JAPAN

1. LaVO, *Back from the Deep*, 140.

2. Rourke, testimony, 2; Rourke, affidavit, 1; Rourke, war crimes testimony, 108.

3. Rocek, videotaped oral history with Robert Wright; Rourke, war crimes testimony, 108.

4. Rocek, videotaped oral history with Robert Wright.

5. Key sources: combinedfleet.com/unyo.htm and combinedfleet.com/chuyo.htm, accessed December 17, 2021.

6. Winton, *Ultra in the Pacific*, 139.

7. Ibid.

8. Ibid., 141–42.

9. Combinedfleet.com/chuyo.htm.

10. Winton, *Ultra in the Pacific*, 143.

11. Ibid.

12. Ibid., 144.

13. Tully, email to author, December 17, 2021.

14. USS *Skate*, McKinney, "Report of War Patrol Number Two," 11.

15. Ibid., 3–4.

16. Joseph Baker, interview with author; J. N. Baker, "The Last Days," 3.

17. Todd, statement, 1.

18. Cooper, telephone interview with author.

19. LaVO, *Back from the Deep*, 141.

20. Moore, *Presumed Lost*, 152; Rikihei, "Aircraft Carrier *Chuyo*'s Distress," 1.

21. USS *Gunnel*, McCain, "Report of War Patrol Number Three," 1–2. McCain was the son of Vice Admiral John McCain, deputy chief of naval operations in late 1943.

22. Ibid., 2.

23. USS *Sunfish*, "Report of Fifth War Patrol," 6.

24. Rikihei, "Aircraft Carrier *Chuyo*'s Distress," 1–2.

NINE ★ FIRST STRIKE

1. Bruckart, "Personal Experiences," 4.

2. Walkup, "Memories of WW II," 71.

3. Ward, interview at Pearl Harbor, 4.

4. USS *Sailfish*, Ward, "Report of Tenth War Patrol," 3.

5. Ibid., 4.

6. Ward, interview with Blair.

7. USS *Sailfish*, Ward, "Report of Tenth War Patrol," 4.

8. Bruckart, "Personal Experiences," 4.

9. USS *Sailfish*, Ward, "Report of Tenth War Patrol," 3.

10. Richardson, interview, 6.

11. Good, *The Submarine* Sailfish, 66.

TEN ★ *CHUYO* IN PERIL

1. Rikihei, "Aircraft Carrier *Chuyo*'s Distress," 2–3.

2. Ibid., 2.

3. Ibid., 3.

4. Edwin Keller, audiotaped interviews with LaVO.
5. Rikihei, "Aircraft Carrier *Chuyo*'s Distress," 3.
6. USS *Sailfish*, Ward, "Report of Tenth War Patrol," 4.
7. Ibid.
8. Richardson, interview, 6.
9. Ward, interview at Pearl Harbor, 6.
10. Monroe-Jones and Green, *The Silent Service in World War II*, 107.
11. LaVO, *Back from the Deep*, 172.
12. Ward, interview at Pearl Harbor, 6.
13. Good, *The Submarine* Sailfish, 68–69.
14. Rikihei, "Aircraft Carrier *Chuyo*'s Distress," 2–3.
15. Rocek, videotaped oral history with Robert Wright.

ELEVEN ★ THIRD STRIKE OF THE *SAILFISH*

1. USS *Sailfish*, Ward, "Report of Tenth War Patrol," 5.
2. Bruckart, "Personal Experiences," 5.
3. Richardson, interview, 8.
4. USS *Sailfish*, Ward, "Report of Tenth War Patrol," 5.
5. Ibid.
6. Rocek, videotaped oral history with Robert Wright.
7. Ibid.
8. Rikihei, "Aircraft Carrier *Chuyo*'s Distress," 3.
9. Ibid.

TWELVE ★ CARRIER DOWN

1. USS *Sailfish*, Ward, "Report of Tenth War Patrol," 6.
2. Ibid.
3. Ibid.
4. Ward, interview with Blair.
5. USS *Sailfish*, Ward, "Report of Tenth War Patrol," 6–7.
6. Ward, interview at Pearl Harbor, 5.
7. USS *Sailfish*, Ward, "Report of Tenth War Patrol," 7.
8. Ibid.
9. Link, *US Submarine Veterans of World War II,* vol. 4, 164–65.
10. Ibid., 7.
11. Rikihei, "Aircraft Carrier *Chuyo*'s Distress," 3.
12. "Saga of a *Sculpin* Survivor," 19, 23.
13. Rikihei, "Aircraft Carrier *Chuyo*'s Distress," 4.
14. Ibid.
15. Rocek, videotaped oral history with Robert Wright.
16. Nevitt, "Submarines vs. *Urakaze.*"
17. Rocek, videotaped oral history with Robert Wright; Rocek, telephone interview with author; "Saga of a *Sculpin* Survivor," 19–20.
18. Nevitt, "Submarines vs. *Urakaze.*"
19. Rikihei, "Aircraft Carrier *Chuyo*'s Distress," 5.
20. "Saga of a *Sculpin* Survivor," 20.
21. Rocek, videotaped oral history with Robert Wright.
22. Ibid.; "Saga of a *Sculpin* Survivor," 20.

23. "Saga of a *Sculpin* Survivor," 20.

24. Rocek, videotaped oral history with Robert Wright.

THIRTEEN ★ *SAILFISH* ON THE PROWL

1. Dillon, personal interview with author, September 30, 2021.

2. Richardson, interview, 9.

3. LaVO, *Back from the Deep*, 169.

4. Richardson, interview, 9.

5. USS *Sailfish*, Ward, "Report of Tenth War Patrol," 8.

6. Pike, "L. C. (Bud) Pike."

7. Richardson, interview, 9; Good, *The Submarine* Sailfish, 77–78.

8. LaVO, *Back from the Deep*, 170.

9. Walkup, "Memories of WW II," 73.

10. USS *Sailfish*, Ward, "Report of Tenth War Patrol," 44; Bruckart, "Personal Experiences," 6.

11. USS *Sailfish*, Ward, "Report of Tenth War Patrol," 57.

12. Bruckart, "Personal Experiences," 2.

13. Accessed combinedfleet.com/Meisho_t.htm on January 4, 2022.

14. Good, *The Submarine* Sailfish, 85.

15. Pike, "L. C. (Bud) Pike."

16. USS *Sailfish*, Ward, "Report of Tenth War Patrol," 17.

17. Ibid., 19.

18. Bruckart, "Personal Experiences," 6.

19. Richardson, interview, 11.

20. Ibid., 39–40; Ward, interview at Pearl Harbor, 8.

21. Accessed combinedfleet.com/YasukuniM_t.htm on January 4, 2022.
22. USS *Sailfish*, Ward, "Report of Tenth War Patrol," 21.
23. Good, *The Submarine* Sailfish, 92.
24. USS *Sailfish*, Ward, "Report of Tenth War Patrol," 57.
25. Ward, interview with Blair.
26. USS *Sailfish*, Ward, "Report of Tenth War Patrol," 63–65.
27. Good, *The Submarine* Sailfish, 92.

FOURTEEN ★ PRISONERS OF WAR

1. Moore, *Presumed Lost*, 29–30.
2. J. N. Baker, "The Last Days," 3.
3. Moore, *Presumed Lost*, 82, 121.
4. Ibid., 121–22.
5. Joseph Baker, interview with author; LaVO, *Back from the Deep*, 158.
6. Edwin Keller, audiotaped interviews with LaVO.
7. Cooper, telephone interview with author.
8. Moore, *Presumed Lost*, 179.
9. "Saga of a *Sculpin* Survivor," 20.
10. LaVO, *Back from the Deep*, 154.
11. Joseph Baker, interview with author.
12. Edwin Keller, affidavit, 3; LaVO, *Back from the Deep*, 157.
13. "Saga of a *Sculpin* Survivor," 20; LaVO, *Back from the Deep*, 156.
14. LaVO, *Back from the Deep*, 158.
15. Moore, *Presumed Lost*, 161–62.
16. Joseph Baker, interview with author.

17. Gamble, *Black Sheep One,* 357; USS *Grenadier* newsletter, 4.

18. Moore, *Presumed Lost*, 245; LaVO, *Back from the Deep*, 159–61; Zucco, affidavit.

19. "Saga of a *Sculpin* Survivor," 21.

20. LaVO, *Back from the Deep*, 163–64.

21. Cooper, telephone interview with author.

22. "Saga of a *Sculpin* Survivor," 22.

23. Ibid., 21.

24. Edwin Keller, audiotaped interviews with LaVO.

25. Rocek, letter to parents, 1944.

26. LaVO, *Back from the Deep*, 181.

27. "Saga of a *Sculpin* Survivor," 21.

28. LaVO, *Back from the Deep*, 167, 179.

FIFTEEN ★ WOLF PACK

1. Dillon Family, *Janet Kugel Dillon*, 2–3.

2. Dillon, personal interview with author, January 8, 2022.

3. Walkup, "Memories of WW II," 76.

4. Knoblock, *Black Submariners in the United States Navy, 1940–1975*, 330.

5. Ibid., 38, 330.

6. "Submarine *Sailfish* Gets Presidential Citation," 6.

7. Dillon, personal interview with author, January 8, 2022.

8. Ward, interview with Blair.

9. Roscoe, *United States Submarine Operations in World War II*, 347–48.

10. "Subs *Bowfin*, *Sailfish* Given High Citations," 17.

11. Good, *The Submarine* Sailfish, 109.
12. Walkup, "Memories of WW II," 77–78.
13. Callanan, oral history interview, 10.
14. Good, *The Submarine* Sailfish, 111.
15. Callanan, oral history interview, 10.
16. Pike, "L. C. (Bud) Pike."
17. Raymond C. Bunt, letter, April 9, 1945, 7; LaVO, *Back from the Deep*, 171.
18. Good, *The Submarine* Sailfish, 111.
19. Walkup, "Memories of WW II," 77–78.
20. Pike, "L. C. (Bud) Pike."
21. Callanan, oral history interview, 13.
22. Dillon, personal interview with author, December 4, 2021.
23. Good, *The Submarine* Sailfish, 113.
24. Link, *US Submarine Veterans of World War II*, vol. 1, 360.
25. Walkup, "Memories of WW II," 80.
26. Ibid., 81.
27. Turver, "On the USS *Sailfish*," 57.
28. Ibid.
29. Good, *The Submarine* Sailfish, 127–28; Walkup, "Memories of WW II," 82.
30. Turver, "On the USS *Sailfish*," 57; Walkup, "Memories of WW II," 84.
31. Walkup, "Memories of WW II," 83–84.
32. USS *Sailfish*, Ward, "Report of Eleventh War Patrol," 6.
33. Ibid., 7; Alden, *U.S. Submarine Attacks During World War II*, 121.
34. Callanan, oral history interview, 14.

35. USS *Sailfish*, Ward, "Report of Eleventh War Patrol," 8.

36. Callanan, oral history interview, 17.

37. Ibid., 18.

38. Ibid., 12; Pike, "L. C. (Bud) Pike," 4.

39. Good, *The Submarine* Sailfish, 137.

40. Tully, email to author, February 13, 2022.

41. USS *Sailfish*, Ward, "Report of Eleventh War Patrol," 13.

42. Ibid.

43. Ibid., 14.

44. Good, *The Submarine* Sailfish, 138–39.

45. USS *Sailfish*, Ward, "Report of Eleventh War Patrol," 17–18.

46. Roberson, interview, 27.

47. Ibid., 20.

48. Richardson, interview, 4.

49. Good, *The Submarine* Sailfish, 142.

50. Roberson, interview, 37–38.

51. Turver, "On the USS *Sailfish*," 57.

SIXTEEN ★ THE MINES OF ASHIO

1. Moore, *Presumed Lost*, 248.

2. Brown, affidavit, 4.

3. Fitzgerald, diary, 52–53; Caverly, interview with author; O'Kane, *Clear the Bridge!*, 463.

4. Brown, affidavit, 4.

5. Ricketts, statement.

6. Kuykendall, telephone interviews with author.
7. LaVO, *Back from the Deep*, 184.
8. Haverland, war crimes testimony, 2.
9. "Saga of a *Sculpin* Survivor," 21.
10. Edwin Keller, audiotaped interviews with LaVO.
11. LaVO, "Footprints in the Sand," 86.

SEVENTEEN ★ LIFEGUARD LEAGUE

1. Good, *The Submarine* Sailfish, 152–53.
2. Ibid., 156–59.
3. Richardson, interview, 1.
4. Dillon, personal interview with author, February 8, 2022.
5. Good, *The Submarine* Sailfish, 163.
6. Dillon, texts to author, January 28, 2022.
7. Good, *The Submarine* Sailfish, 166.
8. Cleaver, *Fabled Fifteen*, 153.
9. Ward, interview with Blair.
10. USS *Sailfish*, Ward, "Report of Twelfth War Patrol," 6; Walkup, "Memories of WW II," 88.
11. Campbell, *Save Our Souls*, 462.
12. Walkup, "Memories of WW II," 88.
13. USS *Sailfish*, Ward, "Report of Twelfth War Patrol," 4.
14. Ibid., 54.
15. Cleaver, *Fabled Fifteen*, 151.
16. Pike, "L. C. (Bud) Pike," 5.

17. USS *Sailfish*, Ward, "Report of Twelfth War Patrol," 48–49.
18. Dillon, text to author, January 28, 2022.
19. Good, *The Submarine* Sailfish, 166.
20. Walkup, "Memories of WW II," 91.
21. Ibid., 92.
22. USS *Sailfish*, Ward, "Report of Twelfth War Patrol," 13–14.
23. Ibid., 15.
24. Tully, email to author, February 13, 2022.
25. Good, *The Submarine* Sailfish, 181; USS *Sailfish*, Ward, "Report of Twelfth War Patrol," 17.
26. USS *Sailfish*, Ward, "Report of Twelfth War Patrol," 17.
27. Good, *The Submarine* Sailfish, 183.
28. Ibid., 183–84.
29. USS *Sailfish*, Ward, "Report of Twelfth War Patrol," 17.
30. Good, *The Submarine* Sailfish, 184.
31. Tully, email to author, February 13, 2022.
32. USS *Sailfish*, Ward, "Report of Twelfth War Patrol," 18; Good, *The Submarine* Sailfish, 185.
33. Walkup, "Memories of WW II," 93.
34. USS *Sailfish*, Ward, "Report of Twelfth War Patrol," 20, 53–54.
35. Ibid., 23.
36. Good, *The Submarine Sailfish*, 187.
37. USS *Sailfish*, Ward, "Report of Twelfth War Patrol," 27–28.
38. Ibid., 27.
39. Ibid., 30.

40. Good, *The Submarine* Sailfish, 188.

41. Roberson, interview, 25.

42. Ibid., 22.

43. USS *Sailfish*, Ward, "Report of Twelfth War Patrol," 30.

44. Raymond C. Bunt, letter, April 9, 1945, 6.

45. Good, *The Submarine* Sailfish, 191.

46. USS *Sailfish*, Ward, "Report of Twelfth War Patrol," 31.

47. Good, *The Submarine* Sailfish, 191.

EIGHTEEN ★ THE LAST NINE MONTHS

1. Lockwood, "Third Endorsement to *Sailfish* Report of Twelfth War Patrol," 1.

2. Dillon, email to author, March 24, 2022.

3. Good, *The Submarine* Sailfish, 192.

4. Ibid., 194.

5. Truman, "Statement by the President Announcing the Use of the A-Bomb at Hiroshima."

6. Pike, oral history; Pike, "L. C. (Bud) Pike," 5.

7. "Saga of a *Sculpin* Survivor," 21.

8. LaVO, "Footprints in the Sand," 88.

9. Rourke, testimony, 2.

10. Wright, war crimes testimony, 1.

11. "Saga of a *Sculpin* Survivor," 21; Rocek, videotaped oral history with Robert Wright.

12. Edwin Keller, papers.

13. Moore, *Presumed Lost*, 257.

14. Cooper, interview with Jason Jewell, 17–18.
15. Cooper, telephone interview with author.
16. Kuykendall, telephone interviews with author.
17. Rocek, videotaped oral history with Robert Wright.
18. Cooper, telephone interview with author.
19. "Saga of a *Sculpin* Survivor," 22.
20. Moore, *Presumed Lost*, 290.
21. LaVO, *Back from the Deep*, 195.
22. Joseph Baker, interview with author.
23. Pike, "L. C. (Bud) Pike," 5.
24. LaVO, *Back from the Deep*, 197.
25. Ibid., 197–98.
26. Ibid., 196; Pike, "L. C. (Bud) Pike," 6.

EPILOGUE

1. Dillon, texts to author, May 24, 2022.
2. LaVO, *Back from the Deep*, 202–3.
3. Ibid., 203–5.
4. Cooper, interview with Jason Jewell, 16.
5. Rocek, videotaped oral history with Robert Wright.
6. Dillon, texts to author, May 22, 2022.

Bibliography

Interviews and Correspondence

Baker, Joseph. Telephone interview with author, February 17, 2007.

Bunt, Raymond C. Jr. Telephone interview with author, February 13, 2022.

Caverly, Floyd M. Telephone interview with author, February 10, 2007.

Cooper, Billie Minor. Telephone interview with author, February 4, 2007.

Dillon, William J. Personal and telephone interviews with and emails and texts to author, September 2021 to June 2022.

Harrison, Royal G., and Susan James (his daughter). Telephone interview with author, February 28, 2022.

Keller, Edwin. Audiotaped interviews with Carl LaVO, circa 1992, courtesy of John Keller and Carl LaVO.

Keller, John. Telephone interviews with and emails to author, July to August 2022.

Kuykendall, Clifford W. Telephone interviews with author, January 20 and January 29, 2007.

LaVO, Carl. Emails to and correspondence and telephone interviews with author, October 21, 2021, to May 6, 2022.

Naquin Tyler, Lorraine. Telephone interview with author, January 26, 2022.

Rocek, George. Telephone interview with author, January 30, 2007.

Thomas, Herbert J. Telephone interview, May 20, 2007.

Tully, Anthony. Personal interview with author, December 10, 2021, and telephone interviews with and emails to author, December 7, 2021, to March 13, 2022.

Oral Histories and Memoirs

Callanan, James B. Oral history interview, April 4, 2004, National Museum of the Pacific War.

Cooper, Bill M. Interview with Jason Jewell, July 26, 2000, Reichelt Oral History Collection (HPUA-2015-00R), Special Collections Number 21420, Florida State University Libraries.

Fitzgerald, John A. Personal diary.

Keller, Edwin. Personal papers, courtesy of Carl LaVO.

Richardson, George, Lt. Cdr. Interview, October 26, 1944, Office of Naval Records and Library.

Roberson, James. Interview, March 8, 1997, University of North Texas Oral History Collection, Number 1169.

Ward, R. E. M., Lt. Cdr. Interview at Pearl Harbor, July 8, 1944, Office of Naval Records and Library.

———. Interview with Clay Blair Jr., courtesy of Renah Miller, A/V Photo Archive Aide, American Heritage Center.

Official Statements and Military Documents

Baker, Cecil Eugene, MoMM1c. War crimes testimony, June 5, 1947, and August 10, 1948.

Baker, J. N., F1c. "The Last Days of the 'Sculpin' (SS-191)," 1945.

Baker, Joseph. Affidavit, June 30, 1948.

Brown, George Estabrook Jr., Lt. Cdr. Affidavit, July 10, 1946, New York, NY.

Erishman, Charles A., Lt. (jg). Signed affidavit, February 2, 1948, New London, CT.

Eskildsen, Leo Aage, ENC, USN. Signed affidavit, July 27, 1948, New London, CT.

Gorman, Michael Thomas, TM3c. Signed affidavit, July 26, 1948, San Diego, CA.

Haverland, William Herbert, CMoMM. War crimes testimony, October 16–17, 1945.

Keller, Edwin Karl Frederick, EM2c. Signed affidavit, August 23, 1948, Record Group 125, Box 2.

Lockwood, C. A. Jr. "Third Endorsement to *Sailfish* Report of Twelfth War Patrol," December 21, 1944.

Murphy, Paul Louis. War crimes testimony, August 21, 1946, New Castle, PA.

Murray, Leo Joseph, ENC. Signed affidavit, July 26, 1948, San Diego, CA.

Peterson, Julius Grant, RM2c. Statement, September 12, 1945, Guam; and affidavit, June 30, 1948, Great Barrington, MA.

Richardson, George F., Captain. Officer biography sheet, Naval History and Heritage Command.

Ricketts, Edward Forest, MoMM2c. Statement, September 14, 1945, Guam.

Rocek, George, MoMM1c. Statement, September 14, 1945, Guam.

Rourke, John Paul, CGM. Statement, September 14, 1945, Guam; testimony, April 22, 1947; affidavit, May 12, 1948; and war crimes testimony, August 10, 1948.

Thomas, Herbert Joseph. Statement, September 14, 1945, Guam.

Todd, Paul A., PhM1c. Statement, September 14, 1945, Guam.

Toney, Harry Ford, TM3c. Statement, September 14, 1945, Guam.

Truman, Harry. "Statement by the President Announcing the Use of the A-Bomb at Hiroshima," August 6, 1945, Harry S. Truman Presidential Library and Museum.

USS *Gunnel*. J. S. McCain Jr. "Report of War Patrol Number Three," January 7, 1944.

USS *Sailfish*. J. R. Moore, "Report of Eighth War Patrol," July 3, 1943; W. R. Lefavour, "Report of Ninth War Patrol," September 20, 1943; R. E. M. Ward, "Report of Tenth War Patrol," January 5,

1944; R. E. M. Ward, "Report of Eleventh War Patrol," September 6, 1944; R. E. M. Ward, "Report of Twelfth War Patrol," December 11, 1944.

USS *Sailfish* deck logs, August 1943–February 1945, RG 24 Records of the Bureau of Naval Personnel, Box 8354, Entry P 118-A1, National Archives and Records Administration.

USS *Sculpin*. "Report of Seventh War Patrol," July 4, 1943; "Report of Eighth War Patrol," September 17, 1943.

USS *Skate*. E. B. McKinney, "Report of War Patrol Number Two," January 7, 1944.

"U.S.S. *Squalus* (SS192) Report of Rescue Operations," May 28, 1939, Naval History and Heritage Command.

USS *Sunfish*. "Report of Fifth War Patrol," December 15, 1943.

Wright, Eldon, EM3c. Statement, September 14, 1945, Guam; and war crimes testimony, 1947.

Wyatt, R. O., GM2c. Statement, September 14, 1945, Guam.

Zucco, Peter, S1c. Statement, September 14, 1945, Guam.

Articles and Memoirs

Brown, George Estabrook. "The Last Engagement."

Bruckart, William L., Cdr., USNR (Ret.). "Personal Experiences Related to the 10th War Patrol of USS *Sailfish* (SS-192)." Privately published essay, July 1, 2002.

Bunt, Raymond C. Personal papers, courtesy of Raymond C. Bunt Jr.

Calogero, James. "Sub *Squalus* Sank 25 Years Ago." *Tallahassee Democrat*, May 24, 1964.

Dienesch, Robert. "Radar and the American Submarine War, 1941–1945: A Reinterpretation." *The Northern Mariner*, vol. XIV, no. 3 (July 2004): 27–40.

Dillon Family. *Janet Kugel Dillon: Stories of Her Life and Treasured Memories*. Privately published family history, March 22, 2007.

Dillon, William J. "Biography of William J. Dillon," unpublished memoir.

Good, John M. "The *Ryuho*'s Last Stand." *Polaris*, August 1993.

Houston, Charles. *Flying with Iron Angels: The Diaries and Memories of Navy Carrier Pilots Fighting the Pacific War in 1944.* Privately published, 2001.

Jaskoviak, Phil. "From Submarines to the Space Race." *American Submariner*, first quarter 2002.

Langenfeld, Tom. "He Served Under the Sea." *Sunday World-Herald Magazine of the Midlands*, February 14, 1965.

LaVO, Carl. "Footprints in the Sand." *Proceedings*, vol. 112/1/995 (January 1986): 85–88.

McKenzie, Jeanine. "The 'Volunteers' of Spritz's Navy." Accessed http://ussseaowl.com/Text/Spritz_Navy.html on April 4, 2023.

Murphy, Walter P. "*Sailfish* vs. *Chuyo*." Unpublished personal narrative, September 6, 1999.

———. "Wedding." Unpublished personal narrative, September 9, 1999.

Nevitt, Allyn D. "Submarines vs. Urakaze." Accessed http://www.combinedfleet.com/subura.htm on November 12, 2021.

Pike, Luverne C. "L. C. (Bud) Pike—U.S. Navy Career, 1942 to 1945." Unpublished memoir, courtesy of Bill Dillon.

Pope, John. "Commander Fred Connaway, USNA Class of '32." Accessed www.usna.com/tributes-and-stories-1932 on January 30, 2022.

Rikihei, Katsura. "Aircraft Carrier *Chuyo*'s Distress." Translation of article supplied by Anthony Tully; accessed http://www5f.biglobe.ne.jp/~ma480/index.htm on January 28, 2012.

Rocek, George. Letters to parents, 1944, courtesy of Carl LaVO.

"Routine Test Dive Turned into Tragedy." *Foster's Daily Democrat*, May 22, 1989.

"Saga of a *Sculpin* Survivor." *Polaris*, December 1979. Courtesy of Submarine Force Museum, Groton, CT.

"Submarine *Sailfish* Gets Presidential Citation." *Honolulu Star-Bulletin*, June 1, 1944.

"Subs *Bowfin*, *Sailfish* Given High Citations." *The Honolulu Advertiser*, July 9, 1944.

"Survivor of Ill-Fated 'Squalus' Describes Its Sinking and Rescue." *The Ottawa Journal*, May 25, 1939.

Tully, Anthony P. "IJN *Chuyo*: Tabular Record of Movement." Accessed www.combinedfleet.com/chuyo.htm on November 12, 2021.

______. "IJN *Chogei*: Tabular Record of Movement." Accessed http://www.combinedfleet.com/Chogei_t.htm on February 3, 2022.

_____. "IJN *Kashima*: Tabular Record of Movement." Accessed http://www.combinedfleet.com/kashima_t.htm on February 3, 2022.

_____. "IJN *Meisho Maru*: Tabular Record of Movement." Accessed http://www.combinedfleet.com/Meisho_t.htm on January 4, 2022.

_____. "IJN *Unyo*: Tabular Record of Movement." Accessed http://www.combinedfleet.com/unyo.htm on December 17, 2021.

_____. "IJN *Yamagu*: Tabular Record of Movement." Accessed http://www.combinedfleet.com/yamagu_t.htm on February 3, 2022.

_____. "IJN *Yasukuni Maru*: Tabular Record of Movement." Accessed http://www.combinedfleet.com/YasukuniM_t.htm on January 4, 2022.

Turver, John. "On the USS *Sailfish*." *US Submarine Veterans of World War II*, vol. 2, 1986.

USS *Grenadier* newsletter, 4: December 1981.

Walkup, Montie D. "Memories of WW II." Privately published memoir, 1991.

Videos

Bayles, Lester. Speech from *Squalus/Sailfish/Sculpin* reunion video, August 1985, courtesy of Carl LaVO.

Bland, Judson. Speech from *Squalus/Sailfish/Sculpin* reunion video, August 1985, courtesy of Carl LaVO.

Ramage, Lawson. Videotaped interview with Robert Hall and Joseph Caruso, 1987, courtesy of Dave Hall.

Rocek, George. Videotaped oral history with Robert Wright at U.S. Submarine Veterans convention, 1993, courtesy of Carl LaVO.

Books

Alden, John D. *U.S. Submarine Attacks During World War II.* Annapolis, MD: Naval Institute Press, 1989.

Blair, Clay Jr. *Silent Victory: The U.S. Submarine War Against Japan.* Philadelphia: J. B. Lippincott Company, 1975.

Campbell, Douglas E. *Save Our Souls: Rescues Made by U.S. Submarines During World War II.* Washington, DC: Syneca Research Group, Inc., 2016.

Cleaver, Thomas McKelvey. *Fabled Fifteen: The Pacific War Saga of Carrier Air Group 15.* Havertown, PA: Casemate, 2020.

Galatin, Admiral I. J. *Take Her Deep! A Submarine Against Japan in World War II.* New York: Pocket Books, 1987.

Gamble, Bruce. *Black Sheep One: The Life of Gregory "Pappy" Boyington.* New York: Ballentine Books, 2003.

Good, John M. *The Submarine* Sailfish. Pittsburgh: Cathedral Publishing, 1997.

Jourdan, David W. *Operation Rising Sun: The Sinking of Japan's Secret Submarine* I-52. Lincoln, NE: Potomac Books, 2020.

———. *The Search for the Japanese Fleet: USS* Nautilus *and the Battle of Midway*. Lincoln, NE: Potomac Books, 2015.

Knoblock, Glenn A. *Black Submariners in the United States Navy, 1940–1975.* Jefferson, NC: McFarland & Company, Inc., 2005.

LaVO, Carl. *Back from the Deep: The Strange Story of the Sister Subs* Squalus *and* Sculpin. Annapolis, MD: Naval Institute Press, 1994.

Link, Robert, ed. *US Submarine Veterans of World War II: A History of the Veterans of the United States Naval Submarine Fleet.* Four volumes. Dallas: Taylor Publishing Company, 1986.

Maas, Peter. *The Terrible Hours: The Greatest Submarine Rescue in History.* New York: Harper Torch, 1999; reprint, 2001.

McCullough, Jonathan J. *A Tale of Two Subs: An Untold Story of World War II, Two Sister Ships, and Extraordinary Heroism.* New York: Grand Central Publishing, 2008.

Mendenhall, Corwin, Rear Admiral, USN. (Ret.). *Submarine Diary: The Silent Stalking of Japan.* Chapel Hill, NC: Algonquin Books of Chapel Hill, 1991.

Michno, Gregory F. *Death on the Hellships: Prisoners at Sea in the Pacific War.* Annapolis, MD: Naval Institute Press, 2001.

———. *USS* Pampanito*: Killer-Angel.* Norman: University of Oklahoma Press, 2000.

Monroe-Jones, Edward, and Michael Green, eds. *The Silent Service in World War II: The Story of the U.S. Navy Submarine Force in the Words of the Men Who Lived It.* Havertown, PA: Casemate, 2012.

Moore, Stephen L. *Battle Surface! Lawson P. "Red" Ramage and the War Patrols of the USS* Parche. Annapolis, MD: Naval Institute Press, 2011.

———. *Presumed Lost: The Incredible Ordeal of America's Submarine POWs During the Pacific War.* Annapolis, MD: Naval Institute Press, 2009.

O'Kane, Richard H., Rear Admiral, USN (Ret.). *Clear the Bridge! The War Patrols of the USS* Tang. Chicago: Rand McNally & Company, 1989.

Parshall, Jonathan, and Anthony Tully. *Shattered Sword: The Untold Story of the Battle of Midway.* Washington, DC: Potomac Books, 2007.

Roscoe, Theodore. *United States Submarine Operations in World War II.* Annapolis, MD: Naval Institute Press, 1949.

Sasgen, Peter T. *Red Scorpion: The War Patrols of the USS* Rasher. Annapolis, MD: Naval Institute Press, 1995.

Winton, John. *Ultra in the Pacific: How Breaking Japanese Codes and Ciphers Affected Naval Operations Against Japan, 1941–45.* Annapolis, MD: Naval Institute Press, 1993.

Index

A

Adams, Joseph Lee Jr., 260
Adinolfe, Nunzio Charles (Nick), 238
Allen, Nelson John (Butch), 66, 72-73, 88, 91, 93
Alvis, Frank Ryals, 10
Anderson, Charles Weldon, 263
Anderson, Edward (Andy), 74, 80, 111, 290
Andrews, Charles Herbert, 50
Apostol, Eugenio, 97
Arnath, Eugene, 90
Arnold, Arlington Reid, 262
Ashio (POW camp 9-B), 218-222, 252-257, 288-292
Azuchi, Takuji, 146-148, 160-161, 166-167, 176-178, 186-187, 190-192, 195-196

B

Baglien, Jerome Warren, 108, 110, 114, 117-120, 170
Bain, Thomas, 51
Baker, Cecil Eugene, 109, 115
Baker, Joseph Nicholas Jr., 84-85, 89-92, 98-99, 101, 104, 107-108, 110, 114-115, 117-118, 120, 137, 143-144, 214-215, 217-219, 252, 254, 292-293, 303, 305
Barnes, Maurice Drummond, 261
Barrera, Maximo, 170, 189, 192, 194
Barry, Edward, 303
Batts, Allen, 226, 274
Bayles, Lester Wallace, 36, 56, 127, 165, 201-202, 206, 209, 211, 233, 235-236, 243, 259, 306
Beidleman, Edgar Melrose Jr., 70
Bells of St. Mary's, 71, 152, 244

Benson, Roy Stanley, 140
Berghausen, Edward Justus II, 52, 123, 126-127, 200, 226, 250, 285
Berry, Warren Rawling, 89, 110, 117, 170
Blair, Leon Nelson, 19, 44, 46, 211
Bland, Judson Thomas (Jud), 6-7, 301
Blatti, Willard Wayne (Bill), 35-36, 55-56, 62, 133, 154, 211, 233
Blundell, Harry Lester, 62, 260, 269
Bontier, Albert Marion, 10, 18, 20
Bowers, Donald Elliot, 295
Boyington, Gregory (Pappy), 219
Bradley, Robert, 247
Bradley, Russell J., 263
Brady, Raymond, 51
Brannum, Bill Clifton, 170
Braun, Claude, 36
Brown, George Estabrook, Jr., 9-11, 14, 66, 71, 73, 75, 80-81, 83, 85, 87, 89, 93-98, 100, 105-106, 108, 111-112, 114, 116, 118, 216-218, 252-254, 292
Brown, Thomas Vincent, 31, 67, 74, 109
Bruckart, William Lee, 45-47, 52, 61-62, 126, 132-133, 150, 152-153, 172, 202-203, 207, 225-226, 303
Bryson, Carl, 7, 59, 303
Bunt, Raymond Charles, 62-63, 122, 133-135, 159, 236, 239, 258, 262, 264, 266, 281, 286-287, 303, 306

C

Callahan, James Bartholomew (Cal), 234-235, 237, 243-244, 303
Campbell, Jack G., 231
Carter, Robert William, 110, 118-119, 170
Caverly, Floyd Merle, 254
Chappell, Lucius (Lu), 9-10, 12-16, 18-20, 84
Charlton, Elmer, 295
Chidori-class patrol boats, 206, 271
Clark, Arthur, 77-78
Coleman, Charles Steele, 90
ComSubPac (see Charles A. Lockwood)
Connaway, Fred, 65-73, 81-84, 86-88, 90-91, 106
Cooper, Billie Minor (Bill), 17-20, 68-69, 71-73, 81, 86-88, 90-92, 101, 104, 111, 144, 216, 218, 220-222, 290-292, 301-302, 305-306
Copeland, Houston Ray, 263
Cowin, Stanley Jr., 51, 55, 126, 131, 150, 154, 158, 172-173, 182, 184, 200, 206, 211, 233, 243, 262, 265, 271
Cravens, Eugene, 4, 7-8, 301
Cromwell, John Philip, 68-70, 72, 85-87, 97, 100, 106
Crytser, William Baker, 60, 153, 173, 211, 225, 233

D

Daubin, Freeland Allan, 24
Davis, Benjamin, 261
Deas, Morris, 210
Defrees, Joseph Rollie Jr., 14, 66, 70, 88, 90-91
Dieterich, Francis Lewis (Frank), 24, 32, 40, 57, 124, 136, 150-154, 159, 162-163, 172, 203, 211, 233, 259
Dillon, Bernard, 28
Dillon, Charles, 28
Dillon, Eleanor, 28
Dillon, Jack, 28
Dillon, James, 28
Dillon, Janet Kugel, 224, 283, 287, 298, 304

Dillon, John Henry, 28, 224
Dillon, Joseph, 295
Dillon, Marilyn, 28
Dillon, Mary Ellen O'Donnell, 28
Dillon, Robert (Bob), 28-29, 224, 227-229
Dillon, Thomas, 28
Dillon, William Joseph (Skip), 21-25, 27-29, 32-43, 54-55, 60-61, 121-125, 127, 136, 150, 153-154, 156, 158-159, 162-163, 172, 183, 199-200, 203, 223-224, 227-229, 233, 235-238, 243-246, 248-249, 259-261, 263, 265-271, 275, 279, 283-287, 295-305
Doritty, Raymond Edward, 32, 36-38
Dublon Island, 107-109, 138
Durbin, Basil, 222
Duva, Ernest Anthony (Tony), 215, 255-256, 292

E

Elliott, Henry Leonidas (Rebel), 110, 117-120, 139, 170
Embury, George Roderic, 88, 90-91
Enola Gay (U.S. Army B-29), 287
Eskildsen, Leo Aage, 110, 112-113
Eto, Toshiyuki, 176-177, 193-194
Evans, Wayne Anthony (Shorty), 52, 126, 131-132, 151, 153, 159, 164-165, 173, 185, 203, 212, 233, 242, 247, 262, 271, 285

F

Farley, Louis C., 51
Fiedler, Eugene Max, 81-83, 97
Fisher, Dale W., 264-265
Fitzgerald, John, 253-254
Formosa Strait, 40, 245, 260, 268
Fox schedules, 21, 125
Freeman, Berley Irving, 295
Fujitsu, Kichitaro, 167
Fukushima, Midori, 176

G

Gabrunas, Philip Joseph, 93, 96-98
Galatin, Ignatius (Pete), 11
Gamel, John Worth, 100, 111, 114
Gaston, David William, 259, 271-272, 278-279, 285
Gato-class submarines, 32
Gebhart, David Ezra, 36
Gerwick, John Day (Jack), 231
Gleeson, Cyril James, 123
Good, John Michael, 57, 122, 127-128, 134, 158-159, 164, 166, 201, 205, 209, 212, 234-237, 240, 244, 247, 250, 258, 260-261, 273-276, 279-280, 282, 286, 295
Goorabian, George, 94-96
Gorman, Michael Thomas, 102, 109, 290, 292
Gray, William Howard, 233, 273, 275, 295
Great Depression, 28, 34, 297, 302-303
Griggs, John Bradford Jr., 42
Guillot, Alexander Benjamin, 90-91

H

Halsey, William Frederick (Bull), 42-43, 260
Harper, James Quinton, 88, 90-92

Harrison, Royal Grace, 46-47, 303, 305
Haug, Leander, 35
Haverland, William Herbert, 93, 97-98, 256
Hawk, Earle Clifford, 49
Hemphill, Richard Earl, 93, 97-98
Hensel, Karl Goldsmith, 39
Hertsgaard, Craig Martell, 226, 229-230, 268, 271, 282, 303
Hertsgaard, Sylvia Gronseth, 226
Hirohito, Emperor, 144, 288
Hiroshima, Japan, 287-288, 290
Hodel, Richard Sullivan, 262-263
Hurt, David Albert, 215

J

Japanese ships:
Akebono (destroyer), 142, 167, 178, 187
Chogei (submarine tender), 70, 84
Chuyo (aircraft carrier), 10-13, 129, 138-143, 145-147, 160-162, 166-170, 174-179, 181, 186-196, 210, 213-214, 217, 295, 300, 305
Gokoku Maru (transport ship), 70
Hagikaze (destroyer), 11
Harukaze (destroyer), 272-273, 276
Haruna (battleship), 245-246
Hiyo (aircraft carrier), 140
Ibarakiken Daiichi Miyashoma Maru (sampan), 14-15
Iburi Maru (freighter), 37
Ishigaki (destroyer), 215
Kaga (aircraft carrier), 12, 26, 183, 210
Kako (heavy cruiser), 26
Kamogawa Maru (aircraft ferry), 26
Kashima (light cruiser), 70
Kinshu Maru (coaster), 242-243
Maya (heavy cruiser), 129, 142, 147, 161, 167, 178, 182-183, 210
Michishio (destroyer), 245
Musashi (battleship), 108
Nitta Maru (cargo liner), 139, 145, 174-175
Nowaki (destroyer), 245
Patrol Boat No. 38, 208, 276
Sazanami (destroyer), 142, 167, 195
Sekko Maru (freighter), 18
Shinju Maru (freighter), 37
Shinten Maru (minelayer), 242
Soryu (aircraft carrier), 183
Taiyo (Japanese carrier), 141
Tama (light cruiser), 208
Tama Maru No. 6 (auxiliary subchaser), 208
Totai Maru (troop transport ship), 204-205
Unyo (aircraft carrier), 10-13, 129, 138-143, 146, 161, 167, 214, 216
Urakaze (destroyer), 142, 162, 166-167, 192-198
Ushio (destroyer), 142, 167
Uyo Maru (troop transport ship), 208
Wakatsuki (destroyer), 70
Yamagumo (destroyer), 70, 73-75, 79-85, 88-92, 98-107, 110, 119, 194, 245
Yawata Maru (cargo liner), 139
Zuiho (aircraft carrier), 129, 142, 145-146, 161, 167, 214
James, Edwin Lafayette, 295
Jarvis, Benjamin Campbell, 39, 42-46, 51
Jeffress, Willard T., 269
Johnson, Albert Joseph, 123
Johnson, Robert William, 32, 38, 57, 62, 125, 129, 154-156-158, 166, 180-181, 183-184, 206, 208, 211, 233-235, 238, 243-244, 248, 260-261, 265-268, 274-275, 282
Johnston Atoll, 69
Jones, Robert, 51

K

Kasuga, Albert Alexander, 269, 286-287
Katoku, Dr., 289
Katsuji, Hattori, 139
Keller, Edwin Karl Frederick (Ed), 30-34, 67-69, 74, 79-80, 82-83, 92-96, 99-100, 103, 106, 109-110, 113-114, 116-119, 137, 144, 161, 215-218, 220-222, 255-257, 289-292, 301, 306
Kelly, Paul Joseph, 57, 125, 158
Kempf, Robert Charles, 224, 238, 269, 295
Kennon, John Bowers Jr., 170
Kitterman, Ralph Randolph Jr., 269
Kuney, Charles, 1, 3, 7
Kure Naval Arsenal (Japan), 139, 197-198
Kuykendall, Clifford Weldon, 255, 291

L

Labrecque, Leon Eugene, 265
Laman, Harold Dewitt, 170, 174
Lang, Joseph Henry, 265
Lefavour, William Robert, 23-24, 39-42, 44-46, 51, 58
Lockwood, Charles Andrews (ComSubPac), 15-16, 21, 39, 41-44, 46, 50-51, 54, 68, 108, 121, 123, 142, 145-146, 149, 208, 210-212, 231, 268, 278, 282, 285, 292
Lohmeier, Marion Howard, 295
Lucas, Emmett, 132-134, 184
Lusk, Gail Cooke, 238
Lyon, William Homer, 62, 202, 212, 233, 259

M

Macek, Matthew Larry, 62, 236, 295, 300
Makley, Philip Charles, 295
Maness, Lloyd B., 2-3, 5, 8
Marcus, Grover Wade, 74, 79
Marcus Island, 130, 134
Marcy, Lincoln, 285, 287
Mare Island Naval Shipyard, 26-27, 30-31, 35, 67, 78, 228
McCain, John Sidney Jr., 145-146
McCarty, Lewis Frederick, 62, 209, 295
McGrath, James Robert, 62
McKinney, Eugene Bradley, 142-143
McLees, Gerald (Gerry), 3, 5-6, 8, 35, 287, 301, 303
McMurtrey, Emerial Afton (Doc), 185
Medal of Honor, 7, 219
Medaris, John, 298
Medeiros, Leonard de, 5-8, 36, 301
Mendel, Joe Francis, 133, 155-157, 159, 164, 166, 184, 240, 248, 275, 278
Mendenhall, Corwin F., 12
Midway, battle of, 12, 210
Midway Island, 15-17, 19, 36, 39, 41, 94, 122-126, 142, 145, 238-239, 250, 258-260, 282-284
Milbourn, Harry Smith Jr., 89
Miller, John Joseph (Saul), 238, 265
Miyazaki, Toshio, 192
Momsen, Charles (Swede), 6, 15, 30, 211, 231, 253, 301
Moore, John Raymond (Dinty), 26-27, 30-39, 43-44
Moore, Weldon Edward (Dinty), 68, 87, 89-90, 97, 99-101, 111, 169-170, 174, 187-188
Moseley's Maulers (wolf pack), 231, 238, 243-244, 249

Moseley, Stanley Page, 231, 243-244, 249
Mosley, Robert David, 131, 210
Moto (Japanese prisoner Hinomoto), 239-241, 244, 251
Mullen, Frank Warren, 209, 261, 263, 287
Mumma, Morton Claire Jr., 8, 25-26
Muinch, George Jr., 263-264
Murphy, Ruth Guenter, 53-54
Murphy, Paul Louis, 111, 115, 290
Murphy, Walter Patrick Jr. (Pat), 53-54, 60-61, 126, 130-134, 136, 153-154, 156-157, 164, 173, 180, 183, 203, 209, 211, 242-243, 247, 259, 271, 278, 287, 303
Murray, Elmon Truett, 68

N

Nagasaki, Japan, 288, 290
Naquin, Oliver Francis, 1-3, 6-8, 25, 301, 306
New London Submarine School, 29-31, 48, 52-54, 59, 63, 283, 286-287
Newton, Killraine Jr., 226-227, 261, 287, 306
Nichols, John, 5
Nimitz, Chester William, 42-43, 141, 210, 232-233
Numajiri, Shigeru ("The Goat"), 220, 254, 288, 290-291

O

Ofuna (POW camp), 213-219, 253-254
Omori (POW camp), 254
O'Kane, Richard Hetherington, 253-254
Operation Galvanic, 68-69
Owen, Richard Salladay, 265

P

Packard, David, 300
Palau Island, 140, 204, 245
Palmer, Robert Wiley, 219
Parr, John, 70, 110, 114-115, 170
Partin, William Henry, 90
Pearl Harbor, 10, 19-21, 25, 31-35, 39, 41-42, 45-47, 50-56, 59-61, 67, 107-108, 121-123, 125, 129, 199, 208, 210, 214, 227-234, 239, 250, 268, 283-286, 292
Pendleton, Charles, 238
Peterson, Julius Grant, 100, 109, 114, 254
Peterson, Richard, 146
Pike, Evelyn Johnson, 224
Pike, Luverne Carl (Bud), 59-60, 62, 93, 122, 126-127, 135, 153, 155-156, 164, 172, 180, 200, 204-205, 211-212, 224-225, 233, 236-237, 242, 244, 266-267, 272-273, 288, 294-296, 300, 303, 306
Pitser, Charles Earl, 90, 92, 108, 110, 117-120, 139, 170
Poppel, William C., 263
Portsmouth Navy Yard, 4, 8, 99, 286-287, 294-295, 301-303

R

Ramage, Lawson P. (Red), 268, 270-271, 278

Ray, James Troy, 124, 128, 152, 154, 157, 164, 171, 180, 200, 204, 210, 212, 269, 272, 278
Red's Rowdies (wolf pack), 270, 278
Reese, Aaron, 11, 300
Richardson, George Floyd (Bud), 52-53, 56, 60, 63-64, 126, 128-131, 135, 149, 152, 156, 163, 171-172, 200-201, 207, 211, 240, 243, 249, 259
Ricketts, Edward Forest, 89, 91-92, 99, 109, 113, 115, 118-119, 217, 254
Ring, Joseph John, 127
Robertson, Henry Keith (Robbie), 124-125, 295
Roberson, James Earl, 248, 250, 281
Rocek, Christina, 78
Rocek, George (Moon), 75-79, 82, 84, 89, 95-96, 99, 107, 110-111, 113, 116, 118-120, 137-138, 145, 161, 167-170, 174-176, 187-189, 192-198, 213-214, 216-222, 256-257, 288-290, 292-293, 300-302, 304-305
Rocek, James, 76, 78, 293
Rocek, Rudy, 78
Rocek, Sylvia, 78
Roosevelt, President Franklin, 8, 25, 232
Rourke, John Paul, 90, 92, 101, 105, 110-112, 114-120, 138, 254, 289
Royal Hawaiian Hotel (Pink Palace), 42-43, 284

S

Sahaj, Joseph, 225-226, 233-235, 237, 247, 262, 271, 274, 280, 287
Saipan Island, 140, 268-270
Santa Cruz, battle of, 139
Sargent, Thomas Andrew, 123, 127, 228, 235
Sargo-class submarines, 4, 32, 74, 83, 237
Sasaki, Kunichi (James; Handsome Harry), 216
Scatuorchio, Dominic Nicholas, 265
Schilling, William Howard, 286
Schroeder, Delbert Eugene, 59-60, 85, 87, 93-95, 100
Scott, John, 140
Seeley, J. C., 265
Sekine, Hideo, 147
Shirley, Dowdy Buel, 68
Shiro, Ono, 73, 75, 79, 82, 84-85, 88, 91, 100-102, 106
Smail, Robert William, 295
Smith, Charles Gold Jr., 100, 104, 110, 114-116, 189, 192, 194
Smith, Laroy Harold, 93, 95
Smith, Thomas S. (Snuffy), 233, 285
Spritz, Charles, 29-31
Suga, Akiji, 196
Sundman, Austin Theodore, 241, 250, 287

T

Taylor, Clifford Gene, 114
Tharp, Samuel M., 262-263
Thomas, Herbert Joseph, 85, 89-90, 99, 101, 104, 110, 113, 117, 290, 305
Todd, Paul Allen (Doc), 87, 105, 111, 119, 144
Tokyo Rose, 38
Tojo (Ki-44 Japanese Army fighter plane),
Tomasaborou, Captain Okura, 160, 162, 166-167, 176-178, 186-187, 190

Tonden, Harry Arthur, 135, 152, 181-182, 204, 235, 295
Toney, Harry Ford, 98-99, 109, 157
Torpedo data computer (TDC), 12, 61, 153-155, 164, 173, 180, 271-272
Torpedo performance, 12, 15-16, 18-19, 123, 140-141, 246
Traxler, Paul Gilbert, 62, 127
Treasure Island (naval station), 27, 32
Truk Atoll, 10-11, 69, 102, 106-115, 129-130, 134, 137-144, 150, 216
Truman, President Harry, 288
Tucker, Joseph Robbins, 37, 39
Turner, Vernon Clark, 231
Turver, John Turton (Doc), 239-240, 251, 262-263, 276, 279-280, 287

U

Ultra, 10, 68, 129-132, 140-142, 149-150
U.S. Navy vessels,
USS *Apogon* (SS-308), 68-69
USS *Arizona* (BB-39), 121, 170
USS *Augusta* (CA-31), 48
USS *Baya* (SS-318), 46
USS *Bergall* (SS-320), 46
USS *Billfish* (SS-286), 51, 231, 233, 238, 249
USS *Bowfin* (SS-287), 232
USS *Brooks* (DD-232), 24
USS *Bushnell* (AS-15), 124, 126
USS *Cabrilla* (SS-288), 141
USS *California* (BB-44), 25
USS *Chester* (CA-27), 71
USS *Enterprise* (CV-6), 262-263
USS *Essex* (CV-9), 263, 265-266
USS *Falcon* (AM-28), 6-7
USS *Franklin* (CV-13), 46
USS *Fulton* (AS-11), 17, 269-270
USS *Greenling* (SS-213), 17-18, 68, 231, 233, 238, 249
USS *Grenadier* (SS-210), 214-216, 218-219, 252-255, 293
USS *Gunnel* (SS-253), 122, 130, 145-146, 278
USS *Gurnard* (SS-254), 49-50
USS *Halibut* (SS-232), 18
USS *Holland* (AS-3), 123
USS *Honolulu* (CL-48), 34
USS M*uskallunge* (SS-262), 15
USS *Nashville* (CL-43), 53
USS *Nautilus* (SS-168), 12, 46, 51-52, 65-66, 210
USS *New Orleans* (CA-32), 25
USS *Odax* (SS-484), 298
USS *Oklahoma* (BB-37), 122
USS *Ozark* (LSV-2), 292
USS *Pampanito* (SS-383), 225
USS *Parche* (SS-384), 268-270, 278-279
USS *Pargo* (SS-264), 53, 62-63
USS *Perch* (SS-176), 215, 293
USS *Pipefish* (SS-388), 259
USS *Pomfret* (SS-391), 270, 278-279, 282-283
USS *Proteus* (AS-19), 250
USCGC *Reliance* (WSC-150), 232, 234
USS *Robalo* (SS-273), 293
USS *Ronquil* (SS-396), 285
USS *S-18* (SS-123), 66
USS *S-26* (SS-131), 48-49, 66
USS *S-28* (SS-133), 231-232, 234, 237
USS *S-40* (SS-145), 71, 225
USS *S-44* (SS-155), 26, 215, 255, 292-293
USS *S-46* (SS-157), 52-53
USS *S-48* (SS-159), 66
USS *Sailfish* (SS-192) *see also Squalus*; 8, 10, 13, 17, 20, 25-35, 43-48,

50-60, 65, 67, 142, 223-232, 284-288, 300-305; eighth war patrol, 21-25, 35-39; ninth war patrol, 39-42; tenth war patrol, 61-64, 121-136, 149-212; eleventh war patrol, 232-251; twelfth war patrol, 260-283; rescues downed aviators, 260-266; attacks on carrier *Chuyo*, 149-158, 162-167, 171-174, 180-184; under depth charge attacks, 26, 37-38, 158-159, 162, 184-185, 204, 206-208, 274-275, 280-281; bombing attacks on, 33, 199-202, 273; Presidential Unit Citation, 227, 232-233, 294; as training submarine, 285-288; decommissioned, 294-295
USS *Sailfish* (SSR-572), 298
USS *Sargo* (SS-188), 57
USS *Sawfish* (SS-276), 23, 130, 142, 267
USS *Sculpin* (SS-191), 4-5, 9-20, 31, 34, 39, 47, 50, 59-61, 64, 300-303; final patrol of, 65-108; survivors of, 141, 144-145, 161-162, 167-170, 174-176, 187-189, 192-198, 213-222, 252-257, 288-294
USS *Sea Leopard* (SS-483), 286-287, 298, 302
USS *Searaven* (SS-196), 68-69, 285
USS *Seawolf* (SS-197), 20
USS *Silversides* (SS-236), 128
USS *Skate* (SS-305), 142-144
USS *Skipjack* (SS-184), 52
USS *Snapper* (SS-185), 54
USS *Spearfish* (SS-190), 57
USS *Sperry* (AS-12), 16, 18, 41
USS *Squalus* (SS-192; see also *Sailfish*), 1-8, 10, 15, 25, 35, 55, 59, 122, 211, 231-232, 238, 287, 294, 298, 300-303
USS *Sunfish* (SS-281), 66, 146
USS *Ralph Talbot* (DD-390), 170
USS *Tang* (SS-306), 253-254, 293
USS *Tarpon* (SS-175), 259
USS *Tennessee* (BB-43), 170, 185
USS *Texas* (BB-35), 48, 66
USS *Trigger* (SS-237), 140, 185
USS *Trout* (SS-202), 259
USS *Tullibee* (SS-284), 255, 291, 293
USS *Tunny* (SS-282), 140
USS *Wasp* (CV-18), 262-265
USS *Whale* (SS-239), 233
USS *Wyoming* (BB-32), 65-66

V

Van Altena, John Paul, 266
Voge, Richard George (Dick), 26, 43
Von Braun, Dr. Wernher, 298-299

W

Wake Island, 130, 134
Walkup, Montie Dewitt, 34-35, 58-59, 150, 166, 201-202, 224-225, 233-234, 236-237, 239-241, 260, 264-265, 269-270, 277, 306
Warburton, Lester, 295
Ward, Frances Larco, 48
Ward, Robert (son), 48
Ward, Robert Elwin McCraner (Bob), 47-64, 122, 124-135, 149-153, 155-159, 162-165, 171-174, 180-186, 199-200, 202-212, 223-224, 226-227, 229-237, 239, 241-249, 259-266, 268-280, 285-287, 298, 300, 302, 306
Warder, Frederick Burdette (Freddy), 41-42

Weade, Claiborne Hoyt, 99
Welsh, William Henry, 68, 101, 104-105
West, Benjamin Freeman, 57, 125
Wetmore, Irving Earl (Dutch), 22, 51-52, 67, 125-126, 129, 149-151, 153, 159, 164-165, 173, 185, 203, 223, 239, 242, 259
Wheeler, Fred Elwood, 57, 122, 127-128, 209, 225, 237, 268
White, Duane Joseph, 67, 89, 110, 117
Whitemore, William Francis, 215, 245
Whitley, Billie (Tex), 240-241
Williams, Bernard Joseph, 295
Wilkin, Warren D., 5
Woody, James Harold, 153, 156, 212, 242, 271-272
Wright, Eldon, 98-99, 104, 111, 289
Wyatt, Robert Orlin, 90, 92, 100, 103, 109, 255

Yamaguchi, Misao, 161
Yokosuka, Japan, 10, 140-141, 167
Yoshida, Shooichi, 192-193
Yoshiro, Katoh, 147, 161, 167
Young, Walton Thomas (Round Belly), 36

Z

Zamperini, Louis Silvi, 218
Ziel, William Rhienhold (Pop), 34-36

About the Author

Stephen L. Moore, a sixth-generation Texan, graduated from Stephen F. Austin State University in Nacogdoches, Texas, where he studied advertising, marketing, and journalism. He is the author of two dozen books on World War II, Vietnam, and Texas history, including *Patton's Payback* and *Blood and Fury*. Parents of three children, Steve and his wife, Cindy, live north of Dallas in Lantana, Texas.